DRESS, DRINKS, AND DRUMS

DRESS, DRINKS, AND DRUMS

FURTHER STUDIES OF SAVAGES AND SEX

BY

ERNEST CRAWLEY

EDITED BY

THEODORE BESTERMAN

METHUEN & CO. LTD.
36 ESSEX STREET W.C.
LONDON

First Published in 1931

PRINTED IN GREAT BRITAIN

TO

HAVELOCK ELLIS

EDITOR'S PREFACE

WHEN *The Mystic Rose* was first put out in 1902, a single modest volume, Mr. Crawley was rewarded by unstinted praise from such men as Dr. Havelock Ellis and M. Salomon Reinach, Dr. E. S. Hartland and M. van Gennep, Dr. W. H. R. Rivers and Professor Westermarck, the last of whom has generously repeated in a recent letter that he considers *The Mystic Rose* "to be one of the most important books on Social Anthropology ever published." But there Mr. Crawley's reward stopped short: his profound insight into the savage mind and his forthright treatment of the psychological problems of sexual anthropology were too far in advance of his time. *The Mystic Rose* failed—failed, that is, to sell; Messrs. Macmillan remaindered it to a bookseller, who very slowly sold off his stock of copies at a few shillings apiece.

But with the passing of time the more recent doctrines in social anthropology, such as those of Professor Malinowski (who has written that *The Mystic Rose* is "a work which appears to me among the best and most important of the psychological studies of primitive custom"), caused students to return to Mr. Crawley's writings with a new perception of their great importance, and by the time of his premature and lamented death in 1924 *The Mystic Rose* was only occasionally obtainable and only at a very high price.

It was a source of the greatest possible gratification to me when I was asked to edit the book for a new edition, but I little expected that after a quarter of a century it would create so large a demand as it has done.   Still less did I anticipate that I should be enabled to edit two volumes of Mr. Crawley's scattered writings on kindred subjects.

In *Studies of Savages and Sex* I brought together nine shorter essays.   In the present volume are assembled three longer studies, the first of which, indeed, is long and important enough to have made a volume in itself.   None of these twelve papers has been previously printed in book-form, and there still remains enough first-rate material to make a third and final volume of essays, should the publishers feel that there is a sufficient demand for it.

As with *Studies of Savages and Sex* I have allowed myself somewhat greater freedom in editing than with *The Mystic Rose*.   I have silently made a good many verbal alterations, omitted and added a number of passages, and generally made slight adaptations to fit the essays for book-form.   Opinions and theories have of course been left intact.   The references to authorities have been verified and reduced to order, and I am also responsible for the Index.

I have again to thank the family of the late Dr. James Hastings and Messrs. T. & T. Clark for permission to reprint from *The Encyclopædia of Religion and Ethics*.

TH. B.

LONDON

CONTENTS

DRESS, DRINKS, AND DRUMS

DRESS, DRINKS, AND DRUMS

I. DRESS

ITS ORIGINS, FORMS, AND PYSCHOLOGY, WITH SPECIAL
EMPHASIS ON THE SEXUAL PSYCHOLOGY

AN analysis of the relations of man's clothing with
his development in social evolution will naturally be
chiefly concerned with psychological categories. When
once instituted, for whatever reasons or by whatever
process, dress became a source of psychical reactions,
often complex, to a greater extent (owing to its more
intimate connexion with personality) than any other
material product of intelligence. Some outline of
the historical development of dress will be suggested,
rather than drawn, as a guide to the main inquiry.
For formal, chronological, or regional histories of
dress, the reader must look elsewhere.[1]

The practical, or, if one may use the term, the
biological uses and meaning of dress, are simple
enough and agreed upon. These form the first state
of the material to be employed by the social consciousness. Its secondary states are a subject in
themselves.

[1] Among such works most warmly to be recommended are Max von Boehn,
*Die Mode : Menschen und Moden vom Untergang der alten Welt bis zum Beginn des
zwanzigsten Jahrhunderts* (Munich 1907-1925, 8 vols.), and the splendid series of
illustrations in Paul Louis de Giafferi, *The History of the Feminine Costume of the
World from the year 531 B.C. to our Century* (New York, Paris [1927]). Among lesser
works of a general kind in English may be mentioned Mary Evans, *Costume Throughout
the Ages* (Philadelphia 1930), and Köhler[2] von Sichart, *A History of Costume* (London
1928). Curiously enough, the bibliography of dress and costume has not yet been
attempted.

I

1. ORIGINS

The primary significance of dress becomes a difficult question as soon as we pass from the institution in being to its earliest stages and origin. For speculation alone is possible when dealing with the genesis of dress. Its conclusions will be probable in proportion as they satisfactorily bridge the gulf between the natural and the artificial stages of human evolution. The information supplied by those of the latter that are presumably nearest to the natural state, to *Protanthropus*, is not in itself a key to the origin of clothing, but, on the other hand, the mere analogy of animal-life is still less helpful. An animal has a natural covering more efficient for the two uses of protection against the environment and of ornamentation as a sexual stimulus. An animal may become adapted to a change, for instance to an Arctic climate, by growing a thick fur which is white. It may be supposed that, to meet a similar change, man invents the use of artificial coverings. But this old argument is contradicted by all the facts.

It may serve, however, to point by contrast the actual continuity of the natural and the artificial stages, the physical and the psychical stages, of our evolution. If we say that man is the only animal that uses an artificial covering for the body, we are apt to forget that even when clothed he is subject to the same environmental influences as in the ages before dress. Again, there is no hint that the approach of a glacial epoch inaugurated the invention of dress. But it is an established fact that the survivors of immigrants to changed conditions of climate and geological environment become physically adapted by some means of interaction, and in certain directions of structure, which are just coming to be recognized. The British settlers in North America have assumed the aboriginal type of the Indian face and head; migrants from lowlands to uplands develop round-headedness; from the temperate zone to the tropics man develops frizzly hair, and so on. The most obvious of these natural adaptations, physiologically produced, to the environment, is pigmentation. The skin of man is graded in colour from the Equator to the Pole. The deeper pigmentation of the tropical skin is a protection against the actinic rays of the sun; the blondness of northern races, like the white colour of Arctic animals, retains the heat of the body.

If we followed the analogy of the animal, we should have to take into account the fact that a mechanical intelligence enables it to obviate certain disadvantages of its natural covering. The animal never exposes itself unnecessarily; its work, in the case of the larger animals, is done at night, not in the glare of the sun. Automatically it acquires an artificial covering in the form of shelter. If man in a natural state followed a similar principle, he would be at no more disadvantage than is the animal. A similar argument applies to the other use mentioned above, namely, sexual decoration. What these considerations suggest is that man was not forced by necessity to invent. The reason is at once deeper and simpler. Again, we get the conclusion that one primary use and meaning of dress is not so much to provide an adaptation to a climate as to enable man to be superior to weather; in other words, to enable him to move and be active in circumstances where animals seek shelter. The principle is implicit in the frequent proverbial comparison of clothing to a house.

Dress, in fact, as a secondary human character, must be treated, as regards its origins, in the same way as human weapons, tools, and machines. Dress increases the static resisting power of the surface of the body, just as tools increase the dynamic capacity of the limbs. It is an extension (and thereby an intension) of the passive area of the person, just as a tool is of the active mechanism of the arm. It is a second skin, as the other is a second hand.

Further, if we take an inclusive view of evolution, admitting no break between the natural and the artificial, but regarding the latter as a sequence to the former, we shall be in a position to accept indications that both stages, and not the former only, are subject to the operation of the same mechanical laws, and show (with the necessary limitations) similar results. These laws belong to the interaction of the organism and the environment, and the results are found in what is called adaptation, an optimum of equilibrium, a balanced interaction, between the two. In this connexion we may take examples from two well-marked stages in the evolution of our subject, the one showing a deficiency, the other a sufficiency, of the artificial covering of the body. A good observer remarks of the Indians of Guiana, not as a result of habituation, but as a first impression of their naked forms, that " it is a most curious but certain fact that these people, even as they wander in the streets of Georgetown, do not appear naked." [1] The other case is that of the Chaco Indians : " The Indian is

---

[1] Sir E. F. Im Thurn, *Among the Indians of Guiana* (1883), p. 194.

perfectly suited to his environment ; even his pictur-
esque costume and the ornamental painting with
which he adorns his body is in perfect harmony with
his surroundings. The colours blend so beautifully
that there is no doubt whatever that the Indian has,
in a very great degree, the idea of fitness and harmony."[1]

If we qualify in the last sentence the word " idea "
by the adjective " unconscious," we shall have a sound
explanation of a very remarkable phenomenon. The
point of the phenomenon is that the evolution of man's
artificial covering maintains a balance or harmony
with the environment, particularly in respect to light,
just as was the case with the naked Indian skins, arrived
at just as mechanically, but through the unconscious
reaction of the retina. Thus there is a real continuity
between the adaptive colour of the chameleon, and
similar cases of so-called protective coloration (which
is primarily merely a mechanical attuning to the
environment), and the harmony which human dress
may show with its surroundings. The selective process has not been conscious, but neither has it been
accidental. It is the result of law. Equally unconscious in its first stages was the adaptation of dress
to temperature.

This brings us no nearer to the origins of dress,
though it clears the ground. Still further to simplify
speculation, we may notice some prevalent hypotheses
on the subject. Dress being a covering, it assumes,
when instituted, all the applicable meanings which the
idea of covering involves. But it by no means follows
that all of these, or even any, were responsible for its
original institution.

[1] W. B. Grubb, *An Unknown People in an Unknown Land : The Indians of the Paraguayan Chaco* (1911), p. 55.

There is, first, the hypothesis that clothing originated in *the decorative impulse*. This has the merit
of providing a cause which could operate through
unconscious intelligence, automatic feeling. Stanley
Hall found that of the three functions of clothing
whose realization and expression he investigated in a
questionnaire—protection, ornament, and Lotzean self-
feeling—the second is by far the most conspicuous in
childhood. The child is not consciously aware of
sex, otherwise this statistical result might be brought
into line with the sexual ornamentation of animals.
And though it is not always safe to press any analogy
between the civilized child and the savage, the savages
known to science are, as a rule, very fond of finery,
absolutely, and not always in relation to the other sex.
The natural man will undergo any trouble, any discom-
fort, in order to beautify himself to the best of his
power. Dandies, Im Thurn remarks, are about as frequent among the Indians as in civilized communities.[1]
At Port Moresby, in New Guinea, young men actually
practise tight-lacing, to be smart and fashionable.[2]
In these spheres, indeed, it is chiefly the young, if
not mere children, who express the impulse to decoration. Of the Dayaks of Borneo a good observer has
remarked that a " love of finery is inherent in the
young of both sexes ; the elderly are less fond of it
and often dress very shabbily, and save up their good
clothes for their offspring." [3]

It is in accordance with the rule among animals
that among primitive peoples the male sex chiefly

---

[1] Sir E. F. Im Thurn, *op. cit.*, p. 199.

[2] A. C. Haddon, *Head-Hunters, Black, White, and Brown* (1901), p. 256.

[3] Low-Roth, " The Natives of Borneo," *Journal of the Anthropological Institute*
(1893), xxii. 41.

assumes decoration. Ornaments among the Indians
of Guiana are more worn by men than by women.
The stock ornamentation is paint; scented oils are
used as vehicles. "A man, when he wants to dress
well, perhaps entirely coats both his feet up to the
ankles with a crust of red; his whole trunk he sometimes stains uniformly with blue-black, more rarely
with red, or he covers it with an intricate pattern of
lines of either colour; he puts a streak of red along
the bridge of his nose; where his eyebrows were till
he pulled them out he puts two red lines; at the
top of the arch of his forehead he puts a big lump of
red paint, and probably he scatters other spots and
lines somewhere on his face." Down is often used
with red paint.[1]

But this analogy is not to be pressed, though it
is sound as far as it goes. It applies, that is, up to a
certain point in social evolution. Beyond that point
the balance inclines the other way, and for the last
five hundred years of European civilization decorative
dress has been largely confined to women. During a
previous period of some centuries—to be regarded
as one of unstable equilibrium—not only did the
curve of luxury in dress reach its highest point, but
there were attempts—spasmodic, it is true—to put
down any tendency towards such luxury on the part
of women, prostitutes being excepted. The previous
stage—one of very considerable length—is still that
of Islām; its significance and origin will concern us
later. Its chief feature was the principle that female
dress should be not ornamental, but protective—of
the rights of the husband. Thus we may infer that,

[1] Sir E. F. Im Thurn, *op. cit.*, pp. 195 ff.

in the latest stage, woman as a sex has not only gained freedom, and the right to fascinate, previously possessed by the courtesan alone, but has also shifted the equilibrium of sex to a more permanent and efficient position. The story of woman's unconscious struggle for a monopoly of beauty in dress thus illustrates an important social movement.

In practical investigation it is difficult to say where clothing ends and ornament begins, or, on the previous hypothesis, where clothing springs out of ornament. Since either may obviously develop into the other when both are instituted, it is idle to examine such cases. Cases where one or the other is absolutely unknown might serve, but there are no examples of this. If an instance, moreover, of the presence of clothing and entire absence of ornament were observed, it would be impossible to argue that clothing cannot be subject to the decorative impulse. In any case, there is the self-feeling, satisfaction in individuality, to be reckoned with, for the impulse to finery is only one phase of it.

The supporters of the ornamentation hypothesis of the origin of dress have an apparently strong argument in the Brazilians and the Central Australians. These peoples possess no clothing in the ordinary sense of the term. But they wear ornament, and on special occasions a great deal of it. Brazilian men wear a string round the lower abdomen, the women a strip of bark-cloth along the perineum, tied to a similar abdominal thread. This is sometimes varied by a small decorative enlargement. The Central Australian man wears a waist-string, to which is tied a pubic tassel. Corresponding to the last in the case of the women is a very small apron. Leaving the waist-string out of account, we have remaining the question of the erogenous centre. In both the decoration hypothesis and the concealment hypothesis this centre is the focus of speculation. If the Australian tassel of the male sex and the leaf-like enlargement of the Brazilian woman's perineal thread are considered superficially, they may appear to be, if not ornaments, at least attractions. But if this be granted, it does not follow that we have here the first application of the idea of dress.

It would be impossible to make out a case to prove that these appurtenances can ever have satisfied the idea of *concealment*, as on the next hypothesis is assumed. This hypothesis is to the effect that male jealousy instituted clothing for married women. Ratzel observes that if clothing was originally instituted for purposes of protection only, the feet and ankles would have been protected first. Clothing, he holds, stands in unmistakable relation to the sexual life. " The first to wear complete clothes is not the man, who has to dash through the forest, but the married woman." The primary function of her dress is to render her unattractive to others, to conceal her body from other men's eyes. In the lower strata of human evolution he considers that dress as a protection from rain and cold is far less common.[1]

But if we may argue from the practice of existing savages, this hypothesis cannot hold even of the origin of female clothing. Only by straining can it be applied to that of men. It is certainly a *vera causa*, at a certain stage in barbarism (the stage when wives became " property "), of the customs of shrouding and veiling

[1] F. Ratzel, *History of Mankind* (1896-1898), i. 93-94.

women, and of confiscating all a maiden's ornaments
and finery when she became a wife. But it does not
explain the origin of the small apron worn in very
early stages, or of the mere thread in the earliest, and
we cannot deny these articles a place in the category of
dress.

A frequent corollary of such views is that modesty
is a result, not a cause, of clothing (so Sergi). But,
as Havelock Ellis observes, " many races which go
absolutely naked possess a highly developed sense of
modesty." [1] Andamanese women " are so modest
that they will not renew their leaf aprons in the presence of one another, but retire to a secluded spot for
this purpose ; even when parting with one of their
bōd-appendages [tails of leaves suspended from the
back of the girdle] to a female friend the delicacy they
manifest for the feelings of the bystanders in their
mode of removing it almost amounts to prudishness " ;
yet they wear no clothing in the ordinary sense.[2] The
Guiana Indians, when they want to change their single
garment, either retire from sight or put the new over
the old, and then withdraw the latter.[3] Modesty is " in
its origins independent of clothing ; . . . physiological modesty takes precedence of anatomical modesty ;
and the primary factors of modesty were probably
developed long before the discovery of either ornaments or garments. The rise of clothing probably
had its first psychic basis on an emotion of modesty
already compositely formed of " these elements.[4]

This last statement, of course, cannot hold of the

[1] H. H. Ellis, *Studies in the Psychology of Sex* (1897), i. 5.

[2] E. H. Man, " The Aboriginal Inhabitants of the Andaman Islands," *Journal
of the Anthropological Institute* (1883), xii. 94, 331.

[3] Sir E. F. Im Thurn, *op. cit.*, p. 194.   [4] H. H. Ellis, *op. cit.*, i. 37.

ultimate genesis of clothing. But, once instituted, it was sure to coincide with emotions of modesty. The general connexion between modesty and dress is a subject of little importance, except in so far as it has involved the creation of false modesty, both individually and socially. Modesty, where there is dress, tends to be concentrated upon it mechanically. When clothing is once established, the growth of the conception of women as property emphasizes its importance, and increases the anatomical modesty of women. Waitz held that male jealousy is the primary origin of clothing, and therefore of modesty. Diderot had held this view. Often married women alone are clothed. It is as if before marriage a woman was free and naked ; after marriage, clothed and a slave. " The garment appears—illogically, though naturally—a moral and physical protection against any attack on his [the husband's] property." [1]

But the fact of dress serving as concealment involved the possibility of *attraction by mystery*. Even when other emotions than modesty, emphasized by male jealousy, intervene, they may work together for sexual attraction. " The social fear of arousing disgust combines easily and perfectly with any new development in the invention of ornament or clothing as sexual lures. Even among the most civilized races it has often been noted that the fashion of feminine garments (as also sometimes the use of scents) has the double object of concealing and attracting. It is so with the little apron of the young savage belle. The heightening of the attraction is indeed a logical outcome of the fear of evoking disgust." [2]

---

[1] H. H. Ellis, *op. cit.*, i. 41.   [2] *Ibid.*, i. 39.

Similarly we find in the most primitive clothing a curious interchange of concealment, protection, decoration, and advertisement. As has been hinted, when an appurtenance has come to be attached to the sexual area, the resulting psychical reactions are significant. In the previous natural stage there is no artificial stimulus ; now there is such an addition to the natural stimulus, first by mere attraction or signification, and later by decoration or veiling. In the mind of the subject also there comes, first, the consciousness of sex, and later the enhancing of self-feeling, which in the case of dress generally, and not merely sexual, is distributed throughout the personality. The subject's material personality is increased by clothing, and his psychical reaction is proportional to this. The result is a rich complex of self-consciousness, modesty, and self-feeling generally, the balance between them varying according to circumstances. But it is highly improbable that such impulses could have led to the invention of dress, much less of mere attachments and appurtenances. Their only means of expression would have been ornament.

Finally, there is the *protection-hypothesis*. Sudden falls in the temperature, rains and winds and burning sunshine, the danger of injuring the feet and the skin of the body generally when in the forest, and the need of body-armour against the attack of insects and of dangerous animals, seem obvious reasons for the invention of dress. But they do not explain the process of invention, which is the main problem. The cloak, the skirt, the apron, cannot have been invented in answer to a need, directly, without any stages. The invention of cloth was first necessary, and this was suggested by some natural covering. The only line of development which seems possible is from protective ligatures. There are numerous facts which apparently point to such an origin of clothing. One of the most characteristic ornaments of savages all over the world is the armlet. It is quite probable that this has an independent origin in the decorative impulse, like the necklace. But here and there we find bands worn round the ankles, knees, wrists, and elbows, the object of which is clearly to protect the sinews and muscles from strains. The pain of a strained muscle being eased by the grip of the hand, the suggestion of an artificial grip might naturally follow, and a system of ligatures would be the result. The Nāgas wear black rings of cane round the knee—as some say, to give strength for climbing.[1] The Malays wear bands and ligatures to protect the muscles and prevent strains, as, for instance, round the wrists and below the knee.[2] Ratzel observes that arm-rings may be useful in striking and warding off blows. But the idea of a cestus is unlikely to be the primary motive for ligatures.[3] The Chacos wear anklets of feathers, chiefly to protect their feet against snake-bites.[4]

Wild peoples, in fact, understand quite well the limitations and the capacity of the human organism in respect to the environment. We may credit them with an adequate system of supplying natural deficiencies, and of assisting natural advantages also. For instance, the Malays explain the object of the papoose for infants as being to prevent the child from

[1] T. C. Hodson, *The Nāga Tribes of Manipur* (1911), p. 23.
[2] Skeat-Blagden, *Pagan Races of the Malay Peninsula* (1906), i. 140.
[3] F. Ratzel, *op. cit.*, i. 99.   [4] W. B. Grubb, *op. cit.*, p. 262.

starting and so straining itself.[1] And it seems probable that there is a connexion between the earlier
use of the ligature and the prevalent custom of wearing metal rings or wire as a decoration. Men and
women of the Watusi wear round the ankles innumerable coils of iron wire, representing a weight of many
pounds. The women wear heavy bracelets of brass.[2]
It is possible, also, that in certain cases dress itself
might have been developed from the same source.
Thus, when we compare the following type of body-
dress with the frequent use, in earlier stages, of a
pliant bough or cane as a girdle, we can imagine the
possibility that the invention of the sheet form of
covering might have been delayed by the extension
of the bandage form. The garment, termed *lumiet*,
of the Sakarang women is a series of cane hoops covered
with innumerable small brass links. The series en-
casing the waist fits close. It sometimes extends right
up to the breasts. The Ulu Ai and Ngkari women
wear eight to ten parallel rows of large brass rings
round the waist. They are strung on rattans, and
fixed to a cane network inside them. Dense coils of
thick brass wire are also worn on the legs.[3]

But the ligature as a primary stage of sheet-clothing
might have developed merely by adding to its breadth.
Given a girdle, we might suppose a natural enlargement of its depth. And among the various bands
used by the lowest peoples there is a gradation of the
kind. The armlets of the Indians of Guiana are broad
cotton bands or string.[4] Yet there is no evidence

[1] W. W. Skeat, *Malay Magic* (1900), p. 335.

[2] L. Decle, "The Watusi," *Journal of the Anthropological Institute* (1894),
xxiii. 425.

[3] Low-Roth, *op. cit.*, xxii. 40-41.   [4] Sir E. F. Im Thurn, *op. cit.*, p. 197.

to show that such a development, from the belt to the kilt, has been the main origin of the skirt form of dress. A skirt supplying its own belt is generally a late modification.

Examination of the earliest peoples inevitably leads to a rejection of the ligature-hypothesis. Every consideration goes to show that the earliest ligature was not intended to support the muscles. It is inconceivable that the use of string in the Guiana example can be intended for such a purpose. In the next place, it must be borne in mind that the chief area of the organism with which dress proper is concerned is the central part of the body, the trunk. Now, the great majority of the lowest peoples known wear no clothes. Shelter is used instead. But there is very commonly a waist-string, and it is more used by men than by women. We assume that the girdle is the point of departure for the evolution of dress, and the mechanism of that departure will be presently discussed. But for the origin of body-clothing it is necessary to find the origin of the girdle. The civilized idea of a girdle is to bind up a skirt or trousers. This is certainly not its object among the earliest peoples, who have nothing to tie up. It might be supposed that the original purpose of the girdle was that of the abdominal belt, useful both as a muscle-ligature and to alleviate the pangs of hunger. But the earliest girdles are merely strings, and string is useless for such purposes. String, moreover, made of grass or vegetable fibre, or animal sinew or human hair, is an earlier invention than the bandage. Its first form was actually natural, the pliant bough or stem.

It is significant that this waist-string is chiefly a male appendage, and that it is worn neither tight nor

very loose. Both facts are explained by the purpose
for which the string is worn. It is neither a bandage
nor a suspender, but a continuous pocket. The
savage finds it indispensable for carrying articles
which he constantly needs, and which otherwise
would encumber his hands. Once fitted with a waist-
string, the body, as a machine, is enormously improved,
being able to carry the artificial aids of manual operations ready for use as occasion requires, without ham-
pering the work of that universal lever, the hand.

We can only speculate vaguely as to the series of
" accidents " which led to the idea of the waist-string.
It was, no doubt, analogous to the series which ended
in the invention of artificial hands in the shape of
weapons and tools, but it was certainly much later in
time. The varied unconscious ideas of holding,
gripping, and encircling, which the muscular experience of the hand imprinted on the brain, might have
evolved the principle and practice of a hold-all round
the trunk, without the occurrence of any fortunate
accidents whatever. The natural position of the
hands when at rest would be rejected by unconscious
reasoning in favour of a more convenient spot, slightly
higher, which would not interfere with the movements of the legs. The downward tapering of the
thigh, moreover, renders it impossible to keep a string
in position. In this connexion it is worth noting
that knee- and ankle-bands are commonly used in
various stages of culture for the purpose of holding
implements.

The waist-string, therefore, being earlier than
clothing proper, and being, as we have suggested,
the point of departure for the wearing of coverings,
we have next to examine the mechanism of the con-

nexion between them. The use of the string as a holder being given, it would serve not only as a pocket, but as a suspender for leaves or bunches of grass, if for any reason these were required. The point to be emphasized here is that the presence of a suspender would suggest the suspension and therefore the regular use of articles for which there had been no original demand. If, for occasional purposes, a decoration or covering was desired, there was the waist-string ready for use. Central as it was, the decoration or covering would fall below it and be thus applied automatically to the perineal region. Similarly, the hair of the head is a natural holder, though much less efficient, and it is used to support leaf-coverings or flower-decorations.

It is unnecessary to enter upon a description of the various zones of the body which require protection, such as the spine at the neck and in the small of the back, against sun and cold, or the mucous membranes of the perineal region, against insects. The use of clothing of certain textures and colours to maintain a layer of air about the skin at a temperature adapted to that of the body, and to neutralize those rays of light which are deleterious to the nervous system and destructive of protoplasm, is also out of place here. We may note, however, that by unconscious selection the evolution of dress has probably followed a thoroughly hygienic course. But no principles of such hygiene, except the very simplest, can have occurred to primitive man. One of the simplest, however, we may admit for tropical races—the use of a protection against insects. The perineal region is most subject to their attacks when man is naked, owing to the sebaceous character of the surface and its relatively higher temperature. These facts, no

doubt, more than anything else, are the explanation
of primitive habits of depilation. But depilation is
not a complete protection. Something positive is
required. The use of bunches of grass or leaves is
natural and inevitable, as soon as there is something
to hold them, namely, the waist-string. A parallel
method is the use of a second string depending from
the waist-string in front and behind, and passing
between the legs. The Brazilian strip of bast used
by women, and the red thread which takes its place
in the Trumai tribe, though they attract attention
like ornaments instead of drawing attention away,
yet, as Von den Steinen also satisfied himself, provide
a protection against insects, a serious pest in the forests
of Brazil.[1] These inter-crural strings protect the
mucous membranes, without, however, concealing
the parts, as do leaves and grass. In the present connexion their chief interest is the use made of the waist-
string. When cloth was invented the first form of
the loin-cloth was an extension of the inter-crural
thread. It may be illustrated from the Indians of
British Guiana, though it is practically universal,
significantly enough, among tropical and sub-tropical
peoples. The Guiana man wears a narrow strip, called
lap ; it is passed between the legs, and the ends are
brought up at back and front and suspended on a rope-
like belt. The women wear an apron, called *queyu,*
hung from a string round the waist. Very young
children, before wearing a cloth, have a string round
the waist. The *lap* is often made of bark, beaten till

---

[1] K. von den Steinen, *Unter den Naturvölkern Zentral-Brasiliens* (Berlin 1894),
pp. 190 f. For other protective coverings for the organs against insects, see Wilken-
Pletye, *Handleiding voor de vergelijkende Volkenkunde van Nederlandsch-Indië* (Leyden
1893), pp. 37-38.

soft.[1] The *lap* method is employed by the Veddas of Ceylon,[2] and by numerous early races throughout the world.

As the various methods of draping and tying developed with man's familiarity with sheet-dress, the later form of loin-cloth naturally superseded the earlier. A length of cloth passed round the waist and between the legs, the ends depending, was both more convenient and more comfortable. In the first place, it supplied a broader bandage, and being two articles in one, was more easily kept in position. This is the familiar and widely prevalent " loin-cloth." Secondly, it supplied a more efficient method of binding the male organs. There is no doubt that the naked male often finds it desirable, for obvious anatomical reasons which do not trouble the animal (whose organs are practically withdrawn into the perineal surface), to confine these parts. Hence, it may be conjectured, the use of a perineal cloth for men and of a mere apron or skirt for women—a distinction of the earliest date and generally maintained. As showing the practice of such confinement, it is enough to point to a common use of the earlier waist-string. The end of the organ is placed under the string, made tight enough to hold it flat against the abdomen.[3]

The development of the apron and skirt is a simple extension (given the suspensory string and the invention of cloth) of the use of leaves hung from the waist. The frequent use of a rear apron as a sitting mat is a later detail, having no influence upon the

[1] Sir E. F. Im Thurn, *op. cit.*, 194.
[2] C. G. and B. Z. Seligmann, *The Veddas* (1911), p. 93.
[3] See Wilken-Pleyte, *op. cit.*, p. 38.

skirt, which developed independently. A frequent
variation is the fringe. A combination of front and
rear aprons no doubt preceded the complete skirt.
When the latter was developed, new methods of suspension were adopted, among them being one similar
to that of the loin-cloth, the upper edge serving as a
bandage. The use of the waist-string by women, for
keeping an inter-crural cloth or tampon in place during
the periods, may be referred to ; but it did not lead
to the development of any article of attire. One
example of its use, however, is instructive, as showing
how a temporary protection may pass into a regular
appendage. Among the majority of the Nyasa tribes
a woman during her periods wears a small piece of
calico corresponding to a diaper. The same is worn
after childbirth. This is the case generally in Nyasaland. But Angoni women " always wear them." [1]

The protection-hypothesis of the origin of dress
may thus be adopted, if we qualify it by a scheme
of development as suggested above. When once instituted as a custom, the wearing of leaves or bark-
cloth upon the abdominal region served to focus
various psychical reactions. One of the earliest of
these was the impulse to emphasize the primary
sexual characters. It is an impulse shown among the
great majority of early races in their observances at
the attainment of puberty, and it is, as a rule, at that
period that sexual dress or ornament is assumed.
Among civilized peoples, in the Middle Ages and in
modern times, the impulse is well marked by various
fashions—the phallocrypt and the tail of the savage
having their European analogues. A less direct but

[1] H. S. Stannus, " Notes on some Tribes of British Central Africa," *Journal of
the Royal Anthropological Institute* (1910), xl. 321.

even more constant instance of the same recognition is the assigning of the skirt to women as the more sedentary, and trousers to men as the more active sex. The suggestion sometimes met with, that the skirt is an adaptation for sexual protection, need only be mentioned to be dismissed. The central Australian pubic tassel and similar appendages will here find significance, but it is improbable that such accentuation was their original purpose. Once instituted for protection, the other ideas followed. Another of these, which at once received an artificial focus, was the emotion of modesty. It has been observed among the higher animals that the female, by various postures, guards the sexual centres from the undesired advances of the male. The assumption of a waist-cloth does not actually serve the same purpose, but it constitutes a permanent psychical suggestion of inviolability. Similarly, the use of any appendage or covering involves the possibility of attraction, either by mere notification, by the addition of decoration, or, later, by the suggestion of mystery.

Further than this speculation as to origins need not be carried. The various forms and fashions of dress, and the customs connected with it, will supply examples of the material as well as of the psychological evolution of the subject.

2. MATERIAL AND FORM

It is proposed to describe the types of human dress and the materials of which it has been composed only so far as is necessary to illustrate the religious and social significance of dress as an index to psychological evolution.

If dress be taken to include anything worn on the
person other than offensive and defensive armour,
there is hardly a single known substance, from iron
to air, which has not for one reason or another been
employed ; while for purposes of decoration or protection against the supernatural, the very utmost
use has been made of the natural covering of the
organism, in the way of hair-dress, skin-painting, and
tatooing, and the wearing of ornaments and amulets
on or in the projecting points of the body, particularly
various orifices. In the earlier stages two features
are prominent—the savage is apt to regard anything
he wears as an ornament, though it may be actually a
protection. Also, the less body-covering there is,
the greater tendency to painting, scarification, and
tatooing. " Having," as Gautier said, " no clothes
to embroider, they embroider themselves." As examples of the earliest stages the following are typical.
The Niam-Niam negress wears a single leaf only, suspended by a string from the waist.[1] The Indians of
Central Brazil wear a string round the lower abdomen.
It is worn after puberty, but it conceals nothing, of
course. The women wear a little strip of bast passing
between the legs ; in some tribes the *uluri*, a trian-
gular decorative piece of bark bast, is worn.[2]

" Except for waist-bands, forehead-bands, neck-
lets, armlets, and a conventional pubic tassel, shell, or,
in the case of the women, a small apron, the Central
Australian native is naked." The waist-string is made
of human hair. The pubic tassel is a fan-shaped
structure of fur-strings, about the size of a five shilling
piece. Being covered at corrobboree times with

[1] F. Ratzel, *op. cit.*, i. 94.
[2] K. von den Steinen, *op. cit.*, pp. 190-191.

gypsum, it serves as a decoration rather than a covering. The Arunta and Luritcha women do not wear even an apron.[1] In the western islands of Torres Straits the men are naked ; the women wear a tuft of grass or split *pandanus* leaves ; for dancing, a short petticoat of shred *pandanus* leaves is worn over this.[2] In Samoa the only necessary garment was, for men and women, an apron of leaves.[3]

The New Ireland men go absolutely naked ; the women wear aprons of grass, suspended from cinctures made of beads strung on threads of aloe leaves. A bonnet of palm leaves is also worn by the women.[4] The Australians of the South show an advance on those of the Centre. The Euahlayi woman's *goomillah* is a waist-string of oppossum-sinew, with strands of hair in front. The Central Australian woman has not even a string. The Euahlayi man's *waywah* is a belt, six inches wide, of sinews and hair, with four tufts. Opossum-skin rugs are worn in winter.[5]

Among the Curetu of the Amazons, the men wore a girdle of woollen thread, but the women were entirely naked.[6] The neighbouring Guaycurus reversed the custom, the men being naked and the women wearing a short petticoat.[7] In other tribes of the same region both sexes were quite nude.[8]

---

[1] Sir W. B. Spencer and F. J. Gillen, *The Native Tribes of Central Australia* (1899), pp. 570, 572.

[2] A. C. Haddon, " The Ethnography of the Western Tribes of the Torres Straits," *Journal of the Anthropological Institute* (1890), xix. 368, 431.

[3] G. Turner, *Samoa a Hundred Years Ago and Long Before* (1884), p. 121.

[4] A. J. Duffield, " On the Natives of New Ireland," *Journal of the Anthropological Institute* (1886), xv. 117.

[5] K. Langloh Parker, *The Euahlayi Tribe* (1905), pp. 120-121.

[6] Sir C. Markham, "A List of the Tribes of the Valley of the Amazons, including those on the Banks of the Main Stream and of all the Tributaries," *Journal of the Royal Anthropological Institute* (1910), xl. 98, 101.

[7] *Ibid.*, xl. 101.   [8] *Ibid.*, xl. 122.

" The costume and ornamentation prevalent with
the Lower Congo men is principally confined to a grass
loin-cloth, and mutilation of the two incisor teeth
of the upper jaw ; the women wear a small apron in
front and behind," and ear decorations of wood and
metal.[1] The Garo petticoat was less than a foot in
depth. To allow freedom of movement it was fastened only at the upper corners.[2] The Wankonda
men wear nothing but a ring of brass wire round the
abdomen. The women wear a tiny bead-work apron,
exactly resembling that of the Kaffirs.[3] The women
at Upoto wear no clothes whatever.[4] In the Short-
lands the men are naked ; the women wear leaves in
a waist-string. In New Britain both sexes are nude.[5]
Of Central Africa, Angus gives as his experience : the
more naked the people and the more to us obscene and
shameless their manners and customs, the more moral
and strict they are in the matter of sexual intercourse.[6]
The fact should be noted, in leaving the subject of
the scantiest form of dress, as being a regular con-
comitant of nakedness.

Variations of the most opposite character in the
same stage of culture are a frequent problem. In
some cases they may be accounted for by foreign influence. But any accident may institute a fashion.
Thus, the Upoto women, as we have just seen, are

[1] H. Ward, " Ethnographical Notes relating to the Congo Tribes," *Journal of
the Anthropological Institute* (1895), xxiv. 293.

[2] E. T. Dalton, *Descriptive Ethnology of Bengal* (1872), p. 66.

[3] Sir H. H. Johnston, *British Central Africa* (1897), pp. 408 ff.

[4] T. H. Parke, *Equatorial Africa* (1891), p. 61.

[5] G. Brown, *Melanesians and Polynesians* (1910), pp. 202, 310.

[6] H. C. Angus, " The ' Chensamwali ' or initiation ceremony of girls, as performed in Arimba Land, Central Africa," *Verhandlungen der Berliner Gesellschaft
für Anthropologie, Ethnologie und Urgeschichte* (1898), p. 479.

entirely nude ; [1] but among the Akikuyu the smallest
girl wears an apron. [2]

In tropical countries the use of *leaves* as occasional
or permanent garments is regular. Several peoples,
such as the East Indian islanders, in Ceram, for example, and the Polynesians, elevated the practice into
an art. Noticeable details are the single-leaf head-
dress, and leaves fixed in arm-bands. The Samoans
wore girdles of *ti*-leaves (*Cordyline terminalis*), gathered
when turning yellow. [3] Adorned with flowers, their
figures were a notable example of adaptation to island
scenery. The Niam-Niam negress wears a leaf tied
to a girdle. [4] Paliyan women are sometimes dressed
in a leaf-girdle only. Gond women wear bunches of
twigs round the waist. The Juángs of Chotā Nāgpur
are famous for their leaf-dresses. When dry and
crackly they are changed for fresh leaves. [5] The
Semangs of the Malay Peninsula wear girdles of leaves.
On festive occasions, ligatures of *Licuala* leaf were used
to hold flowers on the arms ; flowers were also
fastened in the girdle and the head-fillet, both made
of this leaf. The Sakai wear a waist-cord from which
leaves depend in a fringe. [6] This is retained under
the cloth *sarong*. At feasts their dress is like that of
the Semang, a wreath of leaves or a turban of cloth
being indifferently used. The dancing-dress of the
Jakun is made of the leaves of the *serdang* palm, and
consists of an elaborate fringed head-dress, a bandolier,

---

[1] H. Ward, *loc. cit.*

[2] W. Scoresby Routledge and Katherine Routledge, *With a Prehistoric People :
The Akikuyu of British East Africa* (1910), p. 139.

[3] G. Brown, *op. cit.*, p. 315.

[4] F. Ratzel, *op. cit.*, i. 94.

[5] W. Crooke, *Things Indian* (1906), pp. 156-157.

[6] Skeat-Blagden, *op. cit.*, i. 53, 142, 364 ; ii. 118, 124, 136-137.

and belt. Leaf-aprons are still worn by Kōragar women.[1]

Another natural covering is *bark*. "In tropical regions of both hemispheres, where scanty clothing is needed, certain trees weave their inner bark into an excellent cloth, the climax of which is the celebrated *tapa* of Polynesia."[2] Taken from the *wauki*, or paper-mulberry (*Morus papyrifera*),[3] the bark was beaten to a soft consistency. In tropical Africa a species of *Brachystegia* (Order *Leguminosæ*) is generally used as a source of bark-cloth. The bark is made into kilts, cloths, bandboxes, canoes, roofing, and various useful articles.[4] The Guiana Indian wears sandals of the leaf stalk of the *aeta* palm (*Mauritia flexuosa*). They are made in a few minutes, and careful measurements are taken. They wear out in a few hours.[5]

The Kayans use bark-cloth, which they dye red and yellow.[6] Throughout Eastern Asia, the Malay Archipelago, and Polynesia, the girdle of bark-cloth is widely diffused. The Sakai hammer the bark of the *ipoh* tree (*Antiaris toxicaria*) and of the wild breadfruit (*Artocarpus*) so as to expel the sap. It is then washed and dried. The loin-cloth made of this by the Semang is the loin-cloth proper, folded round

[1] J. M. Campbell, "Notes on the Spirit Basis of Belief and Custom," *The Indian Antiquary* (1895), xxiv. 154.

[2] O. T. Mason, "Technogeography, or the Relation of the Earth to the Industries of Mankind," *The American Anthropologist* (1894), vii. 144.

[3] E. Tregear, *Maori Comparative Dictionary* (Wellington, N.Z. 1891), *s.v. tapa ; tapa* is the *kapa* of the Hawaiians.

[4] "Bark Cloth of Uganda," *Journal of the Anthropological Institute* (1893), xxii. 145.

[5] Sir E. F. Im Thurn, *op. cit.*, p. 195.

[6] C. Hose, "The Natives of Borneo," *Journal of the Anthropological Institute* (1894), xxiii. 165.

the waist, and tucked through the front after passing
between the legs. Both this and the women's fringe
of leaves are worn under the Malay *sarong*, where this
has been introduced.[1]

The Woolwa Indians make their clothes, the *tounoo*
and the sleeping-sheet, from the bark of trees. The
women beat this on a smooth log with a mallet shaped
like a club and having grooves which give to the bark-
cloth the texture and appearance of a mesh. The
better sort of garments are made of stout cotton, of
many colours and mixed with the down and feathers
of birds.[2] Watusi women wear bark-cloth fastened
above the breasts and falling below the knees.[3] Formerly the Veddas of Ceylon made bark-cloth from the
riti (*Antiaris innoxia*).[4]

The "shirt-tree" of Brazil is a *Lecythis*. Its
pliant bark is easily stripped. From a length of the
trunk a cyclinder of bark is taken and beaten soft.
Two arm-holes are cut, and it is ready for wear.[5] The
bark of the "sacking-tree" is still used for clothes in
Western India. The men of the Abors of Assam
wear loin-cloths of bark. Bark-cloth was worn by
the ancient Hindu ascetics.[6]

Various circumstances, which need not be here
detailed, make certain peoples adopt *leather* or *fur*
garments. Against cold and rain these are still un-
surpassed. The men of the Akamba wore cloaks of

---

[1] Skeat-Blagden, *op. cit.*, i. 140 ff., 151.

[2] H. A. Wickham, " Notes on the Soumoo or Woolwa Indians," *Journal of the Anthropological Institute* (1895), xxiv. 203-204.

[3] L. Decle, " The Watusi," *Journal of the Anthropological Institute* (1894), xxiii. 425.

[4] C. G. and B. Z. Seligmann, *op. cit.*, p. 93.

[5] F. Ratzel, *op. cit.*, i. 96.

[6] W. Crooke, *op. cit.*, p. 157.

ox-hide before the introduction of trade blankets.[1]
The Masai wore dressed skins before cotton cloth was
introduced.[2] The only garment of a Chaco Indian
woman is a skin petticoat, but in cold weather a mantle
of skins is worn.[3] The Ainus use bear-skins for clothing.[4]
Arctic and sub-Arctic peoples, like the Eskimo, have
made fur-dress into a very perfect covering.

Such ready-made articles of early dress contained
both the suggestion and the material of *manufactured
cloth*. The animal, insect, and vegetable worlds were
gradually exploited for the purpose. Animals like
the sheep and the llama, trees like the palm, have
both supported man and inspired his invention.
Thus from the Mauritia palm the natives of the Orinoco derived wood for building ; from its leaf they
made clothing, fishing nets, and hammocks. Its sap
supplied a fermented drink.[5] Materials which have
complex possibilities are more likely to encourage the
inventive impulse than is sheer necessity. " Weaving is the next art, after agriculture and building,
to acquire economical importance." [6] The hair of
domesticated animals superseded skins ; cotton and
linen superseded leaves, grass-matting, and the rougher
vegetable fibres, palm, aloe, hemp, and the like. With
the introduction of an artificial dress-material the
savage stage of the evolution comes to an end. But
for various reasons many barbarian peoples draw at
times upon the old natural fabrics. In some cases,

---

[1] C. W. Hobley, *Ethnology of the A-Kamba* (Cambridge 1910), p. 40.

[2] A. C. Hollis, *The Masai* (Oxford 1905), p. 301.

[3] W. B. Grubb, *op. cit.*, p. 69.

[4] B. Scheube, " Der Baerencultus und die Baerenfeste der Ainos," *Mittheilungen der Deutschen Gesellschaft bei Süd und Süd-Ostasiens* (Yokohama), xxii. 45.

[5] E. J. Payne, *History of the New World called America* (Oxford 1892), i. 309.

[6] *Ibid.*, i. 369.

like that of the Sakai leaf-girdle, which we considered
above, it is regularly used in combination with woven
material. The earliest stages of the barbarian period
are illustrated by the following typical account of
home-made fabric, dye, and dress. The dress of the
Fulas is " universally the cotton cloths made by themselves out of the plants grown in almost every village ;
it is carded by an instrument, probably imported,
which is very much like a wire brush about 8 inches
by 9 inches, and woven on an ingenious loom." The
cotton is dyed blue with indigo, cultivated by the
natives, and is marked by a white pattern produced
by tying portions of the cloth together before dip-
ping it.[1]

It is significant that in these stages the form of
the material leads to actualization of its possibilities,
and emphasizes simultaneously covering, concealment, and decoration. The third type of the perineal
garment becomes regular : namely, for men, the loin
and inter-crural cloth combined in one length, and
for women the folded petticoat. For example, the
ordinary garment of Fula women is a single cloth,
either folded round and tucked in under the arms
or wound round the waist, leaving the breast exposed.[2]
This type has been largely used by both sexes. In an
extended form it is the *sarong* of the Malays. The
loin-cloth of men is the *maro* of the Polynesians. Both
garments have the same method of fastening—a double
or treble wrapping round the waist. From it have
developed the suspended or belted skirts of women
and kilts of men. A combination of this principle

---

[1] G. F. Scott Elliot, " Some Notes on Native West African Customs," *Journal
of the Anthropological Institute* (1894), xxiii. 80-81.

[2] *Ibid.*, xxiii. 81.

with that of the shoulder-wrap leads to the tunic and robes generally. The toga form of the outer robe is an echo, in its method of wrapping, of the earliest folded garment for the lower body. The loin-cloth proper of the male sex has an extremely wide prevalence.[1] As an example, the *tounoo* of the Woolwa Indians, or *palpra* of the Mosquitos, is a cloth, 24 inches wide, worn by men round the waist, the ends being passed between the legs, and hanging down in front to below the knee.[2] The *tjawat* of the East Indian Islands is a bark cloth or manufactured cloth twice wound round the waist and then passed between the legs from back to front, the end hanging over centrally. It sometimes survives into early civilization, as among the Hindus.

With improvement in cloth and consequent increase in lightness and folding capacity, a modification was made by many peoples, namely, in the omission of the inter-crural method. Externally there is little difference in appearance except for the greater volume of the newer fashion. The two styles are often confused under the term " loin-cloth." The second is the *kain* of the Indonesians, developing into the *sarong* of the Malays.

From the loin-cloth proper were developed drawers and trousers, a type of garment not seldom found among women instead of the petticoat. In all these later extensions of the idea of a loose and modifiable artificial skin, the earliest addition to the natural surface, the primitive waist-string, is still visible. As a girdle and belt it supports various garments ; by

---

[1] See Wilken-Pleyte, *op. cit.*, p. 39.

[2] H. A. Wickham, " Notes on the Soumoo or Woolwa Indians," *Journal of the Anthropological Institute* (1895), xxiv. 203.

creating folds it supplies once more its original purpose as a pocket. Mantles, cloaks, and caps in the
barbarian stages are confined to their particular purpose, protection against rain, wind, and sun. In the
latest civilizations their use becomes regular for out-
door life ; the barbarian cloak is duplicated into the
coat and the overcoat ; the cap into the hat and the
umbrella. Of the tribes of Nyasaland it is reported
that " the amount of clothing worn varies very con-
siderably, from nothing to European garments." [1]
Such a case will serve to combine in one short view
some of the contrasts of the various stages and some
of the principles of dress.

The young children of the Yao and Angoni run
naked. Sometimes one has a strip of cloth suspended
from the waist-string. A man wears a similar loin-
cloth, and a woman an apron, 18 inches deep. Both
are suspended from the waist-string. The more
prosperous men wear calico from the waist to the
knee, wrapped round the body and held by a belt.
Sometimes it is extended to fold across the chest.
Women wear a cloth folded across the upper part of
the chest. Often men and women have two cloths,
one for the waist, the other for the chest. The Angoni
wear the latter toga-fashion, a fold being carried on
the left arm. A chief wears three such togas—blue,
white, and another colour. European calico is now
used ; formerly bark-cloth and skins. Men now
wear a turban, this form of headgear having been
introduced by Arabs. In the house a woman still
wears only a bead apron.[2]

[1] H. S. Stannus, " Notes on some Tribes of British Central Africa," *Journal of the Royal Anthropological Institute* (1910), xl. 320.
[2] *Ibid.*, xl. 320 ff.

In spite of the underlying similarity of principles universally found, dress more than any external feature distinguishes race from race and tribe from tribe. While distinguishing a social unit it emphasizes its internal solidarity. In this latter sphere there is, again, room for individual distinction. Some types of racial and communal costume may be sketched.

The ordinary male attire of the Dayaks of Borneo consists of a *sirat* or waist-cloth, a *labong* or head-dress, and a *takai buriet* or seat-mat ; the full dress consists of the above with the addition of a *klambi* or jacket, and a *dangdong* or shawl. The female attire is a *bidang* or short petticoat ; when out of doors, a *klambi* or jacket is added.[1] The jacket is probably derived from the Muslims ; it is laid aside for work. The *sirat* (*chawat* of the Malays), which is the loin-cloth proper, not the *kain*, is six yards long, but young men wear it as long as twelve or fourteen yards, twisting and coiling it " with great precision round and round their body until the waist and stomach are fully enveloped in its folds. . . . A practised eye can tell in a moment to what tribe or section of a tribe an individual belongs, not merely by the length of his waist-cloth and the way in which it is wound on, but also by its colour and the fashion in which it is decorated at its extremities." The *labong* is a cloth a yard or two in length, and worn as a turban, but one end stands up straight from the forehead. Some wear a cap, *selapok*, made of plaited rush or cane. The *takai buriet* is a small mat tied with string round the waist so as to cover the hindquarters and serve as a portable seat. It is made of split cane. The

---

[1] Low-Roth, " The Natives of Borneo," *Journal of the Anthropological Institute* (1893), xxii. 36, 40.

klambi (*baju* of Malays) is of home-grown cotton.
The sleeves are open under the armpits. There is a
great variety of fashions in the cut and colour of the
klambi. The *dangdong* is slung over one shoulder.
The *bidang* is a petticoat reaching from waist to knee,
folded over in front and tucked in on one side. The
klambi is like that of the men, but larger. Marriageable girls wear chaplets of odoriferous berries.[1]

The Kayan petticoat is open on one side to enable
the wearer to walk with freedom.[2] This is a general
result of the " natural " petticoat folded round the
hips.

The skin garments of North American Indians
comprise a skirt of buckskin with a belt, leggings
attached to the belt, moccasins, socks of sage-brush,
and the skin robe or shawl, generally superseded by
the blanket.[3] The only difference between the dress
of the two sexes is that the women's skirt reaches
below the knee, the men's to the middle of the thigh,
and that the coiffure is not the same.

The male Samoyed wears " a tunic with the hair
inside, which is called the *militza*. It is an ample
garment reaching below the knee, but in cold weather
the Samoyed girds it up round his waist with a leathern
girdle of an unusually decorative character, and thus,
leaving it baggy round the upper part of his body,
secures to himself a layer of warm air." He wears
breeches of deerskin and boots (*pimmies*) of deerskin.
This is " undoubtedly the best form of Arctic boot

---

[1] Low-Roth, " The Natives of Borneo," *Journal of the Anthropological Institute*
(1893), xxii. 36, 37, 38, 40.

[2] C. Hose, " The Natives of Borneo," *Journal of the Anthropological Institute*
(1894), xxiii. 167.

[3] J. Teit, " The Thompson River Indians of British Columbia," *Publications of
the Jesup North Pacific Expedition* (1898), p. 2.

that we know." In severe weather he wears over all
a *sovik*, a larger tunic, with the hair outside, and a
hood.[1]

Among the Malagasy the *salaka* of the men corresponds to the *maro* of Polynesia, the loin-cloth which
is inter-crural; the *kitamby* of the women corresponds to the *paru* of Polynesia, the short apron. The
upper garment is very distinctive. This is the *lamba*,
a toga-like mantle, hung over the left arm by men,
over the right by women. The women wear also an
upper garment or blouse.[2] The Morocco Berbers
wear " a piece of oblong white blanket or dark blue
cotton with a longitudinal slit in the centre for the
head—like the Mexican *poncho*." The women fasten
a skirt-cloth over this on the left hip. A toga-like
arrangement of a light blanket serves as overall. The
khaneef, a thick black waterproof cloak of goat-hair,
with a hood, is the most characteristic garment. On
the back is an assegai-shaped yellow patch denoting
the clan. Round the shaven head is worn a band of
flannel, cotton, or camel-hair.[3]

The dress of Korean women is a pair of very full
white cotton trousers, almost a divided skirt, and over
these a very full skirt, tied under the arms. In summer,
basket-work frames are worn on the arms, back, and
chest, under the robes, to keep the latter clean and
also for the sake of coolness.[4] The trousers of Korean,
Turkish, and the women of various other peoples is

---

[1] Jackson-Montefiore, " Notes on the Samoyads of the Great Tundra," *Journal
of the Anthropological Institute* (1895), xxiv. 402.

[2] W. Ellis, *History of Madagascar* (1838), i. 278-279.

[3] J. E. B. Meakin, " The Morocco Berbers," *Journal of the Anthropological
Institute* (1895), xxiv. 11, 12.

[4] H. S. Saunderson, " Notes on Corea and its People," *Journal of the Anthropological Institute* (1895), xxiv. 303.

probably, as the term " divided skirt " suggests, not lineally descended from the trews, but a later application of the principle to the skirt.

The basis of men's dress in India is the *dhoti*. It is a loin-cloth passed round the loins and between the legs in the universal manner. The typical garment for women is the *sārī*. It may be worn round the shoulders and draped over the head.[1] Ten or fifteen yards long, it is wound round the waist first, and then brought gracefully over the shoulder. A bodice is worn underneath the *sārī*, and some women have adopted the Muhammadan fashion of wearing drawers. The men's upper garment, the *uttarīya*, is worn somewhat like a toga. Generally an under-jacket, *aṅgarakṣa* (body-protector), is worn underneath. A scarf for cold weather is carried on the arm. The long coat of calico, usually worn by servants, apparently is a compromise, like the frock coat elsewhere, between the jacket and the toga. The turban was borrowed from the Muhammadans.[2] In fact, throughout parts of India " all external distinctions have been effaced between Hindus and Musalmāns," the only mark often being that " the former buttons his tunic on the right hand, and the latter on the side of his heart." [3]

The characteristic male attire in Islām consists of the turban, white cotton drawers or full trousers, the *qamīs*, or shirt, the *kaftān*, or coat, the *lungi*, or

---

[1] W. Crooke, *Things Indian* (1906), pp. 158-159 ; Sir M. Monier-Williams, *Brāhmanism and Hindūism* (4th edition, 1891), pp. 395 ff.

[2] Dubois-Beauchamp, *Hindu Manners, Customs, and Ceremonies* (Oxford 1897), p. 326.

[3] W. Crooke, *op. cit.*, p. 163. Mr. Crooke referred the writer to B. Chunder, *Travels of a Hindoo* (1869), ii. 374 ; and J. F. Watson, *Textile Manufactures and Costumes of India* (1866), i. 55.

scarf. The *qamīs* corresponds to the Greek χιτών and the Heb. *ketôneth ;* the *kaftān* to the ἱμάτιον, Heb. *meʿîl.*[1] The turban, generally of muslin, may be from sixty to seventy yards long. The tarbush and the fez are other forms of head-gear.

Pollux gives a classic account of ancient Greek, and Varro of ancient Italian dress.[2] It is significant, sociologically, that the classic type, characterized by the loose tunic and toga, which with some differences was that chiefly affected by the great Oriental races, and is adapted both to the Oriental ideal of repose and to the classic ideal of aristocratic contemplation, was discarded, as the Empire developed into the States of Europe, in favour of what the Greeks styled barbarian dress, chiefly characterized by trousers—a dress adapted to activity. Trousers, the Sanskrit *chalana,* had been connected in India, as now in the East Indian Archipelago, with the dress of warriors and chiefs.[3]

The early Hebrews, like the Egyptians, wore the loin-cloth, originally, according to monuments of the latter, of the *lap* form. Drawers developing from this were first used as a priestly garment. Together with all Semitic peoples and the barbarians of Europe, they differed from Greek peoples in this one garment, though becoming assimilated in the tunic and mantle. The *sādin* was a shirt. Generally it was of the Greek type, and formed indoor dress. Overlapping by means of the girdle, it provided a

[1] T. P. Hughes, " Dress," *Dictionary of Islam ;* see E. W. Lowe, *An Account of the Manners and Customs of the Modern Egyptians* (1846), i. 36.

[2] Pollux, *Onomasticon,* iv, viii ; Varro, *De Ling. Lat.,* v.

[3] Wilken-Pleyte, *Handleiding voor de vergelijkende Volkenkunde van Nederlandsch-Indië* (Leyden 1893), p. 42.

pocket ; it was slit at each side for ease in walking.
The outer garment had two types, the long coat,
corresponding to the ἱμάτιον, and the full-dress
cloak, the me‘îl, worn by wealthy persons and the
priests. Both deserted the toga type in possessing
sleeves. It was similar, generally, to the Chinese
and Muhammadan long coat.[1]

The early Christians wore the ordinary dress of
the country. They always evinced a strong feeling
against luxury, display, and immodesty in dress. This
is to be attributed not merely to their revolt against
Imperial paganism and its luxury and vice, but to
their own class-feeling and class-prejudice, an impulse of the pride in lower class conditions of simplicity
and poverty. This impulse is paralleled in modern
labour and socialist psychology, where the workman's
garb becomes a fetish of caste. Early Christian literature contains stories of Christians being tortured for
refusing to put on garments indicative of idolatry.[2]
All colour was avoided in dress, except the " natural "
colours of the cloth. Under the Frankish Emperors
a prohibition was enacted against the wearing of a
combination of wool and linen.[3] Such ideas gradually
gave way, and the dress of the country, more and
more of the " barbarian " type, even in the south, was
still worn by Christian Europeans without any limitations, country and creed being now identical. Among
details to be noted are the following. In Germany
and Europe generally, till the sixteenth and seventeenth centuries, night garments were not worn ;

---

[1] G. M. Mackie, " Dress," *Dictionary of the Bible ;* I. Abrahams and S. A.
Cook, " Dress," *Encyclopædia Biblica.*

[2] *Acts of Perpetua and Felicitas,* xviii.

[3] See *Capitularium,* vi. 46.

every one slept nude.[1]   Sixty years ago in England the
use of drawers was almost unknown, and was regarded
as immodest and unfeminine.[2]   The tight-fitting hose
were the men's characteristic garment.   The doublet
or jacket was replaced among the academic class by the
long coat.   An extraordinary variety of fashions pre-
vailed from the Middle Ages onwards.   Knee-breeches
later replaced the long hose, and the longer jacket
the doublet.   The peasant's overall, smock, or blouse
goes back to early European times.   Finally, the
modern trousers superseded the knee-breeches.

The evolution of material includes some abnor-
malities of special interest.   Some extreme cases may
be selected to illustrate these.   Among the Central
Australians, human hair is used for various purposes,
expecially for the manufacture of girdles.   The giving
and receiving of it constitute an important right and
duty.   A married man's chief supply is obtained from
his mother-in-law.[3]   The mediæval use of the hair-
shirt as a mode of penance depended on the coarseness
of the fabric for the mortification of the flesh.   Similar
is the use of hempen fabric, sack-cloth, in mourning.
In footgear an analogy is seen in the use of dried peas
to make walking painful.

The famous feather-fabric of the Nahua nations,
who lived in a paradise of gorgeously coloured birds,
was made by skilled artists, termed *amantecas*.   This
feather-cloth, with its brilliantly hued and scintillating
patterns, was used for mantles and dresses by the nobles
and the wealthy, as well as for tapestry and similar

---

[1] W. Rudeck, *Geschichte der öffentlichen Sittlichkeit in Deutschland* (1897), pp.
57, 399.

[2] E. J. Tilt, *Elements of Health* (1852), p. 193.

[3] Spencer-Gillen, *op. cit.*, p. 465.

drapery.[1] The most skilled nation was the Toltec.[2] (Feather cloaks and collars were made also by the Hawaiians.)[3]

The interweaving of precious metal with dress-fabric is a luxurious custom, often merging in superstition. Thus Hindus and Chinese consider it lucky to wear gold, however minute the quantity, in some form on the person.

Colour in dress involves many problems of æsthetic, psychological, and biological importance. Behind fashion in colour there seems generally to be a principle of unconscious adaptation to environment. Æsthetic principles, originally unconscious, were superimposed upon this. The varied symbolism of colour in dress has a psychological foundation. Towards the tropics the tendency to gaudiness becomes marked ; subdued tones are preferred by inhabitants of the temperate zone. Conversely, there is adaptation to racial and individual skin-colour.

The Euahlayi Australians think red to be a " devil's colour." [4] Such cases show an unconscious appreciation of the powerful stimulus of red. Its erotic connexion no doubt explains its frequent use in marriage ceremonies.[5] A natural association of ideas connects white with the purity of virgins and priests. The following are typical cases of doubtful origin. Blue was a sacred colour among the Mayas ; the priests

---

[1] H. H. Bancroft, *The Native Races of the Pacific States of North America* (New York 1875-1876), ii. 488 ff., who gives the authorities on the " feather-mosaic " art and its monuments.

[2] E. J. Payne, *History of the New World called America* (Oxford 1892-1899), ii. 432.

[3] L. Frobenius, *Childhood of Man* (1909), p. 62.

[4] K. L. Parker, *op. cit.*, p. 135.

[5] J. H. Gray, *China* (1878), i. 201.

and the sacred books were clothed in blue. At a certain feast all instruments used in all occupations, and all children, were painted blue.[1] The Yezidis hate blue. Their strongest curse is " May you die in blue garments ! "[2] In the following example a taboo against mixtures may be involved. According to the Atharvaveda a combination of blue and red savoured of witchcraft.[3] Blue and red, however, were worn in the Hebrew high priest's ephod, which was employed for divination.[4]

The special colours of Hindus and Buddhists in Northern India are red and saffron. The Hindu abominates indigo. The Sikh wears blue or white, and abominates saffron. The Musalmān wears indigo, or, if a descendant of the Prophet, green ; never red.[5] Tradition, social inertia, and race-feeling perpetuate such preferences when once established.

Superstitious reasons for wearing a particular colour are probably always secondary, as, for instance, in the following cases from India. For six days before marriage the Indian Musalmān bride wears old tattered yellow clothes, to drive away evil spirits. A wife meeting her husband after a long absence is dressed in yellow. Most Hindus of the West explain the custom of rubbing the body with turmeric in the same way. Among most high-class Hindus the bride's cloth, *vadhūvastra*, is yellow.[6] The Sannyāsī wears yellow clothes.[7] The Lamas of Tibet wear yellow, and yellow is the colour of Buddhist priestly dress universally.

---

[1] H. H. Bancroft, *op. cit.*, ii. 697, 700.

[2] Millingen, *Among the Koords* (1870), p. 277.   [3] W. Crooke, *op. cit.*, p. 165.

[4] Exodus xxviii. 6, et al.   [5] W. Crooke, *loc. cit.*

[6] J. M. Campbell, " Notes on the Spirit Basis of Belief and Custom," *The Indian Antiquary* (1895), xxiv. 156-157.

[7] T. Maurice, *Indian Antiquities* (1806), v. 1008.

A constant tendency may be observed for the colour, as well as the form, of the dress of the sacred world to be the precise opposite of that of the profane. In later stages asceticism is also involved, and simplicity of form is combined with absence of colour in the ordinary priestly garb.

The purple of the Greek world, as worn by the great, and particularly by royal persons, is an expression of super-personality, as distinguished from the abnormal or the contradictory. Royalty among most races wears special colours as well as special dress. For example, the Malay rajas have a monopoly of saffron, for the Malay royal colour is yellow. White is regarded as more exalted and sacred ; it is used to conciliate spirits. It is believed at the same time that the blood of kings is white.[1] As absence of colour, or the " natural " colour of a fabric, implies negation or contraction of personality, so splendour— as in the various shades of crimson used by the ancient world under the one term of " purple "—implies expansion of personality, and is suitable for festal occasions, both sacred and profane.

The negation of splendour is often expressed by black or dark blue. Superstition, when using these, relies upon their minimum of attraction rather than upon any optical adaptation. According to the *Rās Mālā*, dark clothes are a protection against the evil eye.[2] The Gujarāt Musalmān believes that black or indigo clothes keep spirits away.[3] In Roman Catholicism, as elsewhere, blue or violet is a colour symbolic of death. Blue is also connected with the

---

[1] W. W. Skeat, *Malay Magic* (1900), pp. 18, 51.
[2] E. Balfour, *Cyclopædia of India* (4th edition, 1885), v. 29.
[3] J. M. Campbell, *op. cit.*, xxiv. 153.

external attributes of the Virgin Mary, possibly as
mourning her dead Son. Such facts show a senti-
mental adaptation to circumstances. Red and yellow,
being connected with organic growth, are the colours
of well-being, and of the affirmation of energy and
expanded personality ; the blue end of the spectrum
represents the negation of these, in proportion to its
deleterious influence on the organic world. Where
mythological speculation has coloured theology, adaptations in priestly and other garb may occur : blue may
represent the sky ; yellow the sun ; silver the moon ;
red the sacrificial blood, and so on. In social life
colour no less than dress or uniform becomes a distinguishing mark, either by accident or by design.
The gild, the club, the social state (as in the case of
the blue blouse and similar status-garb), even the
seasons of a Church, are represented by colours.

The following adaptations to sacred circumstances
have much the same meaning as the injunction to
wear " decent apparel " on solemn occasions. Among
the various taboos affecting tin-miners in Malaysia is
one forbidding the wearing of black coats, except for
the *pawang*, engineer-in-chief.[1] Local accidents have
much to do with the fixing of such rules. In the
above it is possible that a sympathetic harmony with
the white colour of the sacred metal is alone intended.
In the next case, purity alone may be intended. The
Druid wore a white robe when cutting the mistletoe.[2]
For a similar function the Cambodian priest wears
white.[3]

The following is an excellent example of the prin-

---

[1] W. W. Skeat, *op. cit.*, p. 257.   [2] Pliny, *Historia Naturalis*, xvi. 249-250.
[3] F. Aymonier, " Note sur les coutumes et croyances superstitieuses des
Cambodgiens," *Cochinchine Française* (1883), vi. 136.

ciple of adaptation. The state to which the person is to be assimilated is, no doubt, the succeeding state of cessation of the blood-flow, white being used by way of contrast with red. A ceremonial system, termed *beroemboeng*, is followed by some Dayaks in the case of girls at puberty. The girl is washed, and dressed in white. Then she is incarcerated for a year. During this period she eats only white food ; the hutch in which she lives is of white wood ; at the end she is white herself. A feast is given to celebrate her release ; at this she sucks the blood of a young man through a bamboo.[1]

Green has been used to represent sympathy with the growth of green things upon the earth, as in many agriculture rites and spring ceremonies. As a contrast there is the Black Demeter ; this is " plainly a mythical expression for the bare wintry earth stripped of its summer mantle of green." [2] The use of green is also known to express the non-festal seasons of a religious year. Occasionally green figures as expressive of corruption. The association of green with certain forms of organic decay may explain this.

3. DRESS OF HEAD AND FEET

Foot-gear and head-dress show an evolution as varied, *cæteris paribus*, as dress in general. The constant ideas of dress are seen here, even that of decency. Thus, where special attention is paid to clothing the foot, as among Chinese women, or the face, as among Musalmān women, the resulting modesty is real, but not primary. Decency is a secondary and artificial

---

[1] Low-Roth, " The Natives of Borneo," *Journal of the Anthropological Institute* (1893), xxii. 41-42.

[2] Sir J. G. Frazer, *The Golden Bough* (3rd edition, 1912), viii. 22.

idea, and there is no biological or psychological difference between its application to the foot or the
face and its application to the primary sexual characters.   But in the former there is not, while in the
latter there is, a primary impulse of modesty, the
instinct to protect, though not necessarily to conceal,
the sexual centres.

Most natives in India never wear shoes.   Even
the rich dispense at least with stockings.   Leather is
avoided for reasons of ceremonial purity.[1]   The impulse towards physical cleanliness finds particular
expression in foot-gear.   It is not so obvious in the
case of dress covering the passive areas of the body.
The religious rule of removing the shoes before entering a sacred place is identical with that observed in
social custom, and the original motive is no doubt
merely to avoid carrying dirt or dust into the house
either of God or of man.

Head-dress and coiffure involve ideas of ornament
and distinction in a more marked degree than any
other forms of dress.   In so far as these illustrate the
principles of dress generally, they are here in point.
The Karens wear a head-dress in order to please the
tso, the soul which resides in the head.[2]   The Javanese
wear nothing on the head, which is regarded as holy.[3]
A Zambesi rain-maker never cuts his hair, for fear
the familiar spirits may desert him.[4]   Fashions and
superstitions are equally innumerable in the matter
of coiffure.   No part of the external surface of the

---

[1] Sir M. Monier-Williams, *op. cit.*, p. 396.

[2] E. B. Cross, " The Karens," *Journal of the American Oriental Society* (1854),
iv. 311-312.

[3] Duarte Barbosa, *Description of the Coasts of East Africa and Malabar in the
beginning of the Sixteenth Century* (Hakluyt Society, 1866), p. 197.

[4] *Missions Catholiques* (1893), xxv. 266.

body has been more variously manipulated than the
hair. The coiffure marks differences of race, tribe,
clan, sex, age, and social status.

Flowers in the hair are worn by Dayak women;
the hair is in a knot at the back of the head. Among
Dayak men it is a common practice to grow the back
hair long and shave the front hair.[1] The Kayans of
Borneo shave all the scalp except a large tuft of long
hair which hangs down the back. Hose considers
this to be a last remnant of the Chinese pigtail.[2] The
latter and the Amerindian tuft are the converse of
the priestly tonsure. The hair is either emphasized
by concentration or negated by central denudation.
Similar principles have been applied in the varying
fashions of wearing the beard. Where the hair is
emphasized as a human, or as a masculine or feminine,
character, its æsthetic appeal is parallel to that of
dress, which also emphasizes by various harmonies of
colour and form the æsthetic value of the body.
Especially in woman long hair is regarded as beautiful,
as her glory.[3] From savagery up to modern civilization this attribute has been emphasized by addition,
no less than by decoration.

False hair is regularly worn by the Veddas, who
never brush, or oil, or wash their heads.[4] The latter
fashion, though nearer to the animal, may be an expression of personal pride in the organism, no less
than is scrupulous cleanliness.

The use of the fillet has two purposes—to confine

---

[1] E. L. M. Kühr, " Schetsen uit Borneo's Westerafdeeling," *Bijdragen tot de Taal-, Land- en Volkenkunde van Nederlandsch-Indië* (1896), 6 ser. ii. 65-71.

[2] C. Hose, " The Natives of Borneo," *Journal of the Anthropological Institute* (1894), xxiii. 167.

[3] *Cp.* 1 Corinthians xi. 15.

[4] C. G. and B. Z. Seligmann, *The Veddas* (1911), p. 98.

the hair, and to prevent sweat from reaching the eyes. The protection of the eyes and the spine of the neck from the deleterious rays of the sun has been understood in very early stages. The general tendency in head-gear is towards ornament in the female types, protection in the male. Korean head-gear is remarkable. The men's hats are like inverted flower-pots, with broad, straight brims, similar to the Welsh tall hat. The brims measure two feet across. The hats are made of horsehair, and are varnished. They are stained black, except in half-mourning, when they are string-colour. The court officials wear hats so fantastic that "it is perfectly impossible to describe them." The women wear no head-gear, except fur-caps in winter.[1] Such hats as the Korean and the modern European tall hat are the expression of ideas of the dignity of the head, just as was the crown.

4. ORNAMENTS AND AMULETS

Though dress of the simplest description has an ornamental value, there has always been a precise distinction between dress and ornament. There is little possibility of confusion between them, whether the ornament is directly applied to the body or is actually an addition to the dress, meant to decorate this rather than the wearer. Ornament is often *de rigueur*. No Hindu woman "would dare to hold up her head" unless well provided with eight kinds of ornaments—nose-rings, ear-rings, necklaces, bracelets, armlets, finger-rings, anklets, and toe-rings.[2]

---

[1] H. S. Saunderson, "Notes on Corea and its People," *Journal of the Anthropological Institute* (1895), xxiv. 304.

[2] Sir M. Monier-Williams, *op. cit.*, pp. 396-397.

Lower races are fond of the necklace-method, using shells, seeds, and beads threaded on string. The women of Guiana load themselves with seeds and beads in great ropes.[1] Almost as prevalent is the use of metal cinctures, which subsequently acquire the value of protective armour or amulets. Originally they seem to have been an extension of the ligature-principle.

Amulets are practically innumerable in their variety. They may be worn on the body or on the dress, and are usually abnormal in material. Dress itself may acquire the virtue of an amulet. The Malays write charms on paper or cloth, and wear them next the skin.[2] The Musalmān and Hebrew amulets of sacred texts are familiar examples. The principle employed is that of assimilation of the sacred force by contact. The people of Surinam wear the " strong metal," iron, on their bodies, to acquire its strength.[3] In armour dress reaches the climax of its protective functions.

5. DRESS AS CURRENCY

In the absence of coinage, commercial transactions often take the form of mutual gifts, especially in the case of transactions which are more or less purely financial. At such stages any article representing work and intrinsic value, such as clothing, is an obvious medium for presentation or exchange. In savagery, gifts of clothing are less frequent than gifts of food ;

---

[1] Sir E. F. Im Thurn, *Amongst the Indians of Guiana* (1883), p. 199.

[2] W. W. Skeat, *op. cit.*, p. 567.

[3] K. Martin, " Bericht über eine Reise ins Gebiet des Oberen Surinam," *Bijdragen tot de Taal, Land- en Volkenkunde van Nederlandsch-Indië* (1886), xxxv. 2-4.

in barbarism they are more frequent. The Trojans
placed a robe on the knees of the goddess to induce
her to save their city.[1] In the East Indian Islands
clothes are a frequent offering to the spirits.[2] Blankets were a common gift among the N. American
Indians.[3] To show appreciation of an actor's playing,
the Japanese used to throw their clothes on the stage.
At the end they were purchased by the donors, and
the actor took the money.[4] Blankets form the chief
property of the Kwakiutl and Haidas. They are
treated as money, and lent at interest.[5] A large proportion of the taxes paid by the Nahuas was in the
form of cloths and made-up clothes. The labour involved in providing the tribute was one main aspect
of the *Nahua*, " Rule of Life," which gave the people
their name. Also a considerable amount of dress
was annually expended in sacrifices.[6] The remarkable
institution of the Indians of British Columbia, known
as the *potlatch*, is a distribution of property, such as
blankets, undertaken by each member of society in
turn, according to his status or opportunity. The
system is essentially financial gambling. Similar is
the frequent obligation of the king in early culture to
redistribute the gifts which his subjects make to him.[7]
A *potlatch*, distribution of property, accompanied initiation to the Bear Totem of the Carrier Indians. The
candidate gave presents of clothes to all concerned.[8]

---

[1] Homer, *Iliad*, vi. 87 ff., 302 ff.

[2] F. Valentijn, *Oud en nieuw Oost-Indiën* (1862), iii. 13-14.

[3] J. O. Dorsey, " Mourning and War Customs of the Kansas," *The American Naturalist* (Philadelphia 1885), xix. 678.

[4] L. Kennedy, " Stakes at Games," *Folk-Lore* (1898), ix. 93.

[5] E. J. Payne, *op. cit.*, ii. 376.   [6] *Ibid.*, ii. 465, 476-477.

[7] A. van Gennep, *Les rites de passage* (Paris 1909), p. 43.

[8] A. G. Morice, " Notes Archæological, Industrial and Sociological, on the Western Dénés," *Transactions of the Canadian Institute* (1892-1893), iv. 203-204.

Ornament and currency are interchangeable, Ratzel points out, in early times. There is no safer place for property than the owner's person. But clothing proper is a parallel form of currency, either as made up into garments, or as prepared material. Among the Tlingits, seal and other skins are both worn and circulated as money. The fine mat-garments of the Samoans were their most valuable property, and were used as currency. The Wa-ganda use unbleached calico for the purpose, measuring the unit by the length of the forearm. The Garos use cotton cloth as a medium of exchange.[1] Mat-money is used in the Northern New Hebrides. The mats, which are plaited by women, are called by the same term—*malo*—as women's mat-cloths. They are long, narrow pieces, and the value increases with the folds, which are usually counted in tens. In the Banks Islands, crimson-dyed feathers, the favourite decoration, are used as currency.[2] Formerly braid was so used in the Loyalty Islands. In Florida and Saa, disks of shells are used both as ornaments and as money.[3] In Africa, New Britain, Melanesia, among the Californians, Tlingits, and Eskimo, beads, shells, and the like decorations are used for exchange. The Khalkas discontinued the wearing of their valuable silk scarves, and retained them solely as a form of money.

The famous New Britain shell ornaments, termed *dewarra*, were chiefly in the form of extended collars. The wearing of *dewarra* was abandoned as soon as it was found, on the arrival of Europeans, to have commercial value. The shells were taboo. A man's

---

[1] H. Spencer, *Principles of Sociology* (1876-1896), iii. 387, quoting authorities.
[2] R. H. Codrington, *The Melanesians* (Oxford 1891), pp. 323 ff.
[3] H. Spencer, *op. cit.*, iii. 388 ff.

greatest object in life was to collect as large a hoard as possible. "With *dewarra* they buy their ornaments and their wives ; with *dewarra* they buy themselves free from all troubles and complications ; with *dewarra* they appease their bitterest enemy, even though they may have killed his nearest relative." For daily expenses a man carries about with him a yard or a few fathoms of this money. "The rest is deposited in the *dewarra*-house, a hut specially set apart for keeping the property of all the villagers, the thousands of fathoms belonging to the rich, as well as the smallest savings of the poor. From fifty to a hundred or even two hundred and fifty fathoms are rolled up in a bundle, which is wrapped in bright-coloured leaves. . . . The *dewarra* bank is always guarded by several sentinels." At the death of a capitalist, his *dewarra* is distributed among the depositors. When a man deposits a large amount, the drum is beaten to summon an audience.[1] Shell arm-ornaments are used as currency by the Southern Massim of New Guinea.[2]

Probably the most elaborate type of ornament-currency is that found on Rossel Island, one of the Louisiade group. The monetary system in Rossel operates with two kinds of money : *ndap*, which consists of ground-down and polished pieces of *Spondylus* shell, and *nkö*, the units of which are sets of ten disks of shell, probably made of a giant clam, perforated and strung together. *Ndap* money has twenty-two main intrinsic values, and another series of values in relation to the object desired to be bought ; that is, specific objects can only be bought with pieces of a specific value, and not with pieces of other values

---

[1] L. Frobenius, *op. cit.*, pp. 57-60.
[2] C. G. Seligmann, *The Melanesians of British New Guinea* (1910), p. 513.

made up to the same total value. If a man does not possess a piece of the appropriate value, he borrows one, and makes his repayment with another piece higher in value in proportion to the length of the period of the loan. *Nkö* money, except that it has only sixteen intrinsic values, is similarly used. The far-reaching influence of this elaborate system of ornament-currency can be seen in the fact that the Rossel Islanders can count up to 10,000, whereas their neighbours of Massim find anything above twenty difficult of attainment.[1]

6. DRESS SYMBOLISM

Dress acquires ideal valuations from its various uses, materials, and associations. All languages are full of metaphors recording such ideas. According to the *Śatapatha Brāhmana*, " the priests' fee consists of a hundred garments, for that—to wit, the garment—is man's outward appearance, whence people (on seeing) any well-clad man ask, ' Who can this be ? ' ; for he is perfect in his outward appearance ; with outward appearance he thus endows him." [2] This example well illustrates the idea that dress is both an expression and an extension of personality, in its superficial aspect.

The symbolism of the virgin zone, the girdle, the royal robe and crown, needs no illustration. In rare cases, an article of value used in exchange acquires the virtue of such objects as *regalia* and the Australian *churinga*. The *wampum* of the North American Indians " has, no doubt, grown out of the cords on

---

[1] W. E. Armstrong, *Rossel Island* (Cambridge 1928), *passim*.
[2] *Sacred Books of the East*, xliv. 353.

which were strung shell-beads of divers colours for adorning the neck and arms, and which first served as ornaments, but later circulated in the land as real money. . . . Exchange may have taken place to cement a friendship or a treaty. . . . The *wampum*-belt acquired an extraordinary measure of importance ; in it was evolved a certain kind of documentary script." The speaker at meetings held a *wampum*-belt in his hand. "Brothers," he might say, "with this belt I open your ears that you may hear ; I take care and sorrow from your hearts." At the conclusion of a treaty, tribes exchanged *wampums*, which had a representation of the event woven into them. The Iroquois supported the office of hereditary *wampum*-keeper, who was more or less a depositary of the history of the people. Every year the whole collection was exhibited and explained to the whole tribe.[1]

The eagle-plumes of American warriors' head-dress signified by their numbers and particular marks the achievements of the wearer. Similar marks of honour were made on their garments.[2] It is, however, misleading to characterize such phenomena as dress-language.

Out of the extensive list of metaphors from dress only one or two types can be included in illustration. A proverbial saying of sixteenth-century knighthood contained the phrase, "*Mon harnois ma maison.*"[3] Besides implying the homelessness of the knight-errant, this also involves the application of dress and armour as external shelter no less than as bodily covering. The most prevalent metaphor in all languages, that of dress as a covering, often loses its force as a species of

[1] L. Frobenius, *op. cit.*, pp. 65-69.   [2] *Ibid.*, p. 70.
[3] De la Noue, *Discours politiques et militaires* (Genève 1587), p. 215.

covering, and comes to be a synonym for the genus,
owing to its constant use. In proverbs, the wisdom
of many and the wit of one employs the simplest and
the most complex ideas of dress. In Masailand the
Suahili proverb is used, " to cut out the tunic before
the child is born," equivalent to the English " count-
ing your chickens before they are hatched." [1] A
popular Chinese book of moral instruction says :
" Brothers are like hands and feet. A wife is like one's
clothes. When clothes are worn out, we can substitute those that are new." [2]

The metaphorical wealth of Indian literature suggests two points. In the first place, dress is more
than covering ; it imparts an anthropomorphic value
to the object. According to the Vedic texts on
" Soma," the mixture of *soma* with milk, sour milk,
and barley is a " garment." [3] Water, say the Upani-
sads, is " the dress of breath." [4] In the second place,
there is no doubt that a good deal of mythological
creation is due to metaphor, not as a disease of language, but as a deliberate use of association of ideas
for the purpose of artistic and religious invention.
Metaphors, like those of dress, serve, first, to personal-
ize an object, and then to humanize it. There need
be no confusion between the two uses ; they are
simply two methods of viewing one thing. Nor need
there be any fetishism behind such cases.

On the other hand, the Old Testament and New
Testament use is purely abstract and literary. But
there is no ground for supposing that this is a secondary

[1] A. C. Hollis, *The Masai* (Oxford 1905), p. 245.
[2] *Indo-Chinese Gleaner* (Malacca 1818), i. 164.
[3] A. A. Macdonell, *Vedic Mythology* (Strassburg 1897), pp. 106-107.
[4] *Sacred Books of the East*, i. 74.

stage, and that such metaphors were originally material identifications. The lowest savages, for instance, use metaphors merely as such. The pastures " clothed with flocks " ; the heavens " clothed with blackness " ; a woman " clothed with the sun " ; clothed " with cursing," " with vengeance," " with drowsiness," " with strength and honour " ; and flowers clothing " the grass of the field " [1]—these are examples of Biblical metaphor. Dress-metaphors may be morally applied. Clothed " with salvation," " with righteousness," or " with humility " [2] is a pure metaphor. In Zoroastrian texts it is said that the garments of the soul in the life to come are made from acts of almsgiving.[3] A beautiful metaphor like this is not degraded if it becomes concrete ; it is merely translated into materiality.

The great bifurcation of dress is sexual. Besides the obvious symbolism and metaphor which this involves (as in phrases like " petticoat government " and " wearing the trousers "), there may be mentioned an attempt on the part of asceticism to express the non-sexual idea. The attempt is made both in ideal pictures and in actual priestly garb. The garment selected is the long tunic, which survived here for other reasons, and the colour is white. Thus all indication of primary sexual characters is veiled ; the dress not only covers but replaces the body. White is at once pure, free from " mixture," as a mixture of all colours, and neutral, between splendour and shame.

---

[1] Psalms lxv. 13 ; Isaiah l. 3 ; Revelation xii. 1 ; Psalms cix. 18 ; Isaiah lix. 17 ; Proverbs xxiii. 21, xxxi. 25 ; Luke xii. 28.

[2] 1 Peter v. 5 ; Psalms cxxxii. 9, 16.

[3] *Shāyast lā-Shāyast*, xii. 4, in *Sacred Books of the East*, v. 341.

It has been suggested that the Egyptian *crux ansata*, the symbol of life, is a picture of the loin-cloth.[1] In the Hervey Islands a frequent name for a god is *tatua manava*, "loin-belt."[2] A similar notion is that of the girdle, symbolic of eternity, as the circle is of infinity.

The relation of soul and body is often expressed in terms of dress. The expression may be merely meta-phorical; it may also be real. The body is not only a house or a tomb, as in some early Christian literature; more aptly is it an exactly fitting duplicate, covering the soul. Thus, the body, according to Malay psy-chology, is the *sarong* of the soul. Conversely, the Gnostics spoke of the soul as a "garment." In the one case the inner soul, in the other the outer or filmy soul, seems to be intended.[3] In a famous passage St. Paul combines the metaphors of house and dress in reference to the super-terrestrial body: with this man desires to be "clothed upon," "not for that we would be unclothed, but clothed upon, that mortality might be swallowed up of life." At the same time the body terrestrial is a "house," a "tabernacle."[4] The Déné Indian when sick regains his soul by the following method. His moccasins are stuffed with down and hung up. If the down is warm next morn-ing the soul has entered the shoes, and it may be re-united with the body if the patient puts them on.[5]

[1] A. H. Sayce and H. C. March, "Polynesian Ornament a Mythography: or, a Symbolism of Origin and Descent," *Journal of the Anthropological Institute* (1893), xxii. 314.

[2] H. C. March, *loc. cit.*

[3] Ernest Crawley, *The Idea of the Soul* (1909), pp. 125, 216, quoting authorities.

[4] 2 Corinthians v. 1-4.

[5] A. G. Morice, "The Western Dénés," *Proceedings of the Canadian Institute* (1888-1889), vii. 158-159.

Here the presence of personal warmth, associated with actual wearing, represents the presence of the soul in the dress.

The metaphorical and symbolical applications of the idea of dress thus show an oscillation between very distant extremes, which may be summarized as on the one hand a sheltering house, and on the other hand an almost organic skin.

7. THE SOCIAL PSYCHOLOGY OF DRESS

(a) *The Dress of Mystery*

The results of the free play of the social mind on the subject of dress in magical, religious, and moral opinion and ritual may be introduced by some such observation as that early folklore regards weaving as a mystical art.[1] In other words, the operation has significance, attracts attention, and may inspire wonder. But the ultimate reason is merely that it is outside the normal plane of ordinary human or, more exactly, animal activity. It is not because there is any reference either to dress or to magic.

The invention of fairy tales illustrates, by extravagant emphasis, various ideas connected with dress, but overlaid with that secondary form of magical belief which is merely æsthetic, literary, or generally fanciful. Stories of magical dresses [2] are numerous. The *motif* illustrates either the connexion of dress with personality or the use of dress as a protection, disguise, or honour. There is, for instance, the shirt of snowy whiteness, which turns black when the owner dies.[3] The emphasis on sympathetic connexion is

---

[1] W. Crooke, " The Wooing of Penelope," *Folk-lore* (1898), ix. 124.
[2] *Ibid.*, ix. 129.   [3] M. R. Cox, *Cinderella* (1892), *passim.*

constant. The shirt which never needs mending while the wearer remains faithful [1] is a contrast to the shirt of Nessus.

In German folklore a shirt spun and stitched by a maiden who has kept silence for seven years can undo spells and render the wearer spell-proof.[2] St. Theresa was presented by the Virgin with an invisible cope which guarded her from sin.[3] The clothes and caps which make invisible were familiar subjects of mediæval lore. Malay folklore tells of the cloth, *sansistah kallah*, " which weaves itself, and adds one thread yearly of fine pearls, and when that cloth shall be finished the world will be no more." [4] An old-time raja " wore the trousers called *beraduwanggi*, miraculously made without letting in pieces," also a waistband of flowered cloth, which thrice a day changed colour—" in the morning transparent as dew, at midday of the colour of *lembayong* [purple], and in the evening of the hue of oil." His *sarong* was " a robe of muslin of the finest kind ; . . . it had been woven in a jar in the middle of the ocean by people with gills, relieved by others with beaks ; no sooner was it finished than the maker was put to death, so that no one might be able to make one like it. . . . If it were put in the sun it got damper, if it were soaked in water it became drier." [5]

The idea that dress is a secondary skin, an outer bodily surface, has a connexion with many stories of metamorphosis. A Javanese magician transforms himself into a tiger by means of a miraculous *sarong*, the

[1] W. Crooke, *op. cit.*, ix. 130.

[2] Grimm, *Teutonic Mythology* (1880-1888), iii. 1098-1099.

[3] *The Quarterly Review* (1883), p. 413.

[4] W. W. Skeat, *Malay Magic* (1900), p. 29.   [5] *Ibid.*, pp. 29-30.

Malay garment, half robe and half shirt. This is believed to have such marvellous elasticity that at first it will only cover his great toes, but it stretches till it covers the whole body. It resembles in texture and colour the hide of the Bengal tiger. When it is on, a few muttered charms complete the transformation of the magician into a tiger.[1]

(b) Dress and Personality

One of the simplest cases of association is the idea that a person may be represented by his dress. Dress is here analogous to the name, the effigy, and the image. In China, when a man dies in a foreign land, he is buried in the form of his clothes. The soul is summoned, and then the burial of the evoked soul takes place. In the case, for instance, of an empress in ancient times, her soul was to be evoked " with the aid of her sacrificial robe ; then this robe must be placed on a soul-carriage . . . then the dress must be taken to the sacrificial hall . . . be covered with a corpse-pall, and finally be buried." [2] If the son of a dead Chinese cannot attend the funeral, he is represented by a suit of sackcloth garments carried on a tray in the procession.[3] At a Celebes festival, a woman's and a man's dress represent deceased ancestors.[4] Among the Eskimo the first child born after a death represents the dead man. These namesakes eat and drink the provisions and wear the clothes offered to the dead at feasts, on their behalf. At the

---

[1] W. W. Skeat, *Malay Magic* (1900), p. 161.

[2] J. J. M. de Groot, *The Religious System of China* (Leyden 1892, etc.), iii. 847, 853.

[3] *Ibid.*, i. 193.

[4] B. F. Matthes, *Binnenlanden van Celebes* (1856), p. 5.

end the shades are sent back wearing the spiritual
essence of the clothes, while the gross substance is
kept by the namesakes.[1] When the office of high
priest in Tonga was vacant, the priestly dress was
placed on a chair, and yams were offered to it. It
was regarded as an equivalent for the person.[2] If a
Zulu lightning-doctor is unable to attend a case, he
sends his blanket to be placed in front of the storm as
an equivalent for himself.[3]

Bathing in clothes [4] is a form of ceremonial purification which shows the connexion of dress and person.
If dress is a part of personality, it follows that it must
share in the duties imposed on the natural body.
Similarly, if the soul of a dead person is a replica of
his ordinary personality in life, the soul after the
death of the body is regarded as wearing clothes.
This was, for instance, the case with the Egyptian *ka*.

The anointing of garments is a practice found in
fashion, ritual, and ordinary life.[5] As a detail of
full dress, the wedding garments of the Masai bride
are oiled before being put on.[6] The robes of the
Hebrew high priest, no less than his head and person,
were anointed with the sacred oil.[7] The hygienic
purpose of oiling the skin is also fulfilled by oiling the
garments worn.

In many cases the dress is not merely a representative symbol of the person, but a usable substitute for

[1] E. W. Nelson, "The Eskimo about Bering Strait," *Annual Report of the Bureau of Ethnology* (1899), xviii, pt. i. 363-379, 424-425.

[2] S. S. Farmer, *Tonga and the Friendly Islands* (1855), p. 134.

[3] H. Callaway, *The Religious System of the Amarulu* (Natal 1868), p. 278.

[4] *The Laws of Manu*, xi. 175.

[5] Crawley-Besterman, *Studies of Savages and Sex* (1929), pp. 187 ff.

[6] A. C. Hollis, *op. cit.*, p. 303.

[7] Exodus xxix. 7, 21.

a more or less sacred and therefore unusable reality. A Masai man swears to the truth of a statement " by my sister's garment," a woman " by my father's garment." [1] The converse of this idea may be seen when regalia or royal robes are more sacred than the person of the monarch. These associations, in connexion with the innate love of finery, are concerned in certain observances during sickness and at death. In serious illness, a Mongol's best clothes and ornaments are spread round him in order to tempt the absent soul to return. [2] A similar practice is recorded of the Greenlanders and the Todas. [3] In China " a coat belonging to the sick man, and very recently worn, is suspended on a bamboo." Incantations are performed to induce the errant soul to enter the coat. When the pole turns round in the hands of the holder, the soul has arrived, and the coat is placed on the sick man's body. [4] For the Chinese ceremony of " calling back the dead," the dead man's favourite costume is employed. The idea is to entice the soul into it, for it should be " inclined to slip into such of its garments as it had been proud to wear during life." The dress is held out by a mourner, crying " Ho ! come back." Then, the soul being supposed to have entered, it is placed on the body of the dead man. [5] The Mongols try to persuade the soul of a sick man to return by putting out his best clothes, washed and perfumed. [6] The Maoris enticed the soul of a dead chief by the bait of a piece of its body

[1] A. C. Hollis, *op. cit.*, p. 345.   [2] A. Bastian, *Die Seele* (1860), p. 36.

[3] D. Cranz, *The History of Greenland* (1820), i. 237 ; W. E. Marshall, *A Phrenologist amongst the Todas* (1873), p. 171.

[4] J. Doolittle, *Social Life of the Chinese* (New York 1867), i. 150-151.

[5] J. J. M. de Groot, *op. cit.*, i. 246 ff.

[6] A. Bastian, *op. cit.*, p. 30.

or its clothes, in order to instal it in the *Wahi Tapu*.[1]
Souls are commonly charmed into a cloth or caught
in the same receptacle.[2] The custom of dressing the
dead in his best clothes may often be based on similar
associations (see below).

The principle of impersonation is easily applied
to dress. Particular cases are assimilation to totemic
or other animals, and may be regarded as a fusion of
personalities, or rather the assumption, in the non-
technical sense, of a secondary personality. The
natives of the Upper Congo blacken their faces with
oil and charcoal in resemblance of a species of monkey ;
they explain that by so doing they derive " monkey
cunning." [3] Bechuana warriors wear the hair of a
hornless ox in their hair and the skin of a frog on their
cloak, that they may be as hard to hold as are these
animals.[4] The Bororo of Brazil regard themselves
as being identical with red-plumaged birds. They
decorate themselves with their feathers.[5] All African
tribes, says Schweinfurth (but the statement needs
considerable qualification), imitate in their attire
some animal, especially those for which they have
" reverence." " In this way it frequently happens
that their superstition indirectly influences the habits
of their daily life, and that their animal-worship finds
expression in their dress." [6] Among the Vaydas of

---

[1] R. Taylor, *Te ika a Maui* (2nd edition, 1870), p. 101.

[2] Ernest Crawley, *The Idea of the Soul* (1909), pp. 126, 135-136.

[3] H. Ward, " Ethnographical Notes relating to the Congo Tribes," *Journal of the Anthropological Institute* (1895), xxiv. 293.

[4] E. Casalis, *The Basutos* (1861), p. 272.

[5] K. von den Steinen, *Unter den Naturvölkern Zentral-Brasiliens* (1894), pp. 352, 512.

[6] G. Schweinfurth, *The Heart of Africa* (2nd edition, 1874), i. 406.

Cutch the bridegroom is dressed as a monkey when he goes to the house of the bride.[1]

The purposes of impersonation are naturally manifold, and require no general illustration. When a sick Eskimo child is made to wear a dog's harness, and is consecrated as a dog to the goddess Sedna,[2] the idea is, no doubt, change of condition as resulting from change of personality.

On a similar principle, the Galelareese, concluding that a barren tree is a male, turn it into a female by placing a woman's petticoat upon it.[3]

Assimilation of dress to person has innumerable gradations, passing ultimately into identity or duplication. The principle is complicated by the belief that inanimate objects have souls. There is an Irish belief that the clothes of a dead man wear out more quickly than those of a living man.[4] The Hindus hold that the dress and ornaments of the gods and deified mortals do not decay.[5] Garments, like other inanimate articles, have souls, as in Fijian and Tongan belief.

(c) Magical Associations

All the ideas and practices of sympathetic magic are abundantly illustrated by dress. A few typical cases may be cited. Among the Toradjas of Celebes, when the men are on campaign, those remaining

[1] W. Crooke, *Popular Religion and Folklore of North India* (2nd edition, 1896), ii. 154.

[2] Sir J. G. Frazer, *Totemism and Exogamy* (1910), iv. 208.

[3] M. J. van Baarda, " Fabelen, Verhalen en Overleveringen der Galelareezen," *Bijdragen tot de Taal-, Land- en Volkenkunde van Nederlandsch-Indië* (1895), xlv. 489.

[4] F. D. Bergen, " Burial and Holiday Customs and Beliefs of the Irish Peasantry," *Journal of American Folklore* (1895), viii. 21.

[5] Sir M. Monier-Williams, *op. cit.*, p. 235.

behind may not put off their garments or head-dress, lest the warrior's armour may fall off.[1] The principle of like producing like is frequently applied. A Malay woman explained that her reason for stripping the upper part of her body when reaping rice was in order to make the rice-husks thinner.[2] During the festival of the Mexican " long-haired mother," the maize-goddess, women danced with their long hair unbound, that the tassel of the maize might grow in equal profusion.[3] In a Kashmir story, a weaver offers the king some cloth for a shroud. The king held that the man wished his death.[4] A rain-maker in Mabuiag paints himself white and black, with the explanation " All along same as clouds, black behind, white he go first." A woman's petticoat also is put on to signify clouds.[5] In ancient India, the Brāhman rain-maker wore black garments and ate black food. He had to touch water thrice a day.[6] Generally it is a rule that to make rain the operator must himself be wet, to make dry weather he must be dry. " Who drives fat oxen should himself be fat."

Magical injury is effected upon a person by means of his dress, as having been in contact with or as representing him. The practice of injuring or slaying a man by burning or otherwise destroying fragments of his clothes or food, and the like, is world-wide.[7]

---

[1] Sir J. G. Frazer, *Early History of the Kingship* (1905), p. 61.

[2] W. W. Skeat, *op. cit.*, p. 248.

[3] E. J. Payne, *op. cit.*, i. 421.

[4] J. H. Knowles, *Folktales of Kashmir* (1888), p. 266.

[5] A. C. Haddon, " The Ethnography of the Western Tribes of Torres Straits," *Journal of the Anthropological Institute* (1890), xix. 401.

[6] H. Oldenberg, *Religion des Veda* (Berlin 1894), pp. 420-421.

[7] J. G. F. Riedel, *De Sluik- en kroesharige rassen tusschen Selebes en Papua* (The Hague 1886), pp. 61, 79, 451 ; E. Aymonier, *Le Cambodge* (Paris 1900-1904), p. 166 ; J. Dawson, *Australian Aborigines* (Melbourne 1881), p. 54.

A rejected lover in Burma gets an image of the lady, containing a piece of her clothes or of something she has worn. This is then hanged or drowned.[1] A Wotjobaluk wizard would roast a man's opossum-skin rug before a fire, in order to make him ill or die. The only cure was to soak the rug in water, when the sick man felt cooler and recovered.[2] The Tannese wizard practised a similar method with a cloth which contained the sweat.[3] Prussian folklore has it that if you cannot catch a thief you may get hold of a garment he has dropped in his flight. If this is beaten soundly, the thief falls sick.[4] The last case suggests that the dress is regarded as a part of personality, or an exterior and superficial layer of personality. The practices illustrated above are perhaps better explained on this principle than on the hypothesis that things once in contact retain a magical continuity.

The converse method of enforced assimilation produces intimacy and identity by means of dress. To obtain a favour or to conciliate feeling, a Zulu gets some article or fragment from the person he has in mind, and wears it next his skin.[5]

More numerous are cases of actual transmission of properties by means of dress. A South Slavonian woman who desires a child puts a chemise on a fruitful tree. Next morning she places it on her own person.[6] According to Swiss folklore, the dress of a dead child

---

[1] C. J. F. S. Forbes, *British Burma* (1878), p. 232.

[2] A. W. Howitt, "On Australian Medicine-Men," *Journal of the Anthropological Institute* (1887), xvi. 28-29.

[3] B. T. Somerville, "Notes on some Islands of the New Hebrides," *Journal of the Anthropological Institute* (1894), xxiii. 19.

[4] Tettau-Temme, *Volkssagen Ostpreussens* (Berlin 1837), pp. 383-384.

[5] H. Callaway, *op. cit.*, p. 142.

[6] F. S. Krauss, *Volksglaube und religiöser Branch der Südslaven* (1890), p. 35.

will kill any child who wears it.[1] Such examples need
not be multiplied, but their interpretation cannot
be found merely in the idea of contagion of physical
or magical properties. For early thought it is an
obvious inference that a man's nature " inheres not
only in all parts of his body, but in his dress. . . . Probably the interpretation of odour has led to this belief. If the breath is the spirit or other-self, is not
this invisible emanation which permeates a man's
clothing and by which he may be traced also a part
of his other self ? " [2]

But inference from odour does not, any more than
the idea of contagion, satisfy all the conditions. There
is also, as already suggested, to be taken into account
the general ideas derived from the specific idea of
dress. A garment is an expression of personality,
and, as such, its significance is enforced by its application to other personalities, while this application
receives a concrete meaning and the general idea is
concretely realized from the mere fact that the object
expressive of personality possesses and may retain the
material impress of the person. These ideas enter
into many of the superstitious uses of dress. One or
two types may be cited. The Kayans believe that
to touch a woman's clothes would enervate them and
make them unsuccessful in hunting and war.[3] The
Siamese consider it unlucky to pass under women's
clothes hung out to dry.[4] The Queensland natives
would take off the skin of a slain enemy and cover a
sick man with it, in the hope of curing him.[5] In this

---

[1] H. H. Ploss, *Das Kind* (Leipzig 1876), i. 240.
[2] H. Spencer, *Principles of Sociology* (1876-1896), i. 336.
[3] A. W. Nieuwenhuis, *Quer durch Borneo* (Leyden 1904-1907), i. 350.
[4] A. Bastian, *Die Voelker des oestlichen Asien* (Leipzig 1866-1871), iii. 230.
[5] L. Fison and A. W. Howitt, *Kamilaroi und Kurnai* (1880), p. 223.

and similar cases, as in the practice of blood-drinking, merely the application of organic activity and strength is intended.

It is doubtful if cases like the following imply as much as they seem to do. The desire to have an article clean and new is irreducible, but upon it may be developed habits and beliefs of a mystical nature. The people of Nias, after buying clothes, scrub them carefully in order to rid them of all contagion of the original owners.[1]

The irradiation of ideas of contact has remarkable power and extension, as is shown by beliefs concerning the dress of members of the sacred world. Such garments are impregnated with the *mana* of the wearer, as was Elijah's mantle. But, as pointed out before, metaphors like "impregnated" cannot always be elevated into reasons. The idea that "sanctity," for instance, may inhere in garments as an effluvium or a force is possibly a late explanation, and not the original reason for the practices and beliefs concerned. The Mikado's clothes, by reason of their "sanctity," caused pain and swellings if worn by other persons. Similarly, to avoid injuring others, his eating and drinking vessels were destroyed immediately after use.[2] The garments of a Maori chief would kill any man who wore them. In other words, the chief's *tapu*, inherent in them, had the power of destroying.[3] In Fiji there was a special disease, *kana lama*, caused by wearing the clothes of a chief.[4]

---

[1] Nieuwenhuis-Rosenberg, " Verslag omtrent het Eiland Nias en deszelfs Bewoners," *Verhandelingen van het Bataviaasch Genootschap van Kunsten en Weten-schappen* (1863), xxx. 26.

[2] E. Kaempfer, " History of Japan," in J. Pinkerton, *A General Collection of Voyages and Travels* (1808-1814), vii. 717.

[3] R. Taylor, *op. cit.*, p. 164.

[4] L. Fison, quoted by Sir J. G. Frazer, *The Golden Bough* (3rd edition, 1911-1915, iii. 131.

The principles of ceremonial purity and defilement have produced some remarkable forms of dress and rules of toilette. Among the Mekeo of New Guinea, a woman after childbirth must wear gloves made of coco-nut fibre when pouring water.[1] The Tinné or Déné girl during her first period wears a skin bonnet with fringes reaching to the breast, because the sight of her is dangerous to society.[2]

(d) Personality and State

For the psychology of dress a class of facts relating to murderers and menstruous women, and illustrated by the Eskimo theory of taboo, have an important significance.

It is a frequent rule that persons who have shed blood, or emit blood, shall indicate their state in a peculiar way. Thus, the homicide among the Northern Indians of America had to paint his mouth red before eating.[3] The original intention was probably not protective, but merely an unconscious impulse to adapt the person to the particular state. The idea of protection may be superposed upon this. The Omaha murderer was not allowed to let his robe fly open ; it was to be pulled close about his body, and kept tied at the neck, even in hot weather.[4] Such cases, if their meaning is protective, are perhaps better explained as reactions to a vague and indeterminate impulse to concealment rather than as direct attempts to evade the ghost of the murderer's victim.

[1] Guis, *Missions Catholiques* (1898), xxx. 119.

[2] A. G. Morice, "The Canadian Dénés," *Annual Archæological Report [Ontario]* (1906 for 1905), p. 218.

[3] S. Hearne, *A Journey from Prince of Wales's Fort in Hudson Bay to the Northern Ocean* (1795), p. 204.

[4] J. O. Dorsey, "Omaha Sociology," *Annual Report of the Bureau of Ethnology* (1884 for 1881-1882), iii. 369.

The smearing of the blood-shedder with blood as a means of adaptation to the state of bloodshed is exactly parallel with any investiture with a sacred dress, as a means of adaptation to a sacred state. The " dressing " is a frame to the picture. The Eskimo theory of taboo brings this out. Both personality in general, and particular states of a given personality, form round themselves an expression of their essence. The Eskimo hold that a man who has transgressed taboo appears to animals to be of a dark colour or surrounded by a vapour ; for example, the hands of a menstruous woman appear to be red. This colour becomes attached not only to the soul of the agent, but to the souls of the animals with which he has to do ; in fact, of everything with which he may establish contact. If a child is sick, the *angekok* removes a black attachment from its soul, caused perhaps by the child having taken oil-drippings from the lamp. A dead man's clothes may not be worn, for a hunter wearing them would appear dark and the seals would avoid him.[1]

Behind all this is the instinct against incongruity, mal-adaptation. A hunter must not wear the dress of a dead man or of a mourner ; equally a mourner must not wear the dress of a hunter. The passage from one state to the other, or the transgression of taboo, is not the primary notion. The spiritual garb, resulting from a particular state, is not originally the result of any transgression ; it is an automatic effect of the state, a psychological echo of the adaptation, assimilation, or identification of the individual with his particular condition.

[1] F. Boas, " The Eskimo of Baffin Land and Hudson Bay," *Bulletin of the American Museum of Natural History* (1901), xv. i. 119-126.

Again, it is believed by the Greenlanders that, if a whale fisher wears a dirty dress, or one contaminated by contact with a dead man, the whales will desert the fishing-grounds.[1] In such cases it is probable that there is originally no notion of contamination or contagion at all ; there is merely the incongruity between the full-dress, and complimentary circumstances of the hunt,—the quarry being approached respectfully and regardfully,—and the undress slovenliness of dirty clothes or the ill-omened and tactless reference to death contained in any connexion with a corpse.

The garment of a particular state must be discarded when that state is past. By this means and by bodily " cleansing " transition to the new state or to the normal is effected. The Hebrew high priest after offering the sin-offering had to wash himself and put off the garments he had worn.[2] Similarly the Greek worshipper after an expiation might not enter a city or his house until he had washed himself and his clothes.[3]

Such rules are of world-wide extension. The principle of contamination in its secondary and ordinary meaning cannot cover all the facts. The original meaning of " mixture," and conversely the original meaning of " purity," as an unmixed state, supply an adequate explanation, in the principle of a psychical (and, as expressed in action, a material) adaptation to state. In customs such as the following the original motive is obscure, but the secondary idea of removal of a dangerous effluvium is suggested. Among the Berbers of South Morocco, " persons who have been

---

[1] D. Cranz, *The History of Greenland* (1820), i. 120.
[2] Leviticus xvi. 23-24.   [3] Porphyry, *De abstinentia*, ii. 44.

wrongly accused of a crime sometimes entirely undress themselves in the sainthouse, when going to swear. They believe that, if they do so, the saint will punish the accuser; and I conclude," observes Westermarck, who reports the custom, "that at the bottom of this belief there is a vague idea that the absence of all clothes will prevent the oath from clinging to themselves." [1]

Secondary also is the principle that sacred appurtenances may only be used once; when emptied of their force, they must be destroyed.[2] Nor can we regard as primary the principle that change or removal of dress is a rite of separation from the previous state. The important thing is not the moment of transition (and there is no evidence that any danger is attached to this), but the state itself. Passage from one state to another is marked frequently by change of apparel, but it is unnecessary to labour the point of transition. It is clear that the principle of adaptation to state or circumstance has, as a corollary, the principle of change, which may be more or less emphasized. Thus, the Lapps strip themselves of the garments in which they have killed a bear,[3] just as after any sacred ceremony the participants put off their ceremonial appurtenances. The particular state is over and done with; therefore its exterior adaptation must likewise be removed. Ideas of removing the sacred and dangerous influence are probably secondary.

These considerations, in connexion with the prin-

---

[1] E. Westermarck, *The Origin and Development of the Moral Ideas* (2nd edition, 1917), i. 59.

[2] A. van Gennep, *Les rites de passage* (1909), p. 85.

[3] Sir J. G. Frazer, *The Golden Bough* (3rd edition, 1911-1915), iii. 221.

ciple that solemnity in dress must accompany solemnity
of circumstance and function, may explain the following
types of these customs. For the harvest festival the
two officiating elders of the Nāgas wash carefully and
put on new clothes.[1] The Greeks put on clean clothes
before worship.[2] Before officiating the Shintō priests
of Japan put on clean garments.[3] It is a precept of
Islām that the clothes and person of a worshipper
shall be clean.[4] A Muhammadan " would remove
any defiled garment before he commences his prayer,
or otherwise abstain from praying altogether." [5] In
ancient Christian baptism the novices put off their
garments, and clothed themselves in new white robes.[6]
At the consecration of a Catholic virgin the novice
puts off her ordinary clothes, and puts on the habit
and the veil; also the ring on the finger—the ceremony being actually a marriage to Christ.[7] The putting
away of the skin dress of the noviciate and the assumption of new clothes were part of the " ordination "
of the ancient Brāhman.[8]

Whether the new state is the extraordinary state
of sacredness or the ordinary state of common life,
adaptation to it equally involves change of assimilative
costume, preceded by removal of that previously
worn. In order to assume the crest of the *Lulem*,
the Bear, the Carrier Indian took off all his clothes,
and spent some days and nights in the woods. On

---

[1] T. C. Hodson, *The Nāga Tribes of Manipur* (1911), p. 172.

[2] E. Westermarck, *op. cit.*, ii. 352, citing the authorities.

[3] W. E. Griffis, *Religions of Japan* (1895), p. 85.

[4] E. Sell, *Faith of Islam* (2nd edition, 1896), p. 257.

[5] E. Westermarck, *op. cit.*, ii. 416.   [6] A. van Gennep, *op. cit.*, p. 135.

[7] J. P. Migne, *Encyclopédie Théologique* (1844-1866), xvii; Boissonet, *Dictionnaire des cérémonies et des rites sacrés* (1846), iii. coll. 539 ff.

[8] H. Oldenberg, *Die Religion des Veda* (Berlin 1894), p. 350.

his return he joined in the Bear Dance, in which he was dressed as a bear. During initiation to secret societies in the Congo States, the candidate is naked.[1] In British Central Africa, boys during initiation wear bark-cloth. At the conclusion new clothes are put on. Entrance to the various gilds is marked by a change of costume. Girls after initiation put on new calico.[2] When their initiation ceremonies were over, Kaffir boys were chased to the river, where they washed off the white clay with which their bodies had been painted. Everything about them was burned. They were smeared with the ordinary unguent and were given new karosses.[3]

Frazer has suggested that the practices of depilation, and painting the body white or red, at puberty, are in view of the belief in re-birth.[4] The Kikuyu, for instance, hold that a boy is born again at circumcision, and he pretends so to be.[5] But this idea is *ex post facto*.

When her period is over, a woman puts on new clothes. This is the ordinance of the *Shāyast lā-Shāyast*, of the Mosaic and Hindu law, and of the vast majority of savage and barbarian customary social codes. Thus, the Kharwar woman after her period bathes and washes her clothes.[6] The Thompson Indian girl has the special dress she wore during her seclusion at puberty burnt on her re-entry into

---

[1] L. Frobenius, *Die Masken und Geheimbünde Afrikas* (Halle 1898), pp. 69-70.

[2] H. Stannus, " Notes on some Tribes of British Central Africa," *Journal of the Royal Anthropological Institute* (1910), xl. 296, 297.

[3] J. Maclean, *A Compendium of Kafir Laws and Customs* (Mount Coke 1858), p. 99.

[4] Sir J. G. Frazer, *Totemism and Exogamy* (1910), iv. 230.

[5] *Ibid.*, iv. 228, quoting A. C. Hollis.

[6] W. Crooke, in *North Indian Notes and Queries* (1891), i. 67.

society.[1] At the end of the *hiri*, the annual trading expedition, which partakes of the nature of a solemn pilgrimage, the Koita of New Guinea bathes, anoints himself, and puts on a new *sihi*, loin-cloth. His wife, who has stayed at home, also bathes and puts on new garments.[2]

A sort of mechanical link between purification by lustration and the assumption of new clothes is made by anointing. After childbirth the Kaffir mother is anointed ceremonially with the ordinary fat and red clay.[3] This is equivalent to the resumption of decent apparel.

New clothes express a new state or condition. There is an impulse to rhythmical change in human life, coinciding with later ideas of morality. The Incas, at a purificatory festival which was to banish all evil, shook their clothes, crying " Let the evils be gone ! " [4] In such cases the idea of newness, owing to the contrast between the old state and the new and to the impulsive belief in change as producing good fortune, tends to predominate over the principle of adaptation to the new state. In other words, the important thing is not the succeeding state but the riddance of the old. At the Creek festival of new fruits, the *busk*, new clothes and new utensils were provided by each person ; the old clothes were burned.[5] At the Tongan festival of first-fruits all were clad in

[1] J. Teit, " The Thompson Indians of British Columbia," *Publications of the Jesup North Pacific Expedition* (1898-1900), i. 317.

[2] C. G. Seligmann, *The Melanesians of British New Guinea* (Cambridge 1910), p. 10.

[3] J. Maclean, *op. cit.*, p. 94.

[4] Sir J. G. Frazer, *The Golden Bough*, ix. 130.

[5] W. Bartram, *Travels through North and South Carolina, Georgia, East and West Florida* (Philadelphia 1791), p. 507.

new clothes.[1]   The Hindus wear new clothes at the
festival of the new year, *samvatsarādi*.[2]   The Chinese
ceremony of " raising the head " is the putting on of
special clothes for marriage.   A suit of white body-
clothes of linen is made for both bride and groom.
Brand-new they are, and are worn during the marriage
ceremonies, for on this occasion they themselves " become brand-new people."   The suits are then put
away, only to be worn again in the tomb.[3]   In Korea,
on the 14th day of the first month, anyone entering
upon " a critical year of his life " dresses an effigy of
straw in his own clothes and casts it away.   Fate is
believed to look upon the individual in his new clothes
as another man.[4]

Here the secondary principle of disguise intrudes.
Ideas of disguise by change of dress have been developed in many cases.   Thus, in the seventh month
of pregnancy, a Ceramese woman is rubbed with
dough of seven colours.   A new ornamental *sarong*
is placed on her.   This the husband slices in two
with a sword and immediately runs away.   She is
dressed seven times in seven colours.[5]   The Bulgarian,
to cure scrofula, will creep naked through an arch of
boughs, and then hang his clothes on a tree, donning
other garments.[6]   In Uganda a sick man is made to
jump over a stick, and let his bark-cloth fall off.   The
priest takes the cloth and runs in the opposite direction.[7]

[1] W. Mariner, *An Account of the Natives of the Tonga Islands* (2nd edition, 1818),
ii. 197.

[2] J. E. Padfield, *The Hindu at Home* (Madras 1896), p. 192.

[3] J. J. M. de Groot, *The Religious System of China* (Leyden 1892, etc.), i. 47.

[4] W. E. Griffis, *Corea* (1882), p. 298.

[5] A. S. Buddingh, " Gebruiken bij Javaansche Grooten," *Tijdschrift voor
Neêrland's Indie* (1840), III. ii. 241-242.

[6] A. Strausz, *Die Bulgaren* (Leipzig 1898), p. 414.

[7] J. Roscoe, quoted by Sir J. G. Frazer, *op. cit.*, xi. 181.

Often it is enough to follow the principle of the fantastic as a strong contrast to the previous state which has suffered misfortune. Thus, in South Guinea a sick woman is dressed in a fantastic garb, and her body is painted with streaks of red and white. She then stands in front of her hut brandishing a sword.[1] The last detail is a later stratum. The Mosquito Indians believe that the devil (*Wulasha*) tries to seize the corpse. It is hurried to the grave by four men, who have disguised themselves with paint.[2] A Siberian shaman will paint his face red when about to accompany a soul to the spirit-land, expressly to disguise himself from devils.[3] The Tongans, when at war, changed their costume before every battle by way of disguising themselves.[4] Similarly the king of Israel disguised himself at Ramoth-Gilead.[5]

Disguise may take the form of impersonation, and the agent may be a person or a thing. The people of Minahassa delude the evil spirit by placing on the sick man's bed a dummy dressed in his clothes.[6] Abyssinian kings had a sort of small bodyguard who dressed exactly like their royal master. " So that the enemy may not distinguish him " was the reason assigned.[7]

The protective value of dress is often expressed

---

[1] J. L. Wilson, *Western Africa* (1856), p. 28.

[2] H. H. Bancroft, *The Native Races of the Pacific States of North America* (New York 1875-1876), i. 744-745.

[3] V. V. Radlov, *Aus Sibirien* (2nd edition, Leipzig 1893), ii. 55.

[4] C. Wilkes, *Narrative of the United States Exploring Expedition during the Years 1838-1842* (Philadelphia 1845), iii. 10.

[5] 1 Kings xxii. 30.

[6] N. Graafland, *De Minahassa* (Rotterdam 1869), i. 326.

[7] J. L. Krapf, *Travels, Researches, and Missionary Labours during an Eighteen Years' Residence in Eastern Africa* (1860), p. 454.

merely as that of a covering. Thus, when the angel appeared to Muhammad, he hastened to his house, crying, "Cover me with cloth!" Then God spoke to him : "O thou, enwrapped in thy mantle, arise and warn!" From this point the prophet commenced his composition of the Koran.[1] A Hindu mother passing a haunted place draws her robe over her child. In old Bengal there was a prayer for the protection of children till they were dressed in clothes.[2]

In its sexual and supernatural uses alike the veil protects both the face or head from sight and the eyes from seeing the forbidden or dangerous object. To see and to be seen are often interchangeable, and often combined as media of dangerous influences. In early Arabia handsome men veiled their faces to preserve themselves from the evil eye.[3] Here there is no doubt a combination of subjective and objective methods. The veiling of women and the consequent artificial modesty concerning the exposure of the face are a remarkable characteristic of Muslim social life, and illustrate the secondary habits induced by dress. Ceremonial veiling of a temporary nature is found in the case of puberty, marriage, and widowhood. The novice during initiation to the *Ko'tikili* of the Zuñi wears a veil, and is supposed to see nothing.[4] Similar practices attend initiation to many forms of secret society. The veiling of the bride is more or less universal. A Muslim woman takes the veil, just as does a nun. Momentary veiling occurs in the presence of death and in approaching a deity. Socrates

---

[1] E. Sell, *op. cit.*, p. 5.

[2] *Bombay Gazetteer*, xviii. 441 ; H. T. Colebrooke, *Essays* (1858), i. 213.

[3] J. Wellhausen, *Reste arabischen Heidentums* (2nd edition, Berlin 1897), p. 196.

[4] Mrs. M. C. Stevenson, "The Zuñi Indians," *Annual Report of the Bureau of Ethnology* (1904), xxiii. 103.

and Julius Cæsar veiling their faces at the moment of death typified the Greek and Italian national custom. To interpret, as van Gennep does, these latter cases as rites of passage, with the purpose of separating one's self from the profane world, is fanciful.[1] The habit is more probably a motor reaction to the impulse for concealment before an object of fear. The veil of the bride is a ritual concession to, and a material accentuation of, the sexual character of modesty, rather than a rite of separation from the previous state. To apply the idea of separation from the previous state to the habit of veiling at the moment of death is clearly impossible. In the case of many secret societies veiling is probably intended merely to accentuate the sense of mystery.

In connexion with marriage there are customs of stripping or forcible removal of dress. In some cases these seem to point to a diminution of personality, in others they are preparatory to the assumption of a new dress, often presented by the bridegroom. Among the Roro tribes of New Guinea a nubile girl is tatooed and wears ornaments every day. After marriage, for a few weeks she decorates herself every afternoon. She may not visit her father's village until after a ceremony in which she is stripped of all her finery.[2] The idea, no doubt, is to affirm her subjection to her father's family.

The exchange of presents of dress, a prevalent custom at marriage, may be extended. Thus, the Koita of New Guinea hold the *heni* ceremony when a first-born child is three weeks old. The infant

---

[1] A. van Gennep, *op. cit.*, p. 241 ; also S. Reinach, *Cultes, mythes, et religions* (Paris 1905-1912), i. 299-311.

[2] C. G. Seligmann, *op. cit.*, pp. 266, 270.

is decked with various finery, and is carried by the mother, also dressed up, to her mother's house. Her husband follows her with an empty pot, a spear, a petticoat, and a firestick. After smoking and betel-chewing, the wife of the child's maternal uncle strips the ornaments and clothes from the mother and the child. These and the articles carried by the father become the property of the *raimu* and the *wahia*, the grandfather and grandmother on the maternal side. A return present is given.[1]

Customs which prescribe the wearing of best clothes or of rags illustrate the most important psychological result of the invention of dress. This is a secondary human character, the feeling for dress, and is one aspect (consisting in extension of self-consciousness) of the reaction to extension of personality. It is really distinct from the feeling for ornament and the impulse to protection, but is correlated with the more physical impulse to cleanliness, and the dermal and nervous refinement which dress has introduced into the human organism. Connected with the latter development are various reactions in the spheres of art and etiquette. As we have seen, Stanley Hall finds that of the three functions of clothes—protection, ornament, and Lotze's self-feeling—the second is by far the most conspicuous in childhood.[2] But the sense of personal dignity and physical pride is only learnt in childhood. Of the psychical resultants of dress this adult character is the most signi-

---

[1] C. G. Seligmann, *op. cit.*, p. 71.

[2] G. S. Hall, " Some Aspects of the Early Sense of Self," *American Journal of Psychology* (1898), p. 366. See also, for the social psychology of dress, George van Ness Dearborn, *The Psychology of Clothing* (The Psychological Monographs, No. 112, Princeton 1918). Mr. J. C. Flügel's important *The Psychology of Clothes* (1930) appears as we go to press.

ficant. As Lotze put it, clothes extend the limits of
self and enable the wearer to feel himself to the ex-
tremity of each garment. A precise analogy is found
in the psychology of tools. Add the sexual factor,
and " the mere presence or possession of the article
[of clothing] gives the required sense of self-respect,
of human dignity, of sexual desirability. Thus it is
that to unclothe a person is to humiliate him ; this
was so even in Homeric times, for we may recall the
threat of Ulysses to strip Thersites." [1]

Similarly, to foul a person's garments is a secondarily
direct insult. When the sense of well-being is at a
maximum, fine dress is an expression of it and an
adaptation to it. Also, on momentous occasions a
man of any period will dress very carefully, unconsciously intending to affirm and emphasize his personality. Conversely, to express misery, the negation
of well-being, or humility, a negative form of dress is
employed ; value, colour, and style are at a minimum.
The diminution of personality is echoed by wearing
rags, sackcloth, or colourless or torn or dirty clothes,
which act as adaptations to the negative state. Momentary diminutions of personality can only be expressed
by partial unclothing or by fouling or tearing the
dress. In both cases the dress or its treatment has
a reaction on the psychical state of the individual.

On these foundations luxury and superstition have
erected a mass of fashions. Two typical cases follow.
Great personages in Siam used to wear clothes of a
different colour for each day of the week. As an
example, white was worn on Sunday, yellow on Mon-
day, green on Tuesday, red on Wednesday, blue on
Thursday, black on Friday, violet on Saturday. [2]

[1] H. H. Ellis, *Studies in the Psychology of Sex*, i. 40 ; *Iliad*, ii. 262.
[2] Mgr. Pallegoix, *Description du royaume Thai ou Siam* (Paris 1854), i. 319.

The primary meaning of the dress next cited is not talismanic, but a suggestion of well-being. Its magical content is secondary, and it is therefore considered here particularly. The Chinese *siū i*, " the garment for a long life," is a long gown of valuable silk, blue or red-brown, with a lining of bright blue. It is embroidered all over with gold-thread characters, representing the word "longevity." " It purports, in the first place, to prolong the life of the owner, who therefore frequently wears it, especially on festive occasions, in order to allow the influences of longevity, created by the many characters wherewith it is decorated, to work their full effect upon his person. On the anniversary of his birth he will scarcely ever neglect doing so, it being generally acknowledged among the Chinese that it is extremely useful and necessary then to absorb a good amount of vital energy, in order to remain hale and healthy during the ensuing year. Friends and kinsmen who throng the house to take part in the festivities will then, as a rule, greatly admire the dress and tender their reiterated congratulations to the happy wearer, whose children have been so filial, and so blessed by fate as to have bestowed a present of such delicate and precious description." The longevity garment is generally the gift of children who are filial enough to wish their parent to live long. There is considerable ceremony about the presentation. The garment should be made if possible in a year which has an intercalary month ; such a year naturally has an influence on length. In accordance with Chinese ideas about sympathy between ascendants and descendants, the garment also ensures long life to its wearer's posterity.[1]

---

[1] J. J. M. de Groot, *op. cit.*, i. 61 ff.

In hunting, as in war, the human impulse is to emphasize personality. This is more powerful than the impulse to protection, though the two may be combined. The Dayaks wear as war-dress a basket-work hat, *katapu*, and a jacket of skin or quilted cotton. The crown of the helmet is adorned with feathers or full plumes. The *gagong*, or war-jacket of skin, has the animal's face on the wearer's stomach and its back hanging over his shoulders. It is little defence, though the head is covered with a plate or shell to protect the pit of the stomach.[1]

The mere fact that in all periods social meetings are the occasion for the wearing of best clothes indicates the social significance of dress. Dress loses half its meaning except in relation to society. The principle of extension of personality refers to the individualistic aspect of dress ; the principle of adaptation to state is its social side. The vaguely termed " festival " of lower cultures is expressive of mutual well-wishing and of common well-being. At festivals the Ainus dress in their best clothes. The statement applies to all peoples. The individualistic form of the social meeting is amphitryonic. As is the rule with all peoples, the Guiana Indian, " when expecting guests, grooms himself carefully and puts on his best dress and ornaments, these often, as in this case, consisting only of a narrow waist-cloth by way of dress and of a necklace and armlets of white beads by way of ornament." [2]

A few types of festal dress may be cited from a

---

[1] Low-Roth, " The Natives of Borneo," *Journal of the Anthropological Institute* (1893), xxii. 53.

[2] Sir E. F. Im Thurn, " Anthropological Uses of the Camera," *Journal of the Anthropological Institute* (1893), xxii. 190.

variety which exceeds all other forms of human in-
ventiveness—a fact which illustrates both man's
physical pride and his tendency to shift its focus to
an artificial and variable substitute. The Manipuri
festal head-dress is remarkable. " A white turban
is bound tightly round the head, and over the top
and in front is wound round a *shumzil*, a horn-shaped
construction of cane bound over with cloth or gold
braid, and ending above in a loop and below in three
flat loops which are concealed under the turban. The
shumzil is over a foot high, and curves slightly back-
wards ; from the loop at its end hangs an embroidered
streamer. On each side of the head a plume made
of peacocks' feathers and the tail feathers of the horn-
bill are inserted in the turban. . . . The whole
structure is bound together by a narrow band of red
and white embroidery, wound round and round and
tied under the chin, with ends hanging down nearly
to the waist." [1] On high days Tangkhul men wear
a kilt, and the *luhup* head-dress adorned with toucan
feathers and tresses of hair.[2] The Woolwa Indians
wear on festal occasions coronets made of the curly
head-feathers of the curassow, and on the arms, feathers
of the macaw, or yellow tail-feathers of the *Ostinops
montzuma*.[3] The women wear great masses of beads
round the neck, sometimes occupying the whole space
from the bosom to the chin. A petticoat of bark-
cloth extends below the knee ; it is wrapped round
the loins, and the end is tucked in over the hip.

[1] J. Shakespear, " Notes on the Iron Workers of Manipur and the Annual
Festival in honour of the special Deity Khumlangba," *Journal of the Anthropological
Institute* [1910], xl. 353-354.

[2] T. C. Hodson, *The Nāga Tribes of Manipur* (1911), p. 22.

[3] H. A. Wickham, " Notes on the Soumoo or Woolwa Indians, " *Journal of the
Anthropological Institute* (1895), xxiv. 203.

The exposed parts of the skin are dyed a deep vermilion, the colour being extracted from the pod of the *arnotto* shrub.[1]

The Ackawoi wear for festivals a dress made of the bright, greenish-yellow, young leaves of the Aeta palm (*Mauritia flexuosa*). The Macusi wear a head-dress of bright parrot and macaw feathers, a ruff of black curassow and white egret feathers, and a strip of waist-cloth, as a dancing dress.[2] At the feasts of the dead, Quoireng men wear a " glory." This consists of bands of yellow and red thread, $1\frac{1}{2}$ inches wide, bound round the head. In them are fixed rays of bamboo with feathers inserted, the structure being 18 inches in height.[3]

The negroes of Jamaica hold annually the so-called John Canoe festival. The chief element of this appears to be the dressing-up enjoyed by the participants. The dancers wear painted masks " with slits for the eyes and mouth, white cotton gloves and stockings and white shoes, short, brightly coloured cotton drawers, edged with lace, and a jacket of printed cotton (the favourite colour is a particularly bright rose pink), with a bustle behind and in front." [4]

A notable feature of the South Slav celebration of the festival of St. John is the costumes then worn by the people. Some wear " long, white frieze coats, with white or beautifully worked kerchiefs folded somewhat like those of Italian peasants, and a long white shirt that was often deep with finest openwork at the bottom, sometimes in points of colour, tassels,

---

[1] H. A. Wickham, " Notes on the Soumoo or Woolwa Indians," *Journal of the Anthropological Institute* (1895), xxiv. 204.

[2] Sir E. F. Im Thurn, *op. cit.*, xxii. 195.   [3] T. C. Hodson, *op. cit.*, p. 26.

[4] E. A. Clarke, " The John Canoe Festival in Jamaica," *Folk-lore* (1927), xxxviii. 72.

and pailettes." Others put on "short brown coats of stiff, thick material, elaborately and boldly embroidered in thick circles of green, red, and blue."[1]

The dance is a social language, a motor expression of individuality in society. As a rule, best clothes are worn. Various circumstances often impose different fashions. For ceremonial dancing the Vedda puts on the *hangala*, a white cloth tied round the waist. Formerly leaf-girdles were used.[2] Probably such costumes are merely for the facilitation of movement. In other cases regard is paid to the dance as such. The female dancing dress of the Fulas is elaborate, made of velvet or ornamental cloth, sometimes decked with bells which sound in time to the music.[3]

Meetings of society in its magical or spiritual character are no less marked by fine clothes. The Koran says: "Wear your goodly apparel when ye repair to my mosque."[4] The injunction applies to all religions, with the limitation (due to the difference between well-willing and well-being, and later to the distinction between worshippers and deity) that excess of luxury is forbidden or discouraged. Cleanliness of attire is regularly enjoined, originally, perhaps, for the avoidance not of defilement, material or supernatural, but of mixture of states.

Just as all sacrifice should be precious, so should a dress-wearing victim be well dressed. The human victim sacrificed by the Pawnees was dressed in the richest raiment.[5] The *meriah* of the Khonds was

---

[1] Mrs. N. Huxley Roller, "Notes on some South Slav Beliefs and Festivals," *Folk-lore* (1926), xxxvii. 67, 68.

[2] C. G. and B. Z. Seligmann, *The Veddas* (1911), p. 213.

[3] G. F. Scott Elliot, "Some Notes on Native West African Customs," *Journal of the Anthropological Institute* (1894), xxiii. 81.

[4] *Koran, Sūra,* vii. 29.   [5] Sir J. G. Frazer, *The Golden Bough,* vii. 238.

dressed in a new garment before the sacrifice, anointed, and adorned with flowers.[1] For scapegoats the case may be different. When the image of the god is clothed it necessarily wears the richest raiment (see below).

The connexion of fine dress with well-being, and the estimate of clothing as a necessary of existence,[2] are combined in the Hebrew belief that Jahweh was the ultimate donor of food and raiment.[3] The teaching of Christ against " taking thought " for raiment, illustrated by the natural dress of the lilies of the field,[4] was a wise protest against extravagance in the cult of this secondary body, and a timely rehabilitation of the body itself, no less than of the higher claims of personality.

Diminution of personality is symbolized by various customs of removing part of the dress. In India a low-caste man passing through a high-caste street must take off shoes and turban.[5] That the reason for such uncovering is not the assumption of an unprotected state, by removing a garment of defence, is shown by such a case as the following. All persons when interviewing Montezuma put off their usual costume and " appeared in plain coarse dresses and bare-footed." [6] The modern European fashion of removing the hat is a salutation of respect of a similar order, and not a removal of defence.

A permanent inferiority of person or status is expressed by inferiority of dress. " In Flores the sons even of rich families are dressed like slaves at public

---

[1] S. C. Macpherson, *Memorials of Service in India* (1865), p. 118.

[2] See Isaiah iii. 7.   [3] Genesis xxviii. 20-21.   [4] Matthew vi. 25 ff.

[5] J. Padfield, *The Hindu at Home* (Madras 1896), p. 73.

[6] E. J. Payne, *History of the New World called America* (Oxford 1892-1899), ii. 495.

feasts, so long as the father lives, as also at his funeral. This . . . is apparently the external sign of a strict *patria potestas*, which remains in force till the funeral ; until then the son is the father's slave." [1]   It is a very marked custom of the Mpongwe for the young to show deference to the old.   " They must never come into the presence of aged persons or pass by their dwellings without taking off their hats, and assuming a crouching gait." [2]

An artificial assumption of humility may be employed to emphasize the succeeding magnificence, or to deprecate the ill-luck which may follow pride. For some days before marriage the bride and bridegroom among the Muslims of the N.W. Provinces wear dirty clothes.[3] Such practices may soon take on the ideas connected with disguise and protection from the evil eye. Similar, though of more obscure origin, is the custom, found in old English coronation ceremonies, that the king shall appear in poor garments before he is invested with the royal robes. German peasants dress a child in mean clothes to protect it against the evil eye.   In Egypt the children who are most beloved are the worst clad. A fine lady may often be seen in a magnificent dress, with a boy or girl, her own child, by her side, with its face smeared with dirt, and wearing clothes which look as if they had not been washed for months. The intention is to avoid attracting the evil eye. The method employed is not disguise, but humiliation, negation of well-being, either deprecatory or to escape notice.

---

[1] E. Westermarck, *The Origin and Development of the Moral Ideas* (2nd edition, 1917), i. 602, quoting von Martens.

[2] J. L. Wilson, *Western Africa* (1856), pp. 392-393.

[3] W. Crooke, in *Panjab Notes and Queries* (1886), ii. 960.

The evil eye is stimulated by finery and splendour, and its constant emotion is envy.[1]

Penance and asceticism often coincide in method. Sackcloth is in this connexion the analogue of fasting and humiliation. For penance, Manu prescribes clothes of cow-hair, with the wearer's own hair in braids.[2] Among the rules of penance in mediæval Christendom was the wearing of dirty clothes.[3] An ancient rule for Buddhist monks was that their dress should be made of rags taken from a dust-heap.[4] Early Christian ascetics disdained clothes, and crawled abroad " like animals covered only by their matted hair." [5] Hindu ascetics similarly practised nudity as the least of their mortifications, " until British law interposed to prevent the continuance of the nuisance." [6]

A curious question is raised by certain fashions of cleanliness in connexion with dress. Physical cleanliness is a habit which has undergone evolution, and the fact perhaps suffices as an explanation for the following cases. The ancient Huns and Mongols, and the modern Kalmuks are reported to avoid the washing of their clothes—in the last case, apparently, for religious reasons.[7] The Sūdras of the Carnatic never leave off a suit of clothes when once it has been put on. It drops off as it rots. The custom is said to have been religiously observed, and persons transgressing

---

[1] H. H. Ploss, *Das Kind* (Leipzig 1876), i. 134 ; W. E. Lane, *An Account of the Manners and Customs of the Modern Egyptians* (1846), i. 60.

[2] *Sacred Books of the East* (1886), xxv. 449.

[3] E. Westermarck, *op. cit.*, ii. 356.

[4] H. Kern, *Manual of Indian Buddhism* (Strassburg 1896), p. 75.

[5] W. E. Lecky, *History of European Morals* (1890), ii. 108.

[6] Sir M. Monier-Williams, *Brāhmanism and Hindūism* (4th edition, 1891), p. 395.

[7] K. F. Neumann, *Die Völker des südlichen Russlands* (Leipzig 1847), p. 27 ; J. Georgi, *Russia* (1780-1783), iv. 37.

it and found changing garments before the old set was thoroughly decayed were excluded from the caste.[1] Jenghiz Khan ordered clothes to be worn till they dropped off in tatters. The wearing of clothes in this way is recorded of several peoples. Cold climates encourage such habits.[2] " Poverty," says Wester- marck, " is for obvious reasons a cause of uncleanliness ; ' a starving vulture neglects to polish his feathers, and a famished dog has a ragged coat.' "[3] Cleanliness, again, is frequently a class distinction. Among the Point Barrow Eskimo, as amongst many modern European nations, the poorer people are often careless about their clothes and persons, whereas " most of the wealthier people appear to take pride in being neatly clad."[4] Peoples who are much addicted to bathing are not on that account necessarily cleanly in habits of toilet and dress. The Californian Indians are fond of bathing, but are very uncleanly about their lodges and their clothes.[5] The case of the Australian native, who never takes off his girdle of hair, is rather different ;[6] the analogy here is the non-removal of such articles as rings. Thus, while her husband is alive no Masai woman dares to take off her ear-rings, which are part of the symbols of marriage.[7]

Ideas of ceremonial cleanliness have probably had

---

[1] Dubois-Beauchamp, *Hindu Manners, Customs, and Ceremonies* (Oxford 1897), p. 20.

[2] E. Westermarck, *op. cit.*, ii. 349 ff.

[3] *Ibid., loc. cit.*, quoting B. St. John, *Village Life in Egypt* (1852), i. 187.

[4] J. Murdoch, " Ethnological Results of the Point Barrow Expedition," *Annual Report of the Bureau of Ethnology* (1892 for 1887-1888), ix. 421 ; E. Westermarck, *op. cit.*, ii. 350.

[5] S. Powers, *Tribes of California* (Washington 1877), p. 403.

[6] P. W. Basset-Smith, " The Aborigines of North-West Australia," *Journal of the Anthropological Institute* (1894), xxiii. 327.

[7] A. C. Hollis, *The Masai* (Oxford 1905), p. 283.

an important collateral influence upon the evolution
of habits of cleanliness. Some such idea as the avoidance of mixture of condition and environment may
account for the origin of ceremonial purity, whereas
during the early stages of the evolution of dress there
seems to be no *a priori* reason why clothes, as such,
should be periodically cleaned. The case of the
Sabæans illustrates the connexion between cleanliness of dress and of person. The candidate for the
priestly office is instructed not to dirty himself; and
he must change his dress daily.[1] Given the existence
of a natural impulse to personal and other cleanliness,
its foundation being similar to that of ceremonial
purity—an unconscious preference for clearness and
distinctness in objects, a preference for the thing
itself in its essential, specific, and individual, or unmixed, purity of character—asceticism, when, as is
often the case, encouraging uncleanliness, is a biological
perversion and a social danger. Early Christianity
was largely tainted with this.[2] St. Jerome approves
the observation of Paula, that " the purity of the body
and its garments means the impurity of the soul." [3]

The ritual and emotional removal or tearing of
dress is apparently derived from several motives. The
Hebrew widow repudiating the levirate takes off her
sandal and spits on the ground.[4] In van Gennep's
terminology this is a rite of separation from the
husband's family. Among the ancient Arabs, women
when mourning not only uncovered the face and
bosom, but also tore all their garments. The messenger who brought bad news tore his garments. A

---

[1] N. Siouffi, *Études sur la religion des Soubbas* (Paris 1880), pp. 68-69.
[2] See H. H. Ellis, *Studies in the Psychology of Sex*, iv. ch. 4.
[3] *Ep.* cviii. 713.   [4] " Haliẓah," *Jewish Encyclopædia*.

mother desiring to bring pressure to bear on her son took off her clothes. "A man to whom vengeance was forbidden showed his despair and disapproval . . . by raising his garment and covering his head with it, as was done in fulfilling natural necessities." [1] Among the Chuwashes, Cheremiss, and Wotyaks the husband effects divorce by tearing his wife's veil.[2] Similar customs, especially the rending of the garments to express indignation or repudiation, were prevalent among the Hebrews. The British Columbian expresses indignation against a wrong by destroying a number of blankets, the native currency. His adversary is expected to destroy an equal number to satisfy honour and heal the quarrel.

The rending of garments is perhaps a development from the reflex impulse to destruction generated by anger, indignation, or despair. When it becomes symbolic it may take on the character of a rite of separation, the rending of the garment indicating the severance of a tie or the isolation of the person from calamity or injury. In the Hebrew custom the latter seems to be the prevailing meaning of the rite—a meaning which might naturally be superposed upon an original unconscious reaction to emotions of resentment or sorrow. Stripping, as an indignity or penance, is applied to any person. Thus when his guardian-spirit fails to please him, the Eskimo will strip it of its garments.[3]

---

[1] J. Wellhausen, *Reste arabischen Heidentums* (2nd edition, 1897), pp. 195-196.

[2] J. Georgi, *op. cit.*, i. 42.

[3] L. M. Turner, "Ethnology of the Ungava District, Hudson Bay Territory," *Annual Report of the Bureau of Ethnology* (1894 for 1889-1890), xi. 194.

(e) Dress of the Dead

Like other states, death is marked and solemnized by a change of dress. In modern civilization, the corpse, whether embalmed or not, is swathed or loosely wrapped in linen or cotton cloths, and covered with the garment, if any, most typical of the dead person's official position. In particular cases, customs like that of placing the busby on the coffin involve the idea that official dress is more than individual personality, a special covering representing specialized social functions, whereas lay garments represent generalized.

Among earlier peoples it is the general rule to dress the dead person in his best clothes. Typical cases are the American Indians,[1] Burmans,[2] Tongkingese,[3] Maoris,[4] Greeks,[5] and Chinese.[6] Careful washing and scrupulous toilette are no less significant and prevalent parts of the more or less ceremonial investiture of the dead. Among the Tshi[7] and Ewe[8] peoples the dead body is washed, dressed in the richest clothes, and adorned. The Yorubas dress the corpse in the best raiment. The exposed parts of a woman's body are dyed red. The body is

---

[1] H. R. Schoolcraft, *Historical and Statistical Information respecting the History, Condition, and Prospects of the Indian Tribes of the United States* (Philadelphia 1851-1860), ii. 68 ; H. H. Bancroft, *The Native Races of the Pacific States of North America* (New York 1875-1876), i. 86 ; J. F. Lafitau, *Moeurs des sauvages amériquains* (Paris 1724), ii. 389.

[2] Shway Yoe [Sir J. G. Scott], *The Burman* (1896), ii. 338.

[3] Sir J. G. Scott, *France and Tongking* (1885), p. 97.

[4] R. Taylor, *Te ika a Maui* (2nd edition, 1870), p. 218.

[5] *Folk-lore Journal* (1884), ii. 168-169.

[6] Sir J. G. Frazer, " Certain Burial Customs as illustrative of the Primitive Theory of the Soul," *Journal of the Anthropological Institute* (1886), xv. 75, 86.

[7] A. B. Ellis, *The Tshi-speaking Peoples of the Gold Coast of West Africa* (1887), p. 237.

[8] *Ibid.*, *The Ewe-speaking Peoples of the Slave Coast of West Africa* (1890), p. 157.

wrapped, not in clothes, but in grass mats.[1]   Among
the Koita of New Guinea the dead man is washed,
oiled, and painted ; a new loin-cloth and ornaments
are put on him.[2]   The Malays shroud the dead body
in fine new *sarongs*, sometimes as many as seven.[3]   The
Greenlanders undress a man when at the point of
death, and put his best clothes upon him.[4]   This detail recurs in China.   The Hindus wash, shave, and
dress the corpse in rich garments.[5]

According to Homer, the corpse was covered with
a soft cloth, over which a white robe was placed.[6]   The
Greek dead were shrouded in the handsomest garments
the family could afford ; there was an idea of keeping
them warm on the passage to Hades, and of preventing
Cerberus from seeing them naked.[7]   The modern
Greeks dress the dead in best clothes, but these are
rendered useless by being snipped with scissors or
drenched with oil.[8]

The grave-clothes of a Chinese are arranged round
his dying bed.   His boots are by his feet, his hat by
his head, and so on.   He rejoices in his last moments
of consciousness, " that he will be fashionably attired
in the regions beyond the grave."   It was the old
custom to strip the man of his clothes just before
expiring, and to put the new clothes on, if possible,
before death actually occurred.[9]   The Chinese ritual
of dressing the dead is most elaborate.   The curious

[1] A. B. Ellis, *The Yoruba-speaking Peoples of the Slave Coast of West Africa*
(1894), pp. 156, 158.

[2] C. G. Seligmann, *The Melanesians of British New Guinea* (Cambridge 1910),
p. 159.

[3] W. W. Skeat, *Malay Magic* (1900), p. 397.

[4] D. Cranz, *The History of Greenland* (1820), p. 217.

[5] Dubois-Beauchamp, *op. cit.*, p. 503.   [6] *Odyssey*, xxiv. 293.

[7] Lucian, *de Luctu*, 10.   [8] *Folk-lore Journal* (1884), ii. 168-169.

[9] J. J. M. de Groot, *The Religious System of China* (Leyden 1892, etc.), i. 6.

point is that the corpse is swathed almost as thickly
as an Egyptian mummy, but in suits of clothes, not
bands of cloth. A distinction is made between inner
and outer garments, the former being specially prepared for wear in the grave, the latter being, as a rule,
a person's best or favourite clothes. Five suits of
garments are forbidden, because the number five is a
synonym of evil.[1] Nine and thirteen are usual numbers. Even numbers symbolize the *Yin* part of
Nature, cold, darkness, and evil, they are therefore
avoided; and odd numbers typifying the opposite
blessings are used.[2] Confucius was buried in eleven
suits and one court dress; on his head was a *chang-fu*
cap. But, in accordance with the ancient division
of the dressing into three stages, the body-clothes, the
" slighter " dressing, and the " full " dressing,[3] the
eleven suits comprised the first stage only, and over
them were the " slighter " and the " fuller " dressings.[4]
The clothes are exhibited to those present before each
suit is put on, and the very elaborate rules of the *Li-ki*
about the dressing of the dead are followed.[5] Previously the best or favourite suit is placed round the
dying man. Before being placed on the corpse, the
clothes are put on the chief mourner. He is stripped,
and stands on a tray resting on a chair, " so as not to
pollute the earth " ; he wears a large round hat, " so
as not to pollute heaven." Then each garment is
put upon him in its proper order and afterwards
taken off and put on the corpse. In the case of a
woman, the eldest son, as chief mourner, still has to
put the clothes on.[6] The *Li-ki* explains the custom

---

[1] J. J. M. de Groot, *The Religious System of China* (Leyden 1892, etc.), i. 64.
[2] *Ibid.*, i. 65. [3] *Ibid.*, i. 338-339. [4] *Ibid.*, i. 339.
[5] *Ibid.*, i. 341. [6] *Ibid.*, i. 67-68.

by the analogy of a dutiful son testing a medicine before his father drinks it.[1] As the dressing proceeds the mourners wail and "howl."[2] Wide drawers, lined, for comfort, with silk, are first put on. Stockings and a jacket follow. An ordinary jacket of linen, cotton, or silk, and trousers of the same material come next. A second jacket or even a third—the more there are the more devotion is expressed—may be added. When the body-clothes have been put on, the outer suits follow. The long blue gown of the middle class is a common type. It overlaps to the right, and is buttoned at the side. Over this is a jacket with short sleeves, extending, that is, only to the finger-tips; it is the kind of jacket used in winter as an overcoat. A common skull-cap of silk or horse hair, ordinary shoes and stockings, complete the suit. The costly silk clothes used on festive occasions are preferred by those who possess them. They represent the true sacerdotal attire of the paterfamilias, as high priest of the family.[3] These include an outer and an inner cloak, neither having a collar; the sleeves of the inner cloak project, and are of a horse-hoof shape. The inner is dark blue; for summer wear, white or yellow; the outer is dark blue or brown. A sash is worn round the waist. The boots are of silk. The winter suit alone is used for the dead, even in summer. Women wear their best embroidered clothes, such as the official dress of mandarins' wives, which is the regular bridal costume. It includes a dragon petticoat of green silk, a dragon mantle of red silk, a mantilla of black silk, and boots of red silk. The bride's hood, or phœnix cap, is a quarter-globe of thin twined wire,

---

[1] J. J. M. de Groot, *The Religious System of China* (Leyden 1892, etc.), i. 68.
[2] *Ibid.*, i. 67.   [3] *Ibid.*, i. 46 ff., 49.

covered with butterflies, leaves and flowers of thin
gilt copper, and symbols of felicity, joy, wealth, and
longevity. Great care is taken with the coiffure.[1]

Such is the *tho phao*, attire of the dead. Women,
as a rule, wear the "longevity garment," but men
prefer the true "sacrificial" robes, the *tho phao*.[2]
One prepares them, "the clothing laid out for old
age," at about the age of fifty or sixty. They are
preferably cut out and sewn by a very young woman,
such a person being likely to live long, and part of her
capacity to live "must surely pass into the clothes,
and thus put off for many years the moment when
they shall be required for use."[3]

If these clothes have ever been lent to a friend, not
of one's own clan, they may not be used for their
chief purpose. Another suit must be prepared.
However it may happen, it is a curious fact that the
grave-clothes are often cut carelessly, and merely
pasted, not sewn.[4] Quite poor people use cheap mats.
It is probably Buddhist influence that forbids the use
of leather. Metal buttons may not be used, because
metal is supposed to injure the body during de-
composition.[5]

The bandages of the mummy are a development
(for a particular purpose) from the use of the ordinary
garments of life. In ancient Egypt the gods were
invoked to grant clothing to the dead. The bandaging
of the mummy corresponds in its ritualism very much,
for example, with the Chinese dressing of the corpse.
For instance, a sorrowing husband, reproaching his
wife for haunting him, says : " I have given clothes

---

[1] J. J. M. de Groot, *The Religious System of China* (Leyden 1892, etc.), i.
51-54.

[2] *Ibid.*, i. 63.　　　[3] *Ibid.*, i. 60.　　　[4] *Ibid.*, i. 51.　　　[5] *Ibid.*, i. 65-66.

and bandages for thy burial. I have given to be made for thee many clothes." The application of the swathes was " a divine task." In funeral rituals there are the chapters " of putting on the white bandages," " of putting on the green," and " of the light red and dark red bandages." The quantity used was a " measure of the affection of the relatives." [1]

As a type of simpler customs the following explains itself, and is significant for the whole theory of the subject. The Samoyeds dress the corpse in the clothes he was wearing at death, and wrap the whole in birch bark or deer skins. [2]

Rare cases occur where derogatory garments are applied. The Avestan horror of death and its defilement sufficiently explains the following rule. Zoroastrian law ordained " clothing which is useless ; this is that in which they should carry a corpse." In the case of still useful clothing, which had been touched by a corpse, a very thorough and minute process of cleaning was applied. [3]

When preservatives are not applied to the graveclothes, some peoples periodically renew them. The bodies of the Ccapac-Incas were preserved and clothed, new clothes being supplied as required. [4] At stated periods the Malagasy open the tombs of their ancestors, removing the rotten *lambas* and rolling the bones in new ones. [5]

A simpler method is to place changes of raiment

---

[1] A. Macalister, " Notes on Egyptian Mummies," *Journal of the Anthropological Institute* (1894), xxiii. 103, 107, 111.

[2] Jackson-Montefiore, " Notes on the Samoyads of the Great Tundra," *Journal of the Anthropological Institute* (1895), xxiv. 406.

[3] *Sacred Books of the East* (1880), 269.

[4] E. J. Payne, *op. cit.*, ii. 520-521.

[5] T. T. Matthews, *Thirty Years in Madagascar* (1904), p. 202.

in the grave, just as other articles of use are there
deposited. In Vedic times, clothing and ornaments
were placed with the dead for their use in the life
to come.[1] The Chinese place clothes and silk in
the grave, besides the numerous suits in which the
dead man is clothed.[2] Clothing, according to Pahlavi
texts, was to be put upon the sacred cake of the
" righteous guardian spirit "—both for its use in the
other world.[3] The clothing and weapons deposited
in the Kayan grave are of the highest value, no broken
or damaged article being deemed worthy of a place.[4]
On the other hand, many peoples render such articles
useless by cutting or breaking them before deposition ;
and a principle commonly occurs that in this way the
souls of the articles are released (as is the soul from the
broken body of the dead man), and are thus able to
accompany him to the place of the departed.

There is naturally some doubt as to the condition
of the soul in its super-terrestrial home. Thus the
soul of the Mexican, at death, entered the new life
naked ; [5] whereas the soul of the dead Iroquois wears
" a beautiful mantle " when it departs towards the
other world in the west.[6] The ghost is believed by
Africans to wear the white cloth in which the body
was buried.[7] But, as has been seen, the person in the
life to come wears similar dress to what he wore on
earth. There are refinements ; Christian eschatology

---

[1] A. A. Macdonell, *Vedic Mythology* (Strassburg 1897), p. 165.

[2] J. J. M. de Groot, *op. cit.*, ii. 392, 399.

[3] *Pahlavi Texts*, in *Sacred Books of the East*, v. 383.

[4] C. Hose, " The Natives of Borneo," *Journal of the Anthropological Institute* (1894), xxiii. 165.

[5] E. J. Payne, *op. cit.*, ii. 407.

[6] J. N. B. Hewitt, " The Iroquoian Concept of the Soul," *Journal of American Folk-lore* (1895), viii. 107.

[7] Ernest Crawley, *The Idea of the Soul* (1909), pp. 175, 179.

7

in its popular aspects is inclined to invest the blessed with fine raiment and crowns of gold.

As for the meaning behind these customs, there seems to be, as usual, a series of moral strata or psychological layers. Various emotions might be supposed to be in competition as soon as attention was directed to the dress of a man just dead. Other things being equal, and before ideas of contagion on the one hand and of a future life on the other had been developed, principles of property and feelings of sorrow would first come into play, together with the principle of dress as an adaptation to state. Thus the Samoyed type may be one of the earliest. The corpse retains the garments he wore at death. He is prepared for the new state by the protective (both of external and of internal direction) covering of bark or similar substance which takes the place of the coffin.

Sorrow and affection would make the stripping of the corpse an act impossible for relatives. As the various ideas relating to the state of the dead became clearer, regard would be had to the comfort of the dead. No less than the living they must have the two great necessaries, food and raiment. Naïve examples of the idea are numerous. For instance, the natives of New South Wales wrapped the corpse in a rug, for the expressed purpose of keeping the dead man warm.[1] In Voigtland peasants have been known to put an umbrella and goloshes in the coffin, as a protection against the rainy skies of the other world.[2]

Later still there would supervene the idea, of complex origin, that articles in the house of death must be, like the occupant, broken and soulless. One com-

---

[1] J. Fraser, *The Aborigines of New South Wales* (Sydney 1892), pp. 79-80.

[2] J. A. E. Köhler, *Volksbrauch im Voigtlande* (Leipzig 1867), p. 441.

ponent of this idea is perhaps as early as any, namely, the realization that articles of value, permanently deposited in a place by no means secure, and practically known to be unused, should be rendered useless, to avoid robbery and the attendant distressing results of exhumation.

With the custom of dressing the dead in his richest raiment, and in many suits, the problem becomes less simple. First of all, as soon as the social consciousness realizes that death is a social state, and therefore to be solemnized, a change of garb is necessary. What are significantly termed in various languages " the last offices " express this principle, as well as the feelings of sorrow and affection, and the desire to do honour to the dead, as for the last time. In such conditions it is inevitable that the best of everything should be accorded to him. But another factor perhaps is included in the complex psychosis, at least in the earlier stages. This is economic. In early culture, clothes are property. Just as a man's property is called in and realized at his death, so a similar process is universal in mankind. The dead man is still a member of society; and the most personal and most distinctive of his property fittingly remains with him— his personal attire. Equally fitting is it that this item should be of the best, as representing him in the last of his social functions. By a pathetic paradox he is arrayed in his best clothes, as if to assert his personality and to express it in its highest terms, for the last time, though actually that personality is no more.

It is not likely that the dressing in fine clothes to tempt the departing or absent soul to return has any reference in this connexion. The custom of using many suits of raiment, carried to logical absurdity by the Chinese, is one of those problems that elude all rationalism. There is the analogy of the mummy-swathings, which suggests that the suits may be intended as a protection ; there is also an idea of placing on or with the corpse all his available assets. The custom of dressing the dead in their best clothes, as of placing food with them, has been explained by Frazer as originating " in the selfish but not unkindly desire to induce the perturbed spirit to rest in the grave and not come plaguing the living for food and raiment." [1] But the intellectual atmosphere which the explanation assumes is far from primitive or even from early thought. It represents a late, and somewhat abnormal or excessive, development of spiritualistic belief uncontrolled by social custom or dogma, in fact, an anarchic period of individualistic spiritualist licence.

The dress of the dead seems to preserve only in two or three details the principle of adaptation to state. The reason, no doubt, is that affection and other emotions naturally repudiate the physical actuality of that state, and substitute a moral ideal. But the binding of the corpse, or of its limbs, with cords or ropes, and the later swathing with bandages, accentuate the fact that the body is motionless and the limbs quiescent. At a later stage there might intervene the notion that by these means the possibly dangerous activity of the ghost would be checked. But social habits do not originate from such clear-cut rationalistic motives.

Some sporadic customs have probably an original intention that is not dissimilar. The Koreans fasten

---

[1] Sir J. G. Frazer, " Certain Burial Customs as illustrative of the Primitive Theory of the Soul," *Journal of the Anthropological Institute* (1886), xv. 75.

blinkers over the eyes of the corpse.[1] Various objects, coins and the like, are placed on the eyes of the dead by various peoples. Such habits, no doubt, were in origin intended unconsciously to emphasize, to realize by accentuation, the sightless state of the dead. With this intention is combined the necessity—both from subjective reasons of vague fear of the staring eyes, and from the natural though sympathetic impulse to close them—of mechanically depressing the eyelids after death. Possibly the custom of placing a mask over the face of the dead has a connected origin, as supplying, so to speak, like the swathings of the mummy, a permanent dermal surface over that which is destined to decay. The ancient Aztecs,[2] the earliest Greek peoples,[3] the Aleuts,[4] Shans,[5] and Siamese,[6] masked the faces of the dead, particularly of kings and chiefs. In some cases, as those of the Greeks and the Shans, the mask is of gold or silver.

(f) Mourning Dress

The social significance of dress is well brought out in mourning customs, among which it is the most prominent. The variations are innumerable, but the principles involved are fairly clear. A few types only can be mentioned here.

Among the Masai, as mourning, the wife puts off her ornaments, and the sons shave their heads.[7] As mourning, the Andamanese smear themselves with

---

[1] J. Ross, *History of Corea* (Paisley 1879), p. 325.

[2] H. H. Bancroft, *The Native Races of the Pacific States of North America* (New York 1875-1876), i. 93, ii. 606.

[3] H. Schliemann, *Mycenæ* (1878), pp. 198, 219-223, 311-312.

[4] O. Benndorf, *Antike Gesichtshelme und Sepulcralmasker* (Vienna 1878), *passim*.

[5] A. R. Colquhoun, *Amongst the Shans* (1885), p. 279.

[6] Mgr. Pallegoix, *Description du royaume Thai ou Siam* (Paris 1854), i. 247.

[7] A. C. Hollis, *The Masai* (Oxford 1905), p. 306.

clay,[1] ancient and modern Egyptians throw mud on
their heads.[2] In China the near relatives wear a
mourning dress of brown coarse sackcloth.[3] As regards other clothes, white is the colour of mourning.
The Kiñahs of Borneo " wear bark cloth round their
caps (as we wear crape round our hats) to show they
are in mourning." [4] Among the Gogodara a man's
widow " wears an *atima*, or elongated netted cap and
bodice combined, which covers the head and body to
the waist. It is made for her by her sister or nearest
blood female relative. Modified *atima*, in the form
of skull-caps or netted bands to be worn around the
bottom of *diba*, are made by female relatives of the
deceased for his sons, brothers, and other blood male
relatives. *Atima* are woven from two-ply string of
twisted siniwa bark. A widower wears an *atima*, which
covers the head and neck. On his arms above the
biceps, on his legs below the knees, around his neck,
so as partly to cover his back and chest, he wears
tasselled ornaments made of the cortex of the *biani*
tree. These symbols are called *mamaka*. Around his
waist, and so as to reach almost to his knees, he wears
a shirt made of the same material, which is called *bebe*.
His children by the deceased woman, as well as her
male relatives, wear the modified *atima* above described." [5] In other parts of New Guinea, women in

[1] E. H. Man, " The Aboriginal Inhabitants of the Andaman Islands," *Journal of
the Anthropological Institute* (1883), xii. 143.

[2] Herodotus, *History*, ii. 85; Sir J. G. Wilkinson, *Manners and Customs of the
Ancient Egyptians* (1878), iii. 442.

[3] J. J. M. de Groot, *The Religious System of China* (Leyden 1892, etc.), i. 13 ;
J. Doolittle, *Social Life of the Chinese* (New York 1867), i. 134.

[4] Low-Roth, " The Natives of Borneo," *Journal of the Anthropological Institute*
(1893), xxii. 37.

[5] A. P. Lyons, " Notes on the Gogodara Tribe of Western Papua," *Journal of
the Royal Anthropological Institute* (1926), lvi. 342-343.

mourning wear a net over the shoulders and breast.
In some parts men wear netted vests ; in others, " when
in deep mourning, they envelop themselves with a
very tight kind of wicker-work dress, extending from
the neck to the knees in such a way that they are not
able to walk well." [1] The Koita widow wears fragments of her dead husband's loin-cloth, locks of his
hair and bits of his tools, as a necklace. She is painted
black, and wears a petticoat reaching to the ankles.
Over the upper body she has two netted vests, the
outer ornamented with seeds and feathers. A network cap is on her head. This costume is worn for
six months, after which she is relieved of her mourning
by the *robu momomo* ceremony, and the petticoat is
burnt. The widower is also painted black all over.[2]
Among the Roros, a neighbouring people of New
Guinea, bones of the dead are worn by the mourners.
A dead man's jaw is often worn as a bracelet.[3]

The principle of adaptation in colour is well ex-
emplified. The most frequent colours used are black,
white, dark blue, and the natural colours of, as a rule,
cheap and common fabrics. The mourning colour
in Korea is that of raw hemp or string. For a year
the mourner wears the well-known mourner's hat.
Its shape is that of an enormous toadstool, and the
face is completely hidden.[4] Among the Dayaks of
Borneo, white, " as being the plainest and most un-
pretending, is worn in mourning and during out-door

---

[1] J. Chalmers and W. W. Gill, *Work and Adventure in New Guinea* (1885), pp.
35, 130, 149.

[2] C. G. Seligmann, *The Melanesians of British New Guinea* (Cambridge 1910),
pp. 162-166.

[3] *Ibid.*, pp. 719, 721.

[4] H. S. Saunderson, " Notes on Corea and its People," *Journal of the Anthropological Institute* (1895), xxiv. 304, 306.

labour; it is cheap and will wash." Dark blue is the commonest colour for ordinary wear. A white head-dress is often worn in mourning.[1] Women wear as mourning a deep indigo blue *bidang* petticoat.[2] Among the Tlingits, mourners blacken their faces, and cover their heads with ragged mats.[3] Calabrian women put on a black veil at the moment when a death occurs. At sunset it is taken off.[4] Roman women put on black *pallæ* after a funeral. Black clothes as mourning are the fashion in ancient Greece[5] and Italy,[6] modern Greece,[7] and modern Europe generally. White mourning is recorded for Korea,[8] Tongking, China,[9] Siam,[10] in Imperial Rome for women,[11] and in various parts of modern Europe.[12] In old England, white scarves, hatbands and gloves were worn at the funerals of infants and the unmarried.[13] At Singapore a white sash is worn, but apart from this there is no mourning costume in Malaysia.

Mourners among the Tshi people wear dark blue clothes, which they assume as soon as the burial is over.[14] Among the Yorubas a dark blue head-cloth

---

[1] Brooke Low, *op. cit.*, xxii. 36-37.   [2] *Ibid.*, xxii. 40.

[3] F. Boas, *Fifth Report on the Tribes of N.W. Canada* (1889), p. 41.

[4] V. Dorsa, *La Tradizione Greco-Latina negli usi e nelle credenze popolari della Calabria Citeriore* (Cosenza 1884), p. 91.

[5] Homer, *Iliad*, xxiv. 94; Xenophon, *Hellenica*, i. 798.

[6] J. Marquandt, *Privatleben der Römer* (2nd edition, Leipzig 1886), i. 346.

[7] C. Wachsmuth, *Das alte Griechenland im neuen* (Bonn 1864), p. 109.

[8] J. Ross, *History of Corea* (Paisley [1879]), p. 318.

[9] Sir J. G. Scott, *France and Tongking* (1885), p. 98 (S. Baron, " Description of the Kingdom of Tonqueen," *in* J. Pinkerton, *A General Collection of Voyages and Travels* [1808-1814], ix. 698, describes it as ash-coloured).

[10] Mgr. Pallegoix, *op. cit.*, i. 246.

[11] Plutarch, *Quæstiones Romanæ*, xxvi.

[12] J. A. E. Köhler, *op. cit.*, p. 257.

[13] J. Brand, *Popular Antiquities* (3rd edition, 1870), ii. 283.

[14] A. B. Ellis, *The Tshi-speaking Peoples of the Gold Coast of West Africa* (1887), pp. 240-241.

is worn.[1] Among the Ewes of Dahomey blue baft
is worn, or merely a blue thread is placed round the
arm.[2] This fashion is paralleled by the modern
European custom of wearing a black band round the
sleeve. In parts of Germany blue is worn as mourning
by women[3] and in ancient and modern Egypt a strip
of blue is worn round the head by women at funerals.[4]
Widows on the Slave Coast wear black or dark
blue.[5] Anne Boleyn wore yellow for Catherine of
Aragon.[6] Guatemalan widowers dyed themselves
yellow.[7] Sophocles wore grey or dark blue clothes in
mourning for Euripides.[8] Grey was the mourning
colour of the Gambreiotai.[9]

Simultaneous with change of dress are changes
of bodily appearance, especially of the coiffure. The
practice of cutting the hair short as a sign of mourning is extremely common. On the other hand, some
peoples allow the hair to grow long, as the ancient
Egyptians,[10] the Hindus,[11] the Chinese,[12] and the
Jews.[13]

Mourning as a social state is pre-eminently a suspension of social life; society is avoided, work is

[1] A. B. Ellis, *The Yoruba-speaking Peoples of the Slave Coast of West Africa*
(1894), p. 161.

[2] *Ibid., The Ewe-speaking Peoples of the Slave Coast of West Africa* (1890), p. 160.

[3] C. L. Rochholz, *Deutscher Glaube und Brauch* (Berlin 1867), i. 198.

[4] E. W. Lane, *An Account of the Manners and Customs of the Modern Egyptians*
(1846), ii. 257.

[5] P. Bouche, *La Côte des Esclaves* (Paris 1885), p. 218.

[6] J. Brand, *op. cit.*, ii. 283.

[7] H. H. Bancroft, *The Native Races of the Pacific States of North America* (New
York 1875-1876), ii. 802.

[8] A. Westermann, *Biographi Græci* (Brunswick 1845), p. 135.

[9] *Corpus Inscriptionum Græcarum*, ii. 3562.

[10] Herodotus, *History*, ii. 36.

[11] S. C. Bose, *The Hindoos as they are* (Calcutta 1881), p. 254.

[12] J. H. Gray, *China* (1878), i. 286.

[13] J. Buxtorf, *Synagoga Judaica* (Bâle 1661), p. 706.

discontinued, and the mourner generally is under a
ban. The degrees of mourning depend on the degrees of nearness to the dead. The period of mourning is frequently synchronous with the state of death ;
that is to say, it ends when the corpse is thoroughly
decomposed. Throughout early thought there runs
the idea that a person is not absolutely dead until
every fragment of the viscera has disappeared. At
the end of the time the state of ordinary life is re-
entered in the usual way. Thus, the Ewe people
burn their mourning clothes and put on new raiment
when mourning ends.[1] A widow among the Koossas,
at the end of her month of mourning, threw away her
clothes, washed her whole body, and scratched it with
stones.[2] The last detail is probably merely an extraordinary method of purification. The period of
taboo undergone by murderers among the Omahas
might be needed by the kindred of the victim. The
formula employed was, " It is enough. Begone, and
walk among the crowd. Put on moccasins and wear
a good robe." [3]

The prevalent explanations of mourning dress are
based on the fear of the ghost and of the contagion
of death. Sir James Frazer has suggested that the
painting of the body and the wearing of special costumes by mourners are attempts to disguise themselves so as to escape the notice of the ghost.[4] Professor Westermarck is of opinion that " the latter
custom may also have originated in the idea that a

[1] A. B. Ellis, *The Ewe-speaking Peoples*, p. 160.

[2] H. Lichtenstein, *Travels in Southern Africa* (1803-1806), i. 259.

[3] J. O. Dorsey, " Omaha Sociology," *Annual Report of the Bureau of Ethnology*
(1884), iii. 369.

[4] Sir J. G. Frazer, " Certain Burial Customs as illustrative of the Primitive
Theory of the Soul," *Journal of the Anthropological Institute* (1886), xv. 73.

mourner is more or less polluted for a certain period,
and that therefore a dress worn by him then, being a
seat of contagion, could not be used afterwards." [1]
But such customs originate in unconscious motivation. Of course, concealment may be aimed at,
unconsciously. But several considerations place the
theory of disguise out of court. Savage philosophies
seldom hit on correct explanations ; being *ex post facto*,
they are out of touch with origins. But they do
refer to present conscious motives, which again may
not be the underlying primary reason. The motive
of disguise may often be superposed on some original
unconscious motive, but the following case shows that
the opposite may exist. In some of the Central
Australian tribes it is said that the object of painting
the body of a mourner is to " render him or her more
conspicuous, and so to allow the spirit to see that it
is being properly mourned for." [2] Again, the prevalent custom of wearing the clothes or the bones of
the dead is an absolute negation of the principle of
concealment. On animistic theory these appurtenances should attract the ghost.

Sir James Frazer notes that the customs of blackening the face and of cutting the hair after a death are
observed not only for friends but for slain foes, and
suggests that in the latter case the explanation of their
use as being a mark of sorrow cannot apply. They
may therefore, he adds, be explained as intended to
disguise the slayer from the angry ghost of the slain.[3]
The practice of blackening the body with ashes, soot,

---

[1] E. Westermarck, *The Origin and Development of the Moral Ideas* (2nd edition, 1912-1917), ii. 545.

[2] Spencer-Gillen, *The Native Tribes of Central Australia* (1899), p. 511.

[3] Sir J. G. Frazer, *op. cit.*, xv. 99.

and the like is found in America,[1] Africa,[2] New Guinea,[3] Samoa,[4] and very generally throughout the world. The precise reason for the choice of this medium is obscure.

When spiritualism has once become a part of social belief, such views may enter into the complex of current motives without cancelling the deep-seated original motive of the unconscious mind. Mourning dress, for example, may take on the character of a spiritual armour, as a defence against the evil spirits who often act as a syndicate of death, removing and devouring the souls of the living. At a Chinese funeral the grave-diggers and coffin-bearers tie their shadows to themselves by tying a cloth round their waists.[5] A Northern Indian murderer wraps himself up tightly. The Thompson Indian widow wears breeches of grass to prevent attempts at intercourse on the part of her husband's ghost.[6]

Similarly the principle of contagion may be superposed on the primary meaning of mourning costume. Maoris who had handled a corpse were tabooed, and threw away the special rags they had worn, lest they should contaminate others.[7] It is stated of the Greenlanders that, " if they have happened to touch a corpse, they immediately cast away the clothes they have then on ; and for this reason they always put on their old clothes when they go to a burying. In this they

---

[1] J. Carver, *Travels through the Interior Parts of North America* (1781), p. 407 ; H. H. Bancroft, *op. cit.*, i. 86, 134, 173, 180, 206, 288, 370, ii. 618.

[2] Sir H. H. Johnston, *The River Congo* (1884), p. 426.

[3] Chalmers-Gill, *op. cit.*, pp. 36-37, 149, 266, 286.

[4] G. Turner, *Samoa a Hundred Years and Long Before* (1884), p. 308.

[5] J. J. M. de Groot, *op. cit.*, i. 94, 210-211.

[6] J. Teit, " The Thompson Indians of British Columbia," *Publications of the Jesup North Pacific Expedition* (1898-1900), pp. 331 ff.

[7] Pakeha Maori [E. F. Maning], *Old New Zealand* (1884), pp. 104-114.

agree with the Jews." [1] A Navaho who has touched a corpse takes off his clothes and bathes. [2] Such cases fall into line with other extensive groups of ceremonial observances. For example, at an annual festival the Cherokees flung their old clothes into a river, " supposing then their own impurities to be removed." A Maori, before entering a sacred place, which would *tapu* him, took off his clothes. But the earliest peoples, like the Australians, actually cover themselves with, and otherwise assimilate, the contagion of death.

On the other hand, de Groot holds that mourning costume in China originated in the custom of sacrificing to the dead the clothes worn by the mourner. In the time of Confucius it was the custom for mourners to throw off their clothes while the corpse was being dressed. [3] But this view cannot be seriously entertained.

There are several considerations to be adduced by way of leading up to a more probable explanation. The complex of emotions produced by the death of a near relative may be supposed to be in the primitive mind composed of awe, sorrow, and, to some extent, indignation. In later culture the chief component is sorrowful affection, and mourning costume is regarded as a respectful symbol of this feeling. In the next place, the dead and the living together form a special society intermediate between the world of existence and the world of nothingness. [4]

[1] H. Egede, *A Description of Greenland* (1745), p. 197.

[2] J. Menard *in* H. C. Yarrow, " A Further Contribution to the Study of the Mortuary Customs of the North American Indians," *Annual Report of the Bureau of Ethnology* (1879-1880), i. 123.

[3] J. J. M. de Groot, *op. cit.*, ii. 475-476.

[4] A. van Gennep, *Les rites de passage* (1909), p. 211.

Again, the principle of adaptation to state has to be taken into account. This particular social state calls for particular solemnization. Mourning customs (and, in particular, costumes), says Sir James Frazer, " are always as far as possible the reverse of those of ordinary life. Thus at a Roman funeral the sons of the deceased walked with their heads covered, the daughters with their heads uncovered, thus exactly reversing the ordinary usage, which was that women wore coverings on their heads while men did not. Plutarch, who notes this, observes that similarly in Greece men and women during a period of mourning exactly inverted their usual habits of wearing the hair—the ordinary practice of men being to cut it short, that of women to wear it long." [1] The Mpongwes are very fond of dress, but when in mourning a woman wears as few clothes as possible and a man none at all. [2]

This reversal of habit is better explained on the principles we have assumed than on the principle of disguise. Death is a violent break of social life ; sympathetic adaptation to it necessitates an equally violent suspension or reversal of ordinary costume. Such adaptation coincides with sorrow and indignation on the one hand, and with diminution or negation of personality on the other. A number of customs, of which the following is a type, confirms this. When a death occurs, Tshi women tear their hair and rend their clothes. [3] From this it is but a step to the assumption of torn or ragged clothes and a shorn coiffure.

---

[1] Sir J. G. Frazer, op. cit., xxv. 73.

[2] P. B. Du Chaillu, Exploration and Adventures in Equatorial Africa (1861), p. 9 ; J. G. Wood, Natural History of Man (1868-1870), i. 586.

[3] A. B. Ellis, The Tshi-speaking Peoples of the Gold Coast of West Africa (1887), p. 237.

Sorrow and indignation prompt the mourner to tear
and lacerate both his body and his external coverings ;
sympathy with the state so violently induced prompts
him to deny or humiliate his personality ; this motive
is helped by sorrow.   Absence of colour, as in the hue
of black, or apparent absence, as in white, and variations
of these, as dark blue or self-colour in fabrics, are
material reflexes of this motive of self-negation, which
also coincide with the symbolism of colour as light
and life, and of absence of colour as darkness and death.
A particular case is the adoption of an uncleanly
habit.   Dirty clothes, dirty skin, and unshaven face
were the mourning characters of the Romans. The
custom of blackening the face with ashes has perhaps
the same meaning.   In the primitive camp the most
obvious medium for dirtying the person is, not the
earth, but the ashes of the camp-fire, which with
water form, as does coal-dust in coal-countries, a dye
as well as a defilement.

A paradox similar to one already noted is the result of this adaptation to state ; and sorrow, and with
it an equally praiseworthy intention to honour the
dead, are the feelings which produce it.   The dead
man is dressed in his best, arrayed like Solomon in all
his glory ; for the last time his personality is augmented to superhumanity, while his kin temporarily
assimilate themselves to his actual state, socially substitute themselves for him, and practically negate
and cancel their living personality and abrogate their
social functions.

8. NUDITY AND DRESS

When clothing is firmly established as a permanent
social habit, temporary nudity is the most violent

negation possible of the clothed state. Ceremonial nudity is a complex problem, but the idea of contrast, of an abnormal as contrasted with a normal state, may go far to explain many of its forms. At ceremonies of fumigation the Malay takes off his *sarong*.[1] Such cases are no doubt to be explained in the obvious way ; the purificatory influence has more effect when the body is stripped of all coverings. But other examples of the practice are more obscure. In time of drought, Transylvanian girls strip naked when performing the ritual for rain.[2]   In India the practice is regular.[3] To make rain, Kabui men go on the roof of a house at night, and strip themselves of all clothes. Obscene language is interchanged.[4] To induce rain to fall, Ba-Thonga women strip themselves naked.[5] Baronga women, to make rain, strip themselves of their clothes, and put on instead leaf-girdles or leaf-petticoats and head-dresses of grass.[6] At a festival of Sarasvatī, Bengali students danced naked.[7] A Gujarāt mother whose child is ill goes to the goddess's temple at night, naked, or with only a girdle of *nim* (*Melia*) or *asopato* (*Polyalthea*) leaves.[8]

The principle in the above seems to be that a violent change in the course of Nature may be assisted by a violent change of habit on the part of those con-

---

[1] W. W. Skeat, *Malay Magic* (1900), p. 269.

[2] E. Gerard, *The Land beyond the Forest* (Edinburgh 1888), ii. 40.

[3] *Panjab Notes and Queries*, iii. 41, 115 ; *North Indian Notes and Queries*, i. 210.

[4] T. C. Hodson, *The Nāga Tribes of Manipur* (1911), p. 172.

[5] H. A. Junod, " Les conceptions physiologiques des Bantou Sud-Africains et leurs tabous," *Revue d'ethnographie et de sociologie* (1910), i. 140.

[6] *Ibid.*, *Les Ba-ronga* (Neuchatel 1898), pp. 412 ff.

[7] W. Ward, *A View of the History, Literature, and Religion of the Hindoos* (1817-1820), i. 72 ; *cp.* i. 130.

[8] J. M. Campbell, " Notes on the Spirit Basis of Belief and Custom," *The Indian Antiquary* (1895), xxiv. 265.

cerned. It is adaptation to the desired contrast by instituting a contrast in the officiators. The use of obscene language is, like nudity, a break with the habits of normal life. The use of leaf-girdles is probably no survival of a primitive covering, but merely a method of toning down the violence of the extraordinary state. Similarly, the idea of nakedness is often satisfied by the removal of the upper garment only. Ideas of fertility and outpouring as connected with leaves and with the genital organs are probably later.

The whole subject is illustrated by the following. The headman of certain New Guinea tribes becomes holy before the fishing season. Every evening he strips himself of all his decorations, a proceeding not otherwise allowed, and bathes near the location of the dugongs.[1] An Eskimo may not eat venison and walrus on the same day, unless he strips naked, or puts on a reindeer skin that has never been worn in hunting the walrus. Otherwise his eating gives pain to the souls of the walrus. Similarly, after eating walrus he must strip himself before eating seal.[2]

The principle of assimilation to special circumstances is here conspicuous. Possibly in the New Guinea example the later extension of the principle to assimilation by contact is involved.

Dress being, as will be more fully illustrated below, not only essentially a social habit, but one of the most distinctly social habits that have been evolved, the public removal of garments and nudity generally come under the regulation of custom and law. Dress, like other habits, is a second nature, and social inertia

---

[1] R. E. Guise, " The Tribes inhabiting the Mouth of the Wanigela River, New Guinea," *Journal of the Anthropological Institute* (1899), xxviii. 218.

[2] F. Boas, *Sixth Report on the North-Western Tribes of Canada* (1888), p. 584.

may fix it more securely; hence such curiosities of legalism as the pronouncement of Zoroastrian law, that it is a sin to walk with only one boot on.[1]

The sexual instincts of modesty and attraction give life to the idea of dress, and a balance is seldom exactly attained between them and legalism. In modern times the missionary movement has practically corrupted many a wild race by imposing upon them, as the most essential feature of Christian profession, the regard for clothing developed in a cold climate among peoples inclined to prudery and ascetic ideals; hence a factitious sentiment of hypocritical decency. In other races, legalism has evolved similar conditions. In Uganda it is a capital offence to strip naked.[2] In most European countries " exposure of the person " is a criminal offence. The Roman Catholic Church taught, and still teaches in convent schools, that it is wrong to expose the body even to one's own eyes.[3] " Moslem modesty was carried to great lengths, insufficient clothing being forbidden. . . . The Sunna prescribes that a man shall not uncover himself even to himself, and shall not wash naked—from fear of God, and of spirits; Job did so, and atoned for it heavily. When in Arab antiquity grown-up persons showed themselves naked, it was only under extraordinary circumstances and to attain unusual ends." [4] Such ends have been illustrated above.

Such excess of the idea of decency renders still more powerful both the magical and the superstitious use of nudity and also its sexual appeal. In the

[1] *Pahlavi Texts* in *Sacred Books of the East*, v. 287.
[2] F. Ratzel, *History of Mankind* (1896-1898), i. 94.
[3] H. H. Ellis, *Studies in the Psychology of Sex*, iv. 32, quoting authorities.
[4] J. Wellhausen, *Reste arabischen Heidentums* (2nd edition, 1897), pp. 173, 195.

sphere of art it may be the case that peoples accustomed to nakedness, like the Greeks, employ it as a regular subject for artistic treatment, but it does not necessarily follow that it is better understood than among peoples not so accustomed. It lacks the force of contrast. Similarly in the sexual sphere, both natural modesty and natural expansion may be enhanced by the artificial limitations of decency. In this respect dress plays an important part in social biology. By way of showing the contrast, the African and the European conditions may be sketched.

Of the Wa-taveita, Johnston remarks : " Both sexes have little notion or conception of decency, the men especially seeming to be unconscious of any impropriety in exposing themselves. What clothing they have is worn either as an adornment or for warmth at night and early morning." [1] Of the Wa-chaga he observes : " With them indecency does not exist, for they make no effort to be decent, but walk about as Nature made them, except when it is chilly, or if they wish to look unusually smart, in which cases they throw cloth or skins around their shoulders." [2]

Among Englishmen, a race very observant of the decencies of civilization, Herrick is fairly typical. His attitude to sexual dress is thus described by Havelock Ellis : " The fascination of clothes in the lover's eyes is, no doubt, a complex phenomenon, but in part it rests on the aptitudes of a woman's garments to express vaguely a dynamic symbolism which must always remain indefinite and elusive, and on that account always possess fascination. No one

---

[1] Sir H. H. Johnston, " The People of Eastern Equatorial Africa," *Journal of the Anthropological Institute* (1886), xv. 9.

[2] *Ibid.*, xv. 11.

has so acutely described this symbolism as Herrick, often an admirable psychologist in matters of sexual attractiveness. Especially instructive in this respect are his poems, ' Delight in Disorder,' ' Upon Julia's Clothes,' and notably ' Julia's Petticoat.' ' A sweet disorder in the dress,' he tells us, ' kindles in clothes a wantonness '; it is not on the garment itself, but on the character of its movement that he insists ; on the ' erring lace,' the ' winning wave ' of the ' tempestuous petticoat.' " [1]   Herrick, of course, is dealing with the dynamic quality of dress, but its static meaning is hardly less explicit in the English and European mind.

The significance of dress as an expression of the body will be referred to below in the sexual connexion. Meanwhile the general idea thus illustrated may be regarded as the norm in modern civilization. Its opposite or complementary is the increased value given to legitimate nudity. A movement is even proceeding, particularly in Germany, but to a considerable extent in other countries also, for an extension of this individual privilege into a restricted and occasional social habit—the so-called *Nacktheit* movement.

Such tendencies coincide with the twofold attitude towards the human organism which dress has emphasized—regard for the body in itself and regard for its artificial extension. Periodic social phenomena accentuate one or the other aspect. The Spartan practice of nudity in athletics was based on a reasoned theory of health from exposure and of purity from knowledge. The Papuans have been said to glory in their nudeness, and consider clothing fit only for women. Temporary nudity, when in

[1] H. H. Ellis, *op. cit.*, v. 45-46.

obedience to natural impulse, should be regarded not
as a reversion,[1] still less as a survival of a primitive
state, but as a rhythmical movement. The point is
well illustrated by the use of nudity as a love-charm.

9. DRESS AND SOCIAL GRADE

Dress is the most distinctive expression in a material
form of the various grades of social life. The biological period thus becomes a social period of existence,
and the individual is merged in a functional section of
the community. The assumption of a grade-dress is,
whether explicitly or implicitly, *ipso facto* a social rite—
in van Gennep's term, a rite of aggregation.[2]

(a) Childhood

The swaddling-clothes of infants have their analogue in the earliest cultures, in the form of various
modifications of the papoose-system. In this the
reasons of protection and cleanliness are obvious.
After earliest infancy the children of primitive peoples
are quite naked in the warmer climates. Clothing
proper is first assumed either at puberty or at the age
of six or seven. Probably the former date represents
an earlier stratum of fashion. Children, whether
first clothed at the earlier age or not, assume adult
costume at puberty. In the New Hebrides, girls and
boys are naked till five years of age.[3] Among the
Veddas dress is assumed at the age of six or seven.[4]
Children of well-to-do Hindoos are naked till the

---

[1] As Schurr argues, *Philosophie der Tracht* (Stuttgart 1891), p. 48.

[2] A. van Gennep, *op. cit.*, p. 77.

[3] B. T. Somerville, " Notes on some Islands of the New Hebrides," *Journal of the Anthropological Institute* (1894), xxiii. 7.

[4] C. G. and B. Z. Seligmann, *The Veddas* (1911), pp. 90-91.

third year, those of the poor till about six or seven.[1] Running about uncovered, say the Zoroastrian texts, is no sin, up to the age of fifteen; and it is no sin to be without the sacred girdle till that age.[2]

In cold climates, where the constant purpose of dress is protection, differences of juvenile and adult costume may be reduced. For example, Samoyed children " are dressed precisely as their parents, sex for sex." [3]

There is little to notice in the matter of coiffure in the child-stage. Cases like the following are exceptional. Young Nāga children have the hair shaved. When a girl is of marriageable age, it is allowed to grow long.[4]

(b) Maturity

Examples of the ritual assumption of the adult garb may be confined to a few types. In Florida (Melanesia) the male " wrapper " is assumed with some ceremony at the age of six or seven. In Santa Cruz the adult male dress is ample. Its assumption is celebrated by a feast and pig-killing. Big boys whose parents are too poor to give a feast may be seen going about naked. The custom in the New Hebrides is the same, and after assumption the boy begins to be reserved towards his mother and sisters.[5] The Koita boy of British New Guinea receives his *sihi*, loin-cloth, from his maternal uncle, *raimu*, to whom in return

---

[1] Sir M. Monier-Williams, *Brāhmanism and Hindūism* (4th edition, 1891), p. 397.

[2] *Pahlavi Texts*, in *Sacred Books of the East*, v. 287.

[3] Jackson-Montefiore, " Notes on the Samoyads of the Great Tundra," *Journal of the Anthropological Institute* (1895), xxiv. 404.

[4] T. C. Hodson, *op. cit.*, p. 28.

[5] R. H. Codrington, *The Melanesians* (Oxford 1891), pp. 231 ff.

he owes certain services, such as a share of any fish
or animal he kills. The *raimu* makes the cloth, and
puts it on the boy in the presence of the relatives on
both sides of the family, who then eat together.[1] A
similar ceremony of investiture at puberty is practised
by the Roro tribes.[2] The last initiation of a New
Hebrides boy is the investing of the belt. This is a
broad band of nutmeg bark about six inches wide,
encircling the waist twice and confined by a small
strip of plaited grass. " An underneath strip of
grass cloth or calico supports the very scanty clothing "
of the natives. The belt is therefore an ornament,
corresponding to the *toga virilis*, but usually not
attained (from inability to provide pigs for the feast)
until a man is twenty or older.[3] The old Japanese
made a ceremony for the " breeching " of boys and
the " girdling " of girls.[4]

The Hindu *upanayana* is the investiture with the
sacred thread, which renders a man " twice-born,"
and before which he is not, in religion, a " person,"
not, as it were, individualized, not even named. The
thread is of three slender cotton filaments, white, and
tied in a sacred knot, *brahma-granthi*, each of the three
consisting of three finer filaments. It is consecrated
by *mantras*, and holy water is sprinkled upon it. The
wearer never parts with it. As the Catholic priest
changes his vestments, so the Brāhman alters the
position of the thread. When he worships the gods
he puts it over his left and under his right shoulder ;

---

[1] C. G. Seligmann, *The Melanesians of British New Guinea* (Cambridge 1910),
pp. 67-68, 73.

[2] *Ibid.*, p. 256. [3] B. T. Somerville, *op. cit.*, xxiii. 5.

[4] C. Pfoundes, " On Some Rites and Customs of Old Japan," *Journal of the
Anthropological Institute* (1883), xii. 224.

when he worships ancestors, the position is reversed ;
when he worships saints, it is worn like a necklace.[1]
The earliest mention of this sacred cord, *yajñopavīta*,
of the Brāhman, is perhaps in the Upaniṣads.[2]   Worn
over the left shoulder, its position is altered according
to the particular act in which the wearer is engaged.
This *yajñopavīta* is of one skein when put on the
youth : when he is married it must have three, and
may have five skeins.   An imitation cord is put on
first, then taken off and the real one placed in position.
Then the father covers his own head and that of his
son under one cloth and whispers the Gāyatri prayer.
A new cord is put on every year at the festival in
Śrāvaṇa.   If one touches a Pariah, the cord must
be replaced.   The Sannyāsi, having entered the fourth
or last stage of the Brāhman's life, does not wear the
yajñopavīta.[3]   Manu says that the first birth of a
Hindu is " from his natural mother, the second happens
on the tying of the girdle of Muñja grass, and the
third on the initiation to the performance of a Śrauta
sacrifice." [4]   " Birth " in such contexts as the assumption of the adult state is an almost universal metaphor.
In many well-known instances the metaphor itself has
been translated into ritual, as being a convenient and
impressive mode of affirming the change.   But neither
the metaphor nor the idea of re-birth is the ultimate
reason of initiation ceremonies.

The sacred thread-girdle, the *kōstī*, worn by every
member, male and female, of the Zoroastrian faith,
after the age of fifteen, is a badge of the faithful, a

[1] Sir M. Monier-Williams, *op. cit.*, pp. 360-361, 379.

[2] *Sacred Books of the East*, i. 285.

[3] J. E. Padfield, *The Hindu at Home* (Madras 1908), pp. 76-80.

[4] *The Laws of Manu*, ii. 169.

girdle uniting him or her to Ormazd and his fellows. Bread and water were to be refused to all who did not wear it. It must be made not of silk, but of goat or camel hair ; of seventy-two interwoven filaments ; and it should " three times circumvent the waist." The other garment necessary to salvation was the *sudara*, or sacred shirt, a muslin tunic with short sleeves, worn high, not lower than the hips. At its " opening in front " is a pocket, " the pocket for good deeds." When putting it on the faithful looks at the pocket, asking himself whether it is full. Both shirt and girdle are to be kept on during the night, " for they are more protecting for the body, and good for the soul." To wear the girdle is to gird one's loins " with the Religion." [1]

The distinctive garb of the Athenian *ephebos* was the *chlamys*. It was ceremonially assumed. The Roman boy at sixteen laid aside the *bulla* and the *toga prætexta*, and assumed the white toga of manhood, *toga pura* or *virilis*.[2] The page in mediæval chivalry was made a squire at fourteen. At twenty-one knighthood followed, and new white robes were ceremonially assumed, with a satin vest and a leather collar, over the suit of mail. The Nāga kilt is not assumed till puberty.[3] At puberty the Chaco girl is decorated, and for the first time wears the longer skirt of the women.[4]

There are, of course, exceptions to the rule that the assumption of social dress is a rite. Thus the Mekeo tribes have no ceremony in connexion with

---

[1] *Sacred Books of the East*, iv. 72, 193 ; v. 287, 289.

[2] Cp. as to the significance of the several styles, Léon Heuzey, *Histoire du costume antique d'après des études sur le modèle vivant* (Paris 1922).

[3] T. C. Hodson, *The Nāga Tribes of Manipur* (1911), p. 24.

[4] W. B. Grubb, *An Unknown People in an Unknown Land : The Indians of the Paraguayan Chaco* (1911), p. 177.

the assumption of the male band or the female petticoat.[1] Elsewhere the rite involves such usual complications as the following. Before a boy is circumcised the Masai father puts on a special dress, and
lives secluded in a special hut. On his return he
drinks wine and is called "father of So-and-so."
Then the operation takes place.[2] The designation
of the father points to the fact, expressed by the dress,
that fatherhood, as elsewhere, is a special social grade.

In many examples there is a distinctive dress
worn during the marginal stage of initiation, and discarded at the end for the adult dress proper. Thus,
during the initiation of a Kamilaroi youth he was invested with a kilt of wallaby skin, suspended in front
by a girdle. It is described as a "badge."[3] The
West African boy at initiation is naked and smeared
with clay. He may wear a cap of bark, hiding his
face. Often he pretends at the conclusion of the
sequestration to have forgotten everything and to
know nothing.[4] At initiation A-kamba girls wear
goat-skins.[5] The Déné girl at puberty wore "a sort
of head-dress combining in itself the purposes of a
veil, a bonnet, and a mantlet. It was made of tanned
skin, its forepart was shaped like a long fringe, completely hiding from view the face and breasts; then
it formed on the head a close-fitting cap or bonnet,

[1] C. G. Seligmann, op. cit., p. 491.

[2] A. C. Hollis, The Masai (Oxford 1905), pp. 294-295.

[3] R. H. Mathews, "The Bora, or Initiation Ceremonies of the Kamilaroi
Tribe," Journal of the Anthropological Institute (1895), xxiv. 421.

[4] O. Dapper, Description de l'Afrique (Amsterdam 1670), pp. 288-289; M. H.
Kingsley, Travels in West Africa (1897), p. 531; G. Dale, "An Account of the
Principal Customs and Habits of the Natives inhabiting the Bondei Country,"
Journal of the Anthropological Institute (1896), xxv. 189.

[5] C. W. Hobley, The Ethnology of A-Kamba and other East African Tribes
(Cambridge 1910), p. 70.

and finally fell in a broad band almost to the heels. This head-dress was made and publicly placed on her head by a paternal aunt, who received at once some present from the girl's father. When, three or four years later, the period of sequestration ceased, only this same aunt had the right to take off her niece's ceremonial head-dress. Furthermore, the girl's fingers, wrists, and legs at the ankles and immediately below the knees were encircled with ornamental rings and bracelets of sinew intended as a protection against the malign influences she was supposed to be possessed with." [1]

Entrance into the grade of social puberty is generally equivalent to nubility. Among the Tshi-people a girl announces her eligibility for marriage by dressing up and wearing ornaments. She is escorted through the streets, under an umbrella.[2] Infant betrothal complicates this. In the Northern New Hebrides a girl betrothed in childhood wears nothing except on great occasions. When growing up she is clothed, but in the house wears only the *para* or fringe. In the New Hebrides generally clothing and tatooing are a step towards the marriage of a girl.[3] The Nāga youth, however, is nude until marriage. Only then does he assume the loin-cloth.[4]

Frequently a special dress or modification of the adult dress marks a distinction between maturity and nubility. Among the Koita of New Guinea tatooing

---

[1] A. G. Morice, " The Western Dénés, their Manners and Customs," *Proceedings of the Canadian Institute* (Toronto 1888-1889), 3rd ser. vii. 162-163.

[2] A. B. Ellis, *The Tshi-speaking Peoples of the Gold Coast of West Africa* (1887), p. 235.

[3] R. H. Codrington, *op. cit.*, pp. 233, 241.

[4] R. G. Woodthorpe, " Notes on the Wild Tribes inhabiting the so-called Naga Hills, on our North-East Frontier of India," *Journal of the Anthropological Institute* (1882), xi. 209.

is confined to the women. When a girl is engaged, the region between the navel and the neck, hitherto untouched, is tatooed. Just before marriage the V-shaped *gado* is tatooed between the breasts.[1]

The passage from childhood to youth, and from youth to nubility, is often marked by a change in the mode of wearing the hair. As an example, among Nāga women the coiffure is a mark of status.[2] When children, Reharuna girls have their heads shaved, except for the front and a tuft on the crown; at puberty, the hair is allowed to grow, and is worn in chignon-form; when married, they divide the hair into two large plaits hanging down the back; when they become mothers, they wear these plaits over the breast.

(c) Secondary Social Grades

The distinction of dress is carried into all divisions of society that are secondary to the biological. In India the various castes wear clothes differing both in colour and in cut.[3] In ancient times the law was that the Śūdra should use the cast-off garments, shoes, sitting-mats, and umbrellas of the higher castes.[4] All Brāhmans, as all members of each caste, dress alike, except as regards the quality of material.[5] The turban in India, borrowed from the Muslims, is folded differently according to caste.[6]

The chief epochs in military uniform are marked by metal-armour, which, when rendered obsolete by

---

[1] C. G. Seligmann, *op. cit.*, pp. 73, 76.

[2] T. C. Hodson, *op. cit.*, p. 77; E. Doutté, *Merrâkech* (Paris 1905), pp. 314-315.

[3] Dubois-Beauchanp, *Hindu Manners, Customs, and Ceremonies* (Oxford 1897), p. 20.

[4] *Sacred Books of the East*, ii. 233.

[5] Dubois-Beauchamp, *op. cit.*, p. 356.

[6] Sir M. Monier-Williams, *Brāhmanism and Hindūism* (4th edition, 1891), p. 396.

fire-arms, gave place to the other component, splendour or gaudiness; and lastly, in recent years, by adaptation, for concealment, to the colour of the country, a principle which seems to have been anticipated at various times by the adoption of green uniforms for operations in forest countries. Amongst the Nahuas the standing of warriors was marked by distinctive costumes. The sole test for promotion was the capture of so many prisoners.[1] A secondary motive of splendour in uniform is illustrated by the grotesque costumes often worn in barbarism, in order to strike terror into the enemy. The Nāgas wear tails of hair, which they wag in defiance of the foe. The hair of the head is long and flowing and is supposed to be useful in distracting the aim.[2]

The investiture of a knight in the period of chivalry was practically a sacrament, and the arms were delivered to him by the priest.[3] Even in the mimic warfare of the tournament, the armour was placed in a monastery before the jousting began.[4]

The so-called secret societies of the lower cultures have their closest parallel in the masonic institutions. Mediæval gilds and similar corporations, together with the modern club, are, apart from special purposes, examples of the free play of the social impulse. At the initiation to the Duk-Duk secret society of New Britain the novice receives a ceremonial dress; this terminates the process.[5]

---

[1] E. J. Payne, *History of the New World called America* (Oxford 1892), ii. 481.

[2] R. G. Woodthorpe, " Notes on the Wild Tribes inhabiting the so-called Naga Hills, on our North-East Frontier of India," *Journal of the Anthropological Institute* (1882), xi. 209.

[3] E. Westermarck, *The Origin and Development of the Moral Ideas* (2nd edition, 1912-1917), i. 353, quoting authorities.

[4] Sainte-Palaye, *Mémoires sur l'ancienne chevalerie* (Paris 1781), i. 151.

[5] R. Parkinson, *Dreissig Jahre in der Südsee* (Stuttgart 1907), pp. 532-536.

Throughout barbarian and civilized history professions and offices of every kind have followed the rule of a distinctive costume. Various factors in social evolution tend to reduce these differences in Western civilization by an increasing use of mufti on official occasions, but the inertia of such professions as the legal resists this. In the East, on the other hand, European dress invades the ancient culture, but the assimilation is still problematic. To the Mandarin, for instance, his dress is a second nature.

10. SEXUAL DRESS

(a) The Sexual Background of Dress

The most distinctive social division is the permanent division of sex. Up to puberty this is more or less ignored, and the neutral quality of the previous stage is often indicated by the neutral connotation of the term " child," and by a neutral fashion of child-dress. It is natural that the growth and maturity of the primary sexual characters should give these a prominent place in the principles of the distinguishing garb, and that they should, as it were, mould the dress into adaptive forms. The idea of social sexuality is well brought out in the stories of children failing to distinguish girls from boys when nude. The adaptation of the distinctive feminine and masculine garments, skirt and trousers, to the activity of the respective sexes has already been referred to. The main idea of dress as a material expression in a social form of the psychical reflexes from personality, and, in this case, sexuality, has here particular prominence. To regard the affirmation, by means of dress, of primary sexual characters as intended to attract the attention of the other sex by adorning them is a superficial view. Such intention is secondary, though, of course, it has an important social bearing. Goethe's remark is in point for the consideration of dress as an affirmation of personality : " We exclaim, ' What a beautiful little foot ! ' when we have merely seen a pretty shoe ; we admire the lovely waist, when nothing has met our eyes but an elegant girdle."

Special cases of an intensification of sexual characters may be illustrated by the following. A type of female beauty in the Middle Ages represents forms clothed in broad flowing skirts, and with the characteristic shape of pregnancy. " It is the maternal function, . . . which marks the whole type." [1] The type possibly survived in " that class of garments which involved an immense amount of expansion below the waist, and secured such expansion by the use of whalebone hoops and similar devices. The Elizabethan farthingale was such a garment. This was originally a Spanish invention, as indicated by the name (from *verdugardo*, ' provided with hoops ') and reached England through France. We find the fashion at its most extreme point in the fashionable dress of Spain [2] in the seventeenth century, such as it has been immortalized by Velasquez. In England hoops died out during the reign of George III, but were revived, for a time, half a century later, in the Victorian crinoline." [3] It is curious, but not exceptional to the view here expressed—it is, in fact, corroborative of it, because of the necessity of emphasizing feminine characters which is characteristic

---

[1] Marholm, quoted by H. H. Ellis, *Studies in the Psychology of Sex*, iv. 169.

[2] [But cp. A. Souza, *O Trajo popular en Portugal nos Seculos XVIII e XIX* (Lisboa 1924).]

[3] H. H. Ellis, *loc. cit.*

of the class — that this, like most other feminine
fashions in dress, was invented by courtesans. The
crinoline or farthingale is the culmination of the distinctive feminine garment, the skirt, as a protection
and affirmation of the pelvic character.

Augmentation of the mammary character is similar. In mediæval Europe an exception is found in
a tendency to the use of compressing garments. The
tightening of the waist girth is a remarkable adaptation,
which emphasizes at one and the same time the feminine characters of expansion both of the breasts and
of the abdominal and gluteal regions. " Not only
does the corset render the breasts more prominent ;
it has the further effect of displacing the breathing
activity of the lungs in an upward direction, the ad-
vantage from the point of sexual allurement thus
gained being that additional attention is drawn to
the bosom from the respiratory movement thus imparted to it." [1] The development of the corset in
modern Europe has been traced from the bands, or
fasciæ, of Greek and Italian women. The tight
bodices of the Middle Ages were replaced in the seventeenth and eighteenth centuries by whalebone bodices.
The modern corset is a combination of the *fascia* and
the girdle.[2]

In the sphere of masculine dress and the affirmation
by its means of sexual characters, it is sufficient to note
two mediæval fashions. The long-hose which superseded the barbarian trews and preceded the modern
trousers emphasized most effectively the male attribute and social quality of energy and activity as rep-

---

[1] H. H. Ellis, *Studies in the Psychology of Sex*, iv. 172.

[2] Léoty, *Le Corset à travers les âges* (Paris 1893), quoted by H. H. Ellis, *op. cit.*, iv. 172-173.

resented by the lower limbs, the organs of locomotion. The *braguette*, or codpiece, of the fifteenth and sixteenth centuries is an example of a protective article of dress, originally used in war, which became an article " of fashionable apparel, often made of silk and adorned with ribbons, even with gold and jewels." [1] Its history supplies a modern repetition of the savage phallocrypt, and throws light on the evolution of the ideas of dress.

With regard to secondary sexual characters, sexual dress, itself an artificial secondary sexual character, carries on various adaptations. " The man must be strong, vigorous, energetic, hairy, even rough . . . the woman must be smooth, rounded, and gentle." [2] These characters are echoed in the greater relative coarseness and strength of fabric of masculine dress, and the softness and flimsiness of feminine. A somewhat greater darkness of women is a secondary sexual character ; in this connexion a harmony is unconsciously aimed at ; the tendency is for men to wear darker, and women lighter clothes. Women tend to " cultivate pallor of the face, to use powder," and " to emphasize the white underlinen." [3] The attraction of sexual disparity, so important in sexual selection, reaches its culmination in the matter of clothing, and " it has constantly happened that men have even called in the aid of religion to enforce a distinction which seemed to them so urgent. One of the greatest of sex allurements would be lost and the extreme importance of clothes would disappear at once if the

---

[1] H. H. Ellis, *op. cit.*, iv. 159 ; I. Bloch, *Beiträge zur Aetiologie der Psychopathia Sexualis* (Dresden 1902), i. 159.

[2] H. H. Ellis, *op. cit.*, iv. 208.

[3] *Ibid.*, *loc. cit.*, quoting Kistemaecker.

9

two sexes were to dress alike; such identity of dress has, however, never come about among any people." [1]

The assumption of sexual dress at maturity raises the question of the original meaning of special coverings for the primary sexual characters. Their probable origin in an impulse towards protection against the natural environment has been suggested. When dress becomes more than a mere appendage and produces the reaction of an affirmation of personality, its meaning inevitably becomes richer. The decorative impulse and sexual allurement take their place in the complex. But the chief and the distinctively social factor is always that of affirming by a secondary and artificial integument the particular physiological stage which society transforms into a human grade of communal life. This is well illustrated by such facts as the frequent absence of the skirt, for example, until marriage, and, more significantly, until pregnancy or motherhood. In other cases, as in the frequent confinement of sexual covering to the mammary region, the principle is still logically followed. Thus, among many negro peoples, as the natives of Loango, women cover the breasts especially.[2] Nāga women cover the breasts only. They say it is absurd to cover those parts of the body which every one has been able to see from their birth, but that it is different with the breasts, which appear later.

The evolution of sexual dress involves some side issues of thought and custom which are not without significance.

---

[1] H. H. Ellis, *loc. cit.*, iv. 209. On the phenomenon of interchange of sexual dress, see (*c*) and (*d*) below.

[2] Pechuel-Loesche, " Indiscretes aus Loango," *Zeitschrift für Ethnologie* (1878), x. 27.

The harmony between the ideas of sexual dress and its temporary disuse for natural functions is brought out in many customs and aspects of thought. The following is an instance. The Mekeo tribes of New Guinea have folktales of which the motive is that a man surprising a girl without her petticoat has the right to marry her. After any marriage it is still the custom for the husband to fasten ceremonially the bride's petticoat.[1] The ceremonial loosing of the virgin zone embodies similar ideas.

Savage folklore is full of stories connected with disparity of sexual dress. Difference of custom in different peoples leads to comment when coincidences occur. The Dinka call the Bongo, Mittoo, and Niam-Niam " women " because the men wear an apron, while the women wear no clothes whatever, getting, however, daily a supple bough for a girdle.[2] Sexual disparity, natural and artificial, has often led to speculation. Repudiating the sexual element, Clement of Alexandria argued that, the object of dress being merely to cover the body and protect it from cold, there is no reason why men's dress should differ from women's.[3] The Nāgas of Manipur say that originally men and women wore identical clothes. The first human beings were seven men and seven women. " By way of making a distinction the man made his hair into a knot or horn in front ; the woman behind. The woman also lengthened her waist-cloth, while the man shortened his." As a fact the *dhoti*, loin-cloth, is still the same for both sexes, though worn in

---

[1] C. G. Seligmann, *The Melanesians of British New Guinea* (Cambridge 1910), p. 363.

[2] G. Schweinfurth, *The Heart of Africa* (1878), i. 152.

[3] Clement of Alexandria, *Pædagogus*, ii. 11.

different ways.[1] The waist-cloth differentiates in evolution very simply into either *dhoti* or skirt, both being fastened in the same way, and differing only in length.[2] It is probably a similar accident of national fashion that makes the " longevity garment " of the Chinese identical for both sexes.[3]

Spinning, weaving, dress-making, and connected arts have been the work of women until modern times. Before the rise of organized industry, every family was self-sufficing in the production of clothes for its members. Washing and repairing have been also women's work, equally with cookery. In barbarism, as among the Chaco Indians, all the making of clothes is done by the women. The men's large and cumbersome blankets each take four months to weave.[4]

In the lowest stages each adult prepared and looked after his or her attire. As soon as manufacture began with bark-cloth, the preparation of the material devolved upon women, like other sedentary and domestic arts ; but, since the style of the dress depended not upon measurement and cut, but upon folds and draping, women were not actually the makers of dress. In the ancient civilizations the slave-system of industry was applied in two directions. Skilled male artists were employed irregularly by the luxurious ; while the regular method of domestic manufacture came to include dress-making and tailoring. Among the ancient Greeks and Italians the making of clothes was carried on in the house by the female slaves under the superintendence of the lady of the house. This system gradually gave way to external production,

[1] T. C. Hodson, *op. cit.*, p. 15.　　　　[2] *Ibid.*, p. 27.
[3] J. J. M. de Groot, *The Religious System of China* (Leyden 1892, etc.), i. 63.
[4] W. B. Grubb, *op. cit.*, p. 69.

though female attire still retained its claims upon domestic art up to modern times.

In modern civilization the broad distinction of sexual dress has reasserted itself in the sphere of occupation. The dress of men is prepared by men, that of women by women. Special knowledge rendered this inevitable, as soon as cut and shape superseded draping in both female and male attire. But, as in other arts, the male sex is the more creative, and the luxurious women of modern society are largely catered for by male dress-makers.

In the majority of modern nations the care and repair of the clothes of the family is part of the domestic work of women. The washing of clothes is usually women's work. Yet in Abyssinia it is the man who washes the clothes of both sexes, and " in this function the women cannot help him." [1] In the sphere of industry Chinese men provide another exception.

(b) Wedding Garments

The sexual dress is at marriage intensified by the principle of affirmation, not of sexuality, but of personality. It is an occasion of expansion, of augmentation ; as the social expression of the crisis of love (the culmination of human energy and well-being) it is precisely adapted. Often, for example, the pair assume super-humanity, and are treated as royal persons. A special and distinctive dress for the bride is a widely spread fashion. As a rule, the bride herself is supposed to make the dress. With marriage, housekeeping begins, and, as in Norway, Scotland, India, and elsewhere, the bride supplies the household linen, often including the personal linen of the

---

[1] J. Bruce, *Travels to discover the Source of the Nile* (Edinburgh 1805), iv. 474.

husband. The variety of wedding dress is endless. Frequently each family supplies the other.

In North India the bride's dress is yellow, or red—colours which "repel demons." The Majhwār pair wear white, but after the anointing put on coloured clothes.[1]

English brides wear a white dress. So did Hebrew brides. Old English folklore directed that a bride must wear "Something old, something new, Something borrowed, something blue." [2] The Hindu bridegroom supplies the cloth for the wedding robes of the bride. The fact is (see below) that there is among the Hindus, not merely a dowry, but an interchange of gifts; furniture and clothes being the principal components. When presented, the clothes are put on; this forms a preliminary marriage ceremony.[3] The gorgeous flowered embroidery, *phūlkāri*, of the Jāts is prominent in their wedding dress.

Magnificence, generally, is the characteristic of wedding garments throughout the world; white is frequent, as an expression of virginity. Red is often used, as an unconscious adaptation to the circumstances of expansion.

Special garments or specialized forms of garments are less common than " best clothes " and ornament. The Korean bridegroom-elect, often betrothed at the age of five, wears a red jacket as a mark of engagement.[4] On the day before marriage the Roman

[1] W. Crooke, " The Wooing of Penelope," *Folk-lore* (1898), ix. 125-126 ; *id., The Popular Religion and Folk-lore of Northern India* (new edition, 1896), ii. 28 ff. ; *id., Tribes and Castes,* iii. 425.

[2] *Id.,* " The Wooing of Penelope," ix. 127-128.

[3] J. E. Padfield, *The Hindu at Home* (Madras 1908), p. 116.

[4] H. S. Saunderson, " Notes on Corea and its People," *Journal of the Anthropological Institute* (1895), xxiv. 305.

bride put off the *toga prætexta*, which was deposited
before the Lares, and put on the *tunica recta* or *regilla*.
This was woven in one piece in the old-fashioned
way. It was fastened with a woollen girdle tied in
the knot of Hercules, *nodus Herculeus*.[1] In European
folklore an analogue is to be found in the true lovers'
knot, the idea being a magical and later a symbolical
knitting together of the wedded pair. The hair of
the bride was arranged in six locks, and was ceremonially parted with the *cælibaris hasta*. She wore
a wreath of flowers, gathered by her own hands.[2]

Some cases of investiture follow. On the wedding
night the bride of the Koita people is decorated.
Coco-nut oil is put on her thighs. She wears a new
petticoat. Red lines are painted on her face, and her
armlets are painted. Her hair is combed and anointed
with oil, and in her locks are scarlet *hibiscus* flowers.
The groom wears a head-dress of cassowary feathers ;
his face is painted with red and yellow streaks, and
his ears are decorated with dried tails of pigs.[3] The
Hindu at marriage is invested by the bride's parents
with the two additional skeins necessary to make the
full complement of the *yajñōpavīta*, the sacred thread,
of the married man.[4] The Javanese bridegroom is
dressed in the garments of a chief. The idea is " to
represent him as of exalted rank." [5] The Malays
term the bridegroom *rajasahari*, the " one-day king." [6]

---

[1] Whittuck, " Matrimonium," *Dictionary of Greek and Roman Antiquities*
(3rd edition, 1890).

[2] *Ibid., loc. cit.*   [3] C. G. Seligmann, *op. cit.*, p. 78.

[4] J. E. Padfield, *op. cit.*, p. 123.

[5] J. P. Veth, *Java* (Haarlem 1886-1907), i. 632-635.

[6] G. A. Wilken, " Plechtigheden en Gebruiken bij Verlovingen en Huwelijken
bij de Volken van de Indischen Archipel," *Bijdragen tot de Taal-, Land- en
Volkenkunde van Nederlandsch-Indië* (1889), xxxviii. 424.

The dressing up of both bride and groom and all parties present, for the bridal procession of the Minang-kabauers, is very remarkable.

The bridal veil, originally concealing the face, occurs in China,[1] Korea,[2] Manchuria, Burma, Persia,[3] Russia,[4] Bulgaria,[5] and in various modified forms throughout European and the majority of great civilizations, ancient and modern. In ancient Greece the bride wore a long veil and a garland. The Druse bride wears a long red veil, which her husband removes in the bridal chamber.[6] An Egyptian veil, *boorko*, conceals all the face except the eyes, and reaches to the feet. It is of black silk for married and white for unmarried women.[7] Various considerations suggest that the veil is in origin rather an affirmation of the face, as a human and particularly a sexual glory, than a concealment, though the emphasizing of maidenly modesty comes in as a secondary and still more prominent factor. The veil also serves as an expression of the head and the hair. These are also augmented by various decorations.

The wedding dress often coincides with, or is equivalent to, the grade-dress of the married. The *stola* as a badge of lawful wedlock was the distinctive garment of ancient Roman wives.[8] It was an ample outer tunic in design, and possibly is to be identified

---

[1] J. Doolittle, *Social Life of the Chinese* (New York 1867), i. 79.

[2] W. E. Griffis, *Corea* (1882), p. 249.

[3] J. Anderson, *From Mandalay to Momien* (1876), p. 141 ; J. H. S. Lockhart, " The Marriage Ceremonies of the Manchus," *Folk-lore* (1890), i. 489.

[4] W. R. S. Ralston, *The Songs of the Russian People* (1872), p. 780.

[5] S. G. B. St. Clair and C. A. Brophy, *A Residence in Bulgaria* (1869), p. 73.

[6] G. W. Chasseaud, *The Druses of the Lebanon* (1855), p. 166.

[7] E. W. Lane, *An Account of the Manners and Customs of the Modern Egyptians* (1846), i. 52.

[8] " Stola," *Dictionary of Greek and Roman Antiquities* (1890).

with the bridal *tunica recta*. Among the Hereros, after the wedding meal, the bride's mother puts upon the bride the cap and the dress of married women.[1] The "big garment," ear-rings, and the iron necklace distinguish Masai married women from girls.[2]

Further social stages are marked by distinctive dress, such as pregnancy, motherhood, and, more rarely, fatherhood. As soon as a Wa-taveita bride becomes pregnant, "she is dressed with much display of beads, and over her eyes a deep fringe of tiny iron chains is hung, which hides her and also prevents her from seeing clearly." An old woman attends her, "to screen her from all excitement and danger until the expected event has taken place."[3] Among Cameroon tribes is found the custom of girls remaining naked until the birth of the first child.[4] The bride in South Slavonia used to wear a veil until the birth of the first child.[5] When the birth of twins takes place, the Herero parents are immediately undressed, previously to being specially attired. The detail shows the importance of immediate assimilation to the new state.

After childbirth the mother passes through a stage of recovery, of isolation, with her babe, often expressed by a costume. At its end she assumes the costume of normal life which has been temporarily suspended, or a special costume of her new grade of maternity.

---

[1] J. Irle, *Die Herero* (Gütersloh 1906), pp. 106-107.

[2] A. C. Hollis, *The Masai* (Oxford 1905), p. 282.

[3] Sir H. H. Johnston, " The People of Eastern Equatorial Africa," *Journal of the Anthropological Institute* (1886), xv. 8-9 ; C. New, *Life, Wanderings, and Labours in Eastern Africa* (1874), pp. 360-361.

[4] Hutter, *Nord-Hinterland von Kamerun* (Brunswick 1902), p. 421.

[5] F. S. Krauss, *Sitte und Branch der Südslaven* (Vienna 1885), p. 450.

(c) The Sexual Inversion of Dress

The remarks of Sir James Frazer may introduce this part of the subject, which is curiously large : " The religious or superstitious interchange of dress between men and women is an obscure and complex problem, and it is unlikely that any single solution would apply to all the cases." He suggests that the custom of the bride dressing as a male might be a magical mode of ensuring a male heir, and that the wearing by the wife of her husband's garments might be a magical mode of transferring her pains to the man.[1] The latter mode would thus be the converse of the former. We may also note the importance assigned to the principle of transference or contagion. Such ideas, it may be premised, are perhaps secondary, the conscious reactions to an unconscious impulsive action, whose motivation may be entirely different. The whole subject falls simply into clear divisions, which may be explained as they come.

The Zulu " Black Ox Sacrifice " produces rain. The officiators, chief men, wear the girdles of young girls for the occasion.[2] To produce a change in nature, it is necessary for man to change himself. The idea is unconscious, but its meaning is adaptation. Its reverse aspect is a change of luck by a change of self. The most obvious change is change of sex, the sexual demarcation being the strongest known to society, dividing it into two halves. The following shows this more clearly. In order to avert disease from their cattle, the Zulus perform the *umkuba*. This is the custom of allowing the girls to herd the

---

[1] F. S. Krauss, *The Golden Bough*, iii. 216 ; *id.*, *Totemism and Exogamy* (1910), iv. 248 ff.

[2] H. Callaway, *The Religious System of the Amazulu* (Natal 1868), p. 93.

oxen for a day. All the young women rise early, dress themselves entirely in their brothers' clothes, and, taking their brothers' knobkerries and sticks, open the cattle-pen and drive the cattle to pasture, returning at sunset. No one of the male sex may go near them or speak to them meanwhile.[1] Here a change of officiators, sexually different, produces a change of luck and of nature. Similarly, among the old Arabs, a man stung by a scorpion would try the cure of wearing a woman's bracelets and ear-rings.[2] In Central Australia a man will cure his headache by wearing his wife's head-dress.

On this principle, as a primary reason, a large group of birth customs may be explained. When a Guatemalan woman was lying in, her husband placed his clothes upon her, and both confessed their sins.[3] Here and in the next cases the intention seems to be a change of personality to induce a change of state. When delivery is difficult, a Watubella man puts his clothes under his wife's body,[4] and a Central Australian ties his own hair-girdle round her head.[5] In China the father's trousers are hung up in the room, " so that all evil influences may enter into them instead of into the child." [6] In the last case the dress itself acts as a warning notice, representative of the father's person.

---

[1] E. G. Carbutt, " Some Minor Superstitions and Customs of the Zulus," *Folk-lore Journal* (Cape Town 1880), ii. 12-13.

[2] J. L. Rasmussen, *Additamenta ad historiam Arabum ante Islamismum excerpta ex Ibn Nabatah, Nuveiro atque Ibn Koteibah* (Copenhagen 1821), p. 65.

[3] A. de Herrera, *The General History of the Vast Continent and Islands of America, commonly called the West Indies* (1725-1726), iv. 148.

[4] J. G. F. Riedel, *De sluik- en kroesharige rassen tusschen Selebes en Papua* (The Hague 1886), p. 207.

[5] Spencer-Gillen, *The Native Tribes of Central Australia* (1899), p. 467.

[6] J. Doolittle, *Social Life of the Chinese* (New York 1867), i. 122.

In the following is to be seen the principle of impersonation, the reverse method of change of personality, combined, no doubt, with an impulsive sympathetic reaction, equivalent to a desire to share the pain. In Southern India the wandering Erukalavandhu have this custom—" directly the woman feels the birth-pangs, she informs her husband, who immediately takes some of her clothes, puts them on, places on his forehead the mark which the women usually place on theirs, retires into a dark room, . . . covering himself up with a long cloth." [1]   In Thuringia the man's shirt is hung before the window. In South Germany and Hungary the father's smock is worn by the child, to protect it from fairies. In Königsberg a mother puts her clothes over the child, to prevent the evil *Drud* carrying it off, and to dress a child in its father's smock brings it luck.[2] Among the Basutos, when a child is sick the medicine-man puts a piece of his own *setsiba* garment upon it.[3] In Silesia a sick child is wrapped in its mother's bridal apron. A Bohemian mother puts a piece of her own dress on a sick child. At Bern it is believed that to wrap a boy in his father's shirt will make him strong. Conversely, in some parts of Germany it is unlucky to wrap a boy in his mother's dress.[4]

In the above cases, secondary ideas are clearly present. In particular, the influence of a person's dress, as part of or impregnated with his personality is to be seen.

A holiday being a suspension of normal life, it

[1] J. Cain, in *The Indian Antiquary* (1874), iii. 151.

[2] H. H. Ploss, *op. cit.*

[3] H. Grätzner, " Die Gebrauche der Basutho," *Verhandlungen der Berliner Gesellschaft für Anthropologie, Ethnologie und Urgeschichte* (1877), pp. 77-86.

[4] H. H. Ploss, *op. cit.*

tends to be accompanied by every kind of reversal of
the usual order. Commonly all laws and customs
are broken. An obvious mode of reversal is the adoption of the garments of the other sex. In the mediæval Feast of Fools the priests dressed as clowns or
women.[1] In Carnival festivities men have dressed
up as women, and women as men.[2] In the Argive
Ὑβριστικά festival men wore women's robes and
veils, and women dressed as men.[3] At the Saturnalia,
slaves exchanged positions and dress with their masters,
and men with women. In Alsace, as elsewhere at
vintage festivals and the like, men and women exchange the dress of their sex.[4] In the mediæval
feasts of Purim, the Jewish *Bacchanalia*, men dressed
as women, and women as men.[5] The result, and in
some degree the motive, of such interchange is purely
social, expressive of the desire for good-fellowship
and union.

Numerous cases fall under the heading of sympathetic assimilation. Magical results may be combined with an instinctive adaptation, or may follow
it. In Korea, soldiers' wives " are compelled to wear
their husbands' green regimental coats thrown over
their heads like shawls. The object of this law was
to make sure that the soldiers should have their coats
in good order, in case of war suddenly breaking out.
The soldiers have long ceased to wear green coats,
but the custom is still observed." [6] The explanation
is obviously *ex post facto*. It seems more probable

---

[1] J. A. Dulaure, *Des divinités génératrices* (Paris 1805), p. 315.

[2] J. Brand, *Popular Antiquities* (3rd edition, 1870), i. 36, 66.

[3] Plutarch, *Mulierum virtutes*, 245 E.

[4] W. Mannhardt, *World- und Feldkulte : der Baumkultus der Germanen und ihren
Nachbarstämme* (Berlin 1875-1877), p. 314.

[5] Sir J. G. Frazer, *The Golden Bough*, ix. 363.

[6] H. B. Saunderson, *op. cit.*, xxiv. 303.

that the fashion corresponds to the European custom
of women wearing their husbands' or lovers' colours.
Every autumn the Ngente of Assam celebrate a festival
in honour of all children born during the year.   During
this, men disguised as women or as members of a
neighbouring tribe visit all the mothers and dance in
return for presents.[1]   In the Hervey Islands a widow
wears the dress of her dead husband.   A widower
may be seen walking about in his dead wife's gown.
" Instead of her shawl, a mother will wear on her back
a pair of trousers belonging to a little son just laid
in his grave." [2]   In Timorlaut, widows and widowers
wear a piece of the clothing of the dead in the hair.[3]

The custom is very frequent at pubertal ceremonies
and at marriage festivities.   At the ceremony of *pollo*,
connected with the puberty of their girls, Basuto
women " acted like mad people. . . . They went
about performing curious mummeries, wearing men's
clothes and carrying weapons, and were very saucy
to men they met." [4]   The Masai boy is termed *sipolio*
at his circumcision.   The candidates " appear as
women," and wear the *surutya* ear-rings and long
garment reaching to the ground, worn by married
women.   When the wound is healed they don the
warrior's skins and ornaments, and when the hair has
grown long enough to plait they are styled *il-muran*,
or warriors.[5]   When an Egyptian boy is circumcised,
at the age of five or six, he parades the streets, dressed
as a girl in female clothes and ornaments borrowed

---

[1] A. van Gennep, *Les rites de passage* (Paris 1909), p. 69.

[2] W. W. Gill, *Life in the Southern Isles* (1876), p. 78.

[3] J. G. F. Riedel, *op. cit.*, p. 307.

[4] K. Endemann, " Mittheilungen über die Sotho-Neger," *Zeitschrift für
Ethnologie* (1874), vi. 37 ff.

[5] A. C. Hollis, *op. cit.*, p. 298.

for the occasion. A friend walks in front, wearing round his neck the boy's own writing-tablet. To avert the evil eye a woman sprinkles salt behind.[1] In the old Greek story the boy Achilles lived in Scyros as a girl, dressed as a girl, to avoid being sent against Troy. He bore a maiden name, Issa or Pyrrha.[2]

In such cases we may see, at the initiation to the sexual life and state, an adaptation to it in the form of an assimilation to the other sex.

The principle of sympathetic assimilation is clearly brought out in the following two examples. At the ceremonial burying of the placenta, Babar women who officiate wear men's girdles if the child is a boy, but women's *sarongs* if a girl.[3] At the festival celebrating a birth, Fijian men paint on their bodies the tatoo-marks of women.[4] In West Africa certain tribes have the custom of the groom wearing his wife's petticoat for some time after marriage.[5] In ancient Cos, the groom wore women's clothes when receiving the bride. Plutarch connects the custom with the story of Heracles serving Omphale and wearing a female dress. The Argive bride wore a beard " when she slept with her husband," presumably on the bridal night only. The Spartan bride wore a man's cloak and shoes when she awaited the coming of the bridegroom.[6] In English and Welsh folklore there are cases of dressing the bride in men's clothes.[7]

[1] E. W. Lane, *An Account of the Manners and Customs of the Modern Egyptians* (1846), i. 61-62 ; ii. 279.

[2] Appolodorus, *Bibliotheca*, III. xiii. 8 ; Ptolemæus, *Nova Historia*, i. Cp. Ernest Crawley, " Achilles at Skyros," *The Classical Review* (1893), vii. 243-245.

[3] J. G. F. Riedel, *op. cit.*, p. 355.

[4] T. Williams and J. Calvert, *Fiji and the Fijians* (1858), i. 175.

[5] M. H. Kingsley, *West African Studies* (1901), p. 131.

[6] Plutarch, *Quæstiones Græcæ*, lviii. ; *Mulierum virtutes*, 245 ; *Lycurgus*, xv.

[7] T. Moore, *Marriage Customs* (1814), p. 37.

The custom of inversion of sexual dress is very common at wedding feasts among European peasantry. All these are cases of sympathetic assimilation to the other sex. The principle is brought out by such customs as that mentioned by Spix and Martius, of Brazilian youths at dances with the girls wearing girls' ornaments.[1]

Many cases of the custom at feasts are complicated by various accidents. Sometimes it is meaningless except as a necessity. Among the Torres Islanders women do not take part in ceremonies. Accordingly, at the annual death-dance deceased women are personated not by women but by men, dressed in women's petticoats.[2] In other cases the data are insufficient for an explanation. Thus, at harvest ceremonies in Bavaria, the officiating reaper is dressed in women's clothes ; or, if a woman be selected for the office, she is dressed as a man.[3] At the vernal festival of Heracles at Rome men dressed as women.[4] The choir at the Athenian *Oschophoria* was led by two youths dressed as girls.[5]

Cases occur of change of sexual dress by way of disguise ; it is more frequent in civilization than in barbarism. A Bangala man troubled by a bad *mongoli*, evil spirit, left his house secretly. " He donned a woman's dress and assumed a female voice, and pretended to be other than he was in order to deceive the *mongoli*. This failed to cure him, and in time he returned to his town, but continued to act as a woman." [6]

---

[1] J. B. von Spix and C. F. P. Martius, *Travels in Brazil* (1824), ii. 114.

[2] A. C. Haddon, *Head-Hunters, Black, White, and Brown* (1901), p. 139.

[3] W. Mannhardt, *Mythologische Forschungen* (Strasburg 1884), p. 20.

[4] Lydus, *De Mensibus*, iv. 46 (81).   [5] Photius, *Bibliotheca*, 322a.

[6] J. H. Weeks, " Anthropological Notes on the Bangula of the Upper Congo River," *Journal of the Royal Anthropological Institute* (1910), xl. 370-371.

The last detail and the psychological analysis of modern cases suggest that a congenital tendency towards some form of inversion is present in such cases. On the face of them, we have to account for the choice of a *sexual* change of dress.

A Koita homicide wears special ornaments and is tatooed. The latter practice is otherwise limited to the female sex.[1] Women's dress may involve the assumption of women's weakness and similar properties. The King of Burma suggested to the King of Aracan to dress his soldiers as women. They consequently became effeminate and weak.[2] The Lycians, when in mourning, dressed as women. Plutarch explains this rationalistically, as a way of showing " that mourning is effeminate, that it is womanly and weak to mourn. For women are more prone to mourning than are men, barbarians than Greeks, and inferior persons than superior." [3] If the document is genuine, we may apply to the Lycians the principle adopted in regard to mourning costume generally. The state of mourning is an absolute suspension, and it may come to be regarded as an absolute reversal or inversion of the normal state of life.

Death, the negative of life, has taken place and made a violent break with the tenor of existence ; hence such an adaptation as an inversion of sexual dress. Occasions might well be conceived when, if change of attire was desired, the only obvious attire presenting itself would be that of the other sex.

One of the most complex cases, at first appearance,

---

[1] C. G. Seligmann, *The Melanesians of British New Guinea* (Cambridge 1910), p. 130.

[2] T. W. Lewin, *Wild Races of South-Eastern India* (1870), pp. 137-138.

[3] Plutarch, *Consolatio ad Appolonium*, 22 ; Valerius Maximus, xii. §§ 6, 13.

10

is that of the adoption of feminine dress by priests, shamans, and medicine-men. Where for various mythological reasons an androgynous deity exists, it is natural that the attendant priests should be sympathetically made two-sexed in their garb, and even that the worshippers should invert their dress. Sacrifice was made to the Bearded Venus of Cyprus by men dressed as women, and by women dressed as men.[1]

As a rule, however, the deity is an invention intended, unconsciously enough, to harmonize with a traditional habit of priestly life. This particular habit is of wide extension, and involves a whole genus of psychoses. Some examples may precede analysis.

Chukchi shamans commonly dress as women.[2] The *basir* of the Dayaks make their living by witchcraft, and are dressed as women.[3] The priestesses, *blians*, of the Dayaks dressed as men. Sometimes a Dayak priest marries simultaneously a man and a woman.[4] Among both the Northern Asiatic peoples and the Dayaks it frequently happens that a double inversion takes place, so that of the wedded priestly pair the husband is a woman and the wife a man. It is said by the Koryaks that shamans who had changed their sex were very powerful.[5] The Illinois and Naudowessie Indians regarded such men as had " changed their sex " as *manitous* or supernaturally gifted persons.[6] But

---

[1] Macrobius, *Saturnalia*, III. vii. 2 ; Servius, on Virgil, *Aeneid*, ii. 637.

[2] W. Jochelson, " The Koryak Religion and Myths," *Publications of the Jesup North Pacific Expedition* (Leyden, New York 1908), vol. vi. part 1, pp. 52-53.

[3] A. Hardeland, *Dajacksch-deutsches Wörterbuch* (Amsterdam 1859), *s.v.*

[4] J. Pijnappel, " Beschrijving van het westelijke gedeelte van de Zuid- en Oosterafdeeling van Borneo (de Afdeeling Sampit en de Zuidkust)," *Bijdragen tot de Taal-, Land- en Volkenkunde van Nederlandsch Indië* (1860), new ser. iii. 330 ; S. St. John, *Life in the Forests of the Far East* (2nd edition, 1863), i. 62.

[5] W. Jochelson, *loc. cit.*

[6] J. Marquette, *Récit des voyages* (Albany 1855), pp. 53-54.

it is unnecessary to assume that the practice is intended to acquire special magical powers attributed
to women. This idea may supervene. Possibly the
fantastic nature of the change itself, as mere change,
has had some influence.

Patagonian sorcerers, chosen from children afflicted
with St. Vitus' dance, wore women's clothes. Priests
among the Indians of Louisiana dressed as women.[1]
In the Pelew Islands a remarkable change of sex was
observed. A goddess often chose a man, instead of a
woman, to be her mouthpiece. In such cases the
man, dressed as a woman, was regarded and treated
as a woman. One significance of this is in connexion
with the Pelewan social system. Sir James Frazer
regards this inspiration by a female spirit as explaining
other cases when sex is exchanged, as with the priest-
hoods of the Dayaks, Bugis, Patagonians, Aleuts, and
other American Indian tribes.[2] It is stated of some
North American cases that the man dreamed he was
inspired by a female spirit, and that his " medicine "
was to live as a woman.[3] In Uganda Mukasa gave
oracles through a woman, who when she prophesied
wore clothes knotted in the masculine style.[4] The
legends of Sardanapalus (Assur-bani-pal) and Heracles,
as well as the cases of the priests of Cybele and the
Syrian goddess, would come under the explanation.[5]
Heracles' priest at Cos wore a woman's raiment when
he sacrificed. The story of Heracles himself may be

---

[1] A. Bastian, *Der Mensch in der Geschichte* (Leipzig 1860), iii. 309-310.

[2] J. Kubary, " Die Religion der Pelauen," in A. Bastian, *Allerlei aus Volks- und Menschenkunde* (Berlin 1888), i. 35 ; Sir J. G. Frazer, *The Golden Bough*, vi. 253.

[3] Maximilian Prince zu Wied, *Reise in das innere Nord-Amerika* (Coblenz 1839-1841), ii. 133.

[4] J. Roscoe, in Sir J. G. Frazer, *op. cit.*, vi. 257.

[5] Sir J. G. Frazer, *op. cit.*, vi. 257-259.

a reminiscence of such effeminate priests, who were priest-gods. Dionysus Pseudanor is a similar embodiment of the principle.

Eunuchs in India are sometimes dedicated to the goddess *Huligamma*, and wear female dress. Men who believe themselves to be impotent serve this goddess, and dress as women in order to recover their virility.[1] A festival was given among the Sioux Indians to a man dressed and living as a woman, the *berdashe* or *i-coo-coo-a*. " For extraordinary privileges which he is known to possess he is driven to the most servile and degrading duties, which he is not allowed to escape ; and he, being the only one of the tribe submitting to this disgraceful degradation, is looked upon as ' medicine ' and sacred, and a feast is given to him annually." [2]

Among the iron-workers of Manipur, the god Khumlangba is attended by priestesses, *maibi*. But a man is sometimes taken possession of by the god. He is then known as *maiba*, and wears at ceremonies the dress of a *maibi*, viz. white cloth round the body from below the arms, a white jacket, and a sash. A fine muslin veil covers the head. " The *maibi* is looked on as superior to any man, by reason of her communion with the god ; and therefore if a man is honoured in the same way he assumes the dress of the *maibi* as an honour. If a man marries a *maibi*, he sleeps on the right of her, whereas the ordinary place of a woman is the right, as being the inferior side. It appears that women are more liable to be possessed

---

[1] Fawcett, in *Journal of the Anthropological Society of Bengal* (1854), xi. 343.

[2] G. Catlin, *Letters and Notes on the Manners, Customs, and Condition of the North American Indians* (1876), ii. 214-215.

by the god, and the same may be observed among all
the hill tribes of these parts." [1]

The *nganga*, medicine-men, of the Bangala, in
certain ceremonies after a death, for the purpose of
discovering the slayer, dress up as women.[2] Off the
coast of Arracan there were " conjurers " who dressed
and lived as women. On the Congo a priest dressed
as a woman and was called Grandmother.[3] The
Nahanarvals, a tribe of ancient Germany, had a priest
dressed as a woman. Men of the Vallabha sect win
the favour of Krishna by wearing their hair long
and generally assimilating themselves to women. The
practice is even followed by rajas.[4] Candidates for
the *areo* society of Tahiti were invested with the dress
of women.[5]

There is no doubt that these phenomena are cases
of sexual inversion, congenital or acquired, partial or
complete. Any idea of inspiration by female deities
or the reverse is secondary, as also the notions of
assimilation of priest to goddess, or of marriage of a
priest to a god. The significant fact is that throughout history the priesthood has had a tendency towards
effemination.

Sexual inversion has especially obtained among
the connected races of North Asia and America. It
is marked by inversion of dress. " In nearly every
part of the continent [of America] there seem to

---

[1] J. Shakespear, " Notes on the Iron Workers of Manipur and the Annual
Festival in honour of the Special Deity Khumlangba," *Journal of the Royal Anthropological Institute* (1910), xl. 354.

[2] J. H. Weeks, " Anthropological Notes on the Bangala of the Upper Congo
River," *Journal of the Royal Anthropological Institute* (1910), xl. 388.

[3] J. B. Labat, *Relation historique de l'Ethiopie Occidentale* (Paris 1732), ii. 195 ff.

[4] Sir M. Monier-Williams, *Religious Life and Thought in India* (1883), p. 136.

[5] W. Ellis, *Polynesian Researches* (1859), i. 324.

have been, since ancient times, men dressing themselves in the clothes and performing the functions of
women." [1]   Thus in Kadiak " it was the custom for
parents who had a girl-like son to dress and rear him
as a girl, teaching him only domestic duties, keeping
him at woman's work, and letting him associate only
with women and girls." [2]   A Chukchi boy at the age
of sixteen will often relinquish his sex. He adopts a
woman's dress, and lets his hair grow. It frequently
happens that in such cases the husband is a woman
and the wife a man. " These abnormal changes of
sex . . . appear to be strongly encouraged by the
shamans, who interpret such cases as an injunction of
their individual deity." [3]   A similar practice is found
among the Koryaks. [4]

Among the Sacs there were men dressed as women. [5]
So among the Lushais and Caucasians. [6]   Among the
former, women sometimes become men. When asked
the reason, a woman so changed said " her *khuavang*
was not good, and so she became a man." [7]   In Tahiti
there were men, called *mahoos*, who assumed " the
dress, attitude, and manners of women." [8]   So among
the Malagasy (the men called *tsecats*), the Ondonga
in South-West (German) Africa, and the Diakité-Sar-
racolese in the French Sūdan. [9]   Of the Aleut *schupans*

---

[1] E. Westermarck, *The Origin and Development of the Moral Ideas* (2nd edition,
1912-1917), ii. 456, quoting the authorities.

[2] *Ibid.*, ii. 457, quoting Davydov.   [3] *Ibid.*, ii. 458, quoting Bogoraz.

[4] W. Jochelson, *op. cit.*, pp. 52-53.

[5] W. H. Keating, *Narrative of an Expedition to the Source of St. Peter's River*
(1825), i. 227-228.

[6] T. H. Lewin, *Wild Races of South-Eastern India* (1870), p. 255 ; J. Reineggs,
Allgemeine historisch-topographische Beschreibung des Kaukasus (Gotha, etc., 1796-
1797), i. 270.

[7] " The Lushais at Home," *The Indian Antiquary* (1903), xxxii. 413.

[8] J. Turnbull, *A Voyage round the World in the Years 1800-1804* (1813), p. 382.

[9] E. Westermarck, *op. cit.*, quoting authorities.

Langsdorff wrote : " Boys, if they happen to be very handsome, are often brought up entirely in the manner of girls, and instructed in the arts women use to please men ; their beards are carefully plucked out as soon as they begin to appear, and their chins tatooed like those of women ; they wear ornaments of glass beads upon their legs and arms, bind and cut their hair in the same manner as the women." [1] Lisiansky described them also and those of the Koniagas : " They even assume the manner and dress of the women so nearly that a stranger would naturally take them for what they are not. . . . The residence of one of these in a house was considered as fortunate." Apparently the effemination is developed chiefly by suggestion beginning in childhood.[2] In Mexico and Brazil there was the same custom. In the latter these men not only dressed as women, but devoted themselves solely to feminine occupations, and were despised. They were called *cudinas,* which means " circumcised." [3] Holder has studied the *boté* (" not man, not woman ") or *burdash* (" half man, half woman ") of the North-West American tribes. The woman's dress and manners are assumed in childhood. Some of his evidence suggests that the greater number are cases of congenital sexual inversion. " One little fellow, while in the Agency boarding-school, was found frequently surreptitiously wearing female attire. He was punished, but finally escaped from school and became a *boté,* which vocation he has since followed." [4] The

[1] G. H. von Langsdorff, *Voyages and Travels in Various Parts of the World, During the Years 1803-1807* (1813-1814), ii. 47.

[2] U. Lisiansky, *A Voyage round the World* (1814), p. 199.

[3] C. F. P. von Martius, *Beiträge zur Ethnographie und Sprachenkunde Amerika's zumal Braziliens* (Leipzig 1867), i. 74.

[4] A. B. Holder, in *New York Medical Journal,* 7 December, 1889.

i-wa-musp, man-woman, of the Indians of California
formed a regular social grade. Dressed as women,
they performed women's tasks. "When an Indian
shows a desire to shirk his manly duties, they make
him take his position in a circle of fire ; then a bow
and a ' woman-stick ' are offered to him, and he is
solemnly enjoined . . . to choose which he will, and
ever afterward to abide by his choice." [1] Something
analogous is recorded of the ancient Scythians and
the occurrence of a θήλεια νοῦσος among them.[2]

Some of the above cases, difficult to disentangle
accurately, are not so much cases of congenital inversion as of general physical weakness. It is a remarkable aspect of certain types of barbarous society that
the weak males are forced into the grade of women,
and made to assume female dress and duties. Such
a practice may, of course, induce some amount of
acquired inversion. Payne has suggested that their
survival was due to advancement in civilization, and
that later they formed a nucleus for the slave-class.[3]

The occurrence of a masculine temperament in
women is not uncommon in early culture. In some
tribes of Brazil there were women who dressed and
lived as men, hunting and going to war.[4] The same
practice is found in Zanzibar [5] and among the Eastern
Eskimo.[6] Shinga, who became Queen of Congo in
1640, kept fifty or sixty male concubines. She always

---

[1] S. Powers, *Tribes of California* (Washington 1877), pp. 132-133.

[2] Herodotus, *History*, i. 105 ; iv. 67.

[3] E. J. Payne, *History of the New World called America* (Oxford 1892), ii. 16-17.

[4] M. de Gandavo, *Historia de Santa Cruz* (1837), pp. 116-117.

[5] O. Baumann, " Conträre Sexual-Erscheinungen bei der Neger-Bevölkerung
Zanzibars," *Verhandlungen der Berliner Gesellschaft für Anthropologie, Ethnologie,
und Urgeschichte* (1899), pp. 668-669.

[6] W. H. Dall, *Alaska and its Resources* (1870), p. 139.

dressed as a man, and compelled them to take the names and dress of women.[1] Classical antiquity has many similar cases of queens wearing men's armour in war, and of women fighting in the ranks, either temporarily, or permanently, as the Amazons. The last case, on the analogy of the West African cases of women's regiments, may be based on fact.[2]

In modern civilization the practice of women dressing as men and following masculine vocations is no less frequent than was in barbarism the custom of effemination of men. Women of masculine temperament are by no means a rare phenomenon to-day, and the balance of sexual reversal has thus changed.

There remain to be considered two classes who form more or less definite social grades, and in some cases are distinguished by dress. These are old men and women.[3] After the menopause, women, as the Zulus say, "become men," and the customs of *hlonipa*, or sexual taboo, do not apply to them any longer.[4] Often, instead of the dress of matrons, savage and barbarous women after the menopause dress as men. For instance, in Uripiv (New Hebrides) an old widow of a chief lived independently, and "at the dances painted her face like a man and danced with the best of them."[5] Often they engage in war, consult with the old men, as well as having great influence over their own sex.

---

[1] W. W. Reade, *Savage Africa* (1863), p. 364.

[2] Pausanias, *Descriptio Græciæ*, ii. 21 ; Apollonius Rhodius, *Argonautica*, i. 712 ; Ptolemy, in Photius, *Bibliotheca*, 150, v. 33 ; Pomponius Mela, *Chorographia*, i. 19 ; A. B. Ellis, *The Ewe-speaking Peoples of the Slave Coast of West Africa* (1890), pp. 183, 290.

[3] See A. van Gennep, *Les rites de passage* (Paris 1909), p. 207.

[4] H. Callaway, *The Religious System of the Amazulu* (Natal 1868-1870), p. 440.

[5] B. T. Somerville, "Notes on some Islands of the New Hebrides," *Journal of the Anthropological Institute* (1894), xxiii. 7.

Various enactments, both in semi-civilized custom and in civilized law, have been made against inversion of dress. A typical decision is that of the Council of Gangra (A.D. 370) : " If any woman, under pretence of leading an ascetic life, change her apparel, and instead of the accustomed habit of women take that of men, let her be anathema." The point is noticeable that asceticism here, in the absence of a neutral garb, has recourse to the male dress. Such enactments and the modern laws on the subject are based on the Heb. law of Deuteronomy xxii. 5, and the Christian of 1 Corinthians xi. 6, but they embody a scientifically sound principle.

(d) The Sexual Exchange of Dress

This custom is frequent between friends, lovers, betrothed, and as a marriage rite. It is analogous to an exchange of any objects serving as mutual gifts, and its ultimate origin is to be found in this natural and obvious practice. Originally, therefore, it is outside the sphere of the psychology of dress proper ; but it at once assumes various ideas of dress, often in an intensified form.

In Homer's story Glaucus and Diomed exchanged armour and became brothers-in-arms.[1] Among the Khamptis an exchange of clothes " gives birth to or is a sign of amity." [2] In Amboyna and Wetar and other islands lovers exchange clothes in order, as it is reported, to have the odour of the beloved person with them.[3] In European folklore it is a very frequent

---

[1] Homer, *Iliad*, vi. 235-236.

[2] H. B. Rowney, *Wild Tribes of India* (1882), p. 162.

[3] J. G. F. Riedel, *De sluik- en kroesharige rassen tusschen Selebes en Papua* (The Hague 1886), pp. 447, 67, 300, 41.

custom that bride and bridegroom exchange head-
dress.[1] The Ainu youth and girl after betrothal wear
each other's clothes.[2] In South Celebes the bridegroom at a certain stage of the ceremonies puts on
the garments which the bride has put off.[3] Among
the mediæval Jews of Egypt a custom is recorded of
the bride wearing helmet and sword, and the groom
a female dress.[4] At a Brāhman marriage in South
India the bride is dressed as a boy and another girl
is dressed to represent the bride.[5]

The secondary idea which is prominent in these
customs is that of union by means of mutual assimilation. This is shown by such cases as the following.
In Buru a family quarrel is terminated by a feast.
The father of the injured woman puts on the shoulders
of her husband some of his own family's clothes;
the husband puts on him a cloth he has brought for
the purpose.[6] Among the Masai murder may be
" arranged " and peace made between the two families
by the offices of the elders. " The family of the mur-
dered man takes the murderer's garment, and the
latter [the family of the murderer] takes the garment
of one of the dead man's brothers." [7]

A later stage of development is marked by ideas
of contagion of ill-will, or of the conditional curse.
By way of making a guarantee of peace, Tahitian

[1] Baron I. and Baroness O. von Reinsberg-Düringsfeld, *Hochzeitsbuch* (Leipzig 1871), *passim*.

[2] J. Batchelor, *The Ainu and their Folk-lore* (1892), p. 142.

[3] B. F. Matthes, *Bijdragen tot de Ethnologie van Zuider-Celebes* (The Hague 1875), p. 35.

[4] Sepp, *Althayerischer Sagenschatz* (Munich 1876), p. 232.

[5] E. Thurston, *Ethnographic Notes in Southern India* (Madras 1906), p. 3.

[6] J. G. F. Riedel, *op. cit.*, p. 23.

[7] A. C. Hollis, *The Masai* (Oxford 1905), p. 311.

tribes wove a wreath of green boughs furnished by
both parties, and a band of cloth manufactured in
common, and offered both to the gods, with curses on
the violator of the treaty.[1]   To establish that contact with a person which serves as a " conductor " of
conditional curses, in the Moorish institution of *l-'ar*,
it is enough to touch him with the turban or the dress.[2]
The Biblical story is not a case of indignity by mutilation of garments, but a magical act of guarantee.
When Hanun, King of Ammon, cut off half the beard
and half the clothes of David's ambassadors when he sent
them back, he wanted a guarantee of friendly relations.
His wise men, Sir James Frazer observes, would be
muttering spells over these personal guarantees while
David was on his way.[3]

Similarly, possession or contact ensures sympathy,
whether by mere union or by the threat of injury.
In the Mentawey Islands, " if a stranger enters a
house where children are, the father or some member
of the family present takes the ornament with which
the children decorate their hair, and hands it to the
stranger, who holds it in his hands for a while and then
returns it."   The procedure protects the children
from the possibly evil eye of the visitor.[4]

Union in marriage and other rites is commonly
effected by enveloping the pair in one robe, or by
joining their garments together.   In South Celebes
the ceremony of *ridjala sampú* consists in enveloping
them in one *sarong*, which the priest casts over them

---

[1] W. Ellis, *Polynesian Researches* (1859), i. 318.

[2] E. Westermarck, *op. cit.*, i. 586 ;   cp. *Encyclopædia of Religion and Ethics*, iv.
372.

[3] 2 Samuel x. 4 ;   Sir J. G. Frazer, *The Golden Bough*, iii. 273.

[4] H. von Rosenberg, *Der Malayische Archipel* (Leipzig 1878), p. 198.

like a net.[1] The Tahitians [2] and the Hovas of Madagascar [3] have the same custom. The Dayak *balian* throws one cloth over the pair.[4] Among the Toba-Bataks the mother places a garment over them.[5] A similar ceremony among the Nufoors of Doreh is explained as a symbol of the marriage " tie." [6] In north Nias the pair are enveloped in one garment.[7]

Among the Todas, the man who ceremonially sleeps with a girl before puberty covers her and himself with one mantle.[8] The Hindu bride and groom are tied together by their clothes, in the " Brahma knot." It is the same knot as is used in the sacred thread. The tying is repeated at various points in the ceremonies. The *mangalasūtra*, or *tāli*, is a cord with a gold ornament, worn round the married woman's neck, as a European wears a wedding-ring ; and its tying is a binding rite. The bride and groom both don wedding clothes during the ceremonies.[9] The Bhillalas tie the garments of the bride and groom together.[10] Previously to the ceremony of *ridjala sampú* the clothes of the Celebes pair are sewn together—the rite of *ridjai-kamma parukusenna*.[11]

In connexion with marriage the custom is hardly

[1] B. F. Matthes, *op. cit.*, pp. 31, 33-34.

[2] W. Ellis, *op. cit.*, i. 117-118, 270, 272 ff.

[3] J. Sibree, *Madagascar and its People* (1870), p. 193.

[4] F. Grabowsky, " Die Orang bukit oder Bergmenschen von Mindai in Südost-Borneo," *Das Ausland* (1885), viii. 785.

[5] W. Ködding, " Die Battaker auf Sumatra," *Globus* (1888), liii. 91.

[6] J. L. Hasselt, *Gedenkboek van een vijf-en-twintig jarig zendelingsleven op Nieuw-Guinea, 1862-1887* (Utrecht 1888), p. 42.

[7] H. Sundermann, *Die Insel Nias* (Berlin 1884), p. 443.

[8] W. H. R. Rivers, *The Todas* (1906), p. 503.

[9] J. E. Padfield, *The Hindu at Home* (Madras 1908), pp. 124 ff.

[10] W. Kincaid, " The Bheel Tribes of the Vindhyan Range," *Journal of the Anthropological Institute* (1880), ix. 403.

[11] B. F. Matthes, *op. cit.*, pp. 31 ff.

intended to unite the woman to the man's family and
the man to the woman's.[1]   More probably it merely
assimilates the two individuals ; while, from the social
point of view, it unites their respective sexual grades.

It is remarkable that many ceremonies of initiation, particularly those in which a spiritual fatherhood
and sonship is established, are analogous in method
to a marriage rite. Thus the *guru* of the Deccan
Mhārs, when initiating a child, covers the child and
himself with one blanket.[2]

Cases where the rite has one side only are natural,
but are apt to take on the character of an act of acquisition and possession. In the Sandwich Islands the
bridegroom casts a piece of *tapa* over the bride, this
constituting marriage.[3]   It is analogous to the Hindu
" giving cloth." In Arabian times to cast a garment
over a woman was to claim her. This explains the
words of Ruth.[4]   In Malachi ii. 16 " garment " is
equivalent to " wife." [5]   A similar idea obtains in
other circumstances, the dress having the force of a
personal representative. The Southern Massim have
a custom that a woman may save a man's life when
struck down if she throws her *diripa*, grass-petticoat,
over him.[6]

---

[1] As van Gennep holds (*op. cit.*, p. 246).   On the whole subject of exchange of
dress and similar practices, and on the sexual psychology underlying them, see Crawley-
Besterman, *The Mystic Rose* (2nd edition, 1926), *passim ;* and for these practices in
the East Indies, see G. A. Wilken, " Plechtigheden en Gebruiken bij Verlovingen en
Huwelijken bij de Volken van de Indischen Archipel," *Bijdragen tot de Taal-, Land-
en Volkenkunde van Nederlandsch-Indië* (1886), xxxv. 140-219 ; (1889), xxxviii.
380-460.

[2] *Bombay Gazetteer*, xviii. 441.

[3] W. Ellis, *op. cit.*, iv. 435.   [4] Ruth iii. 9.

[5] W. Robertson Smith, *Kingship and Marriage in Early Arabia* (2nd edition,
1903), p. 105.

[6] C. G. Seligmann, *The Melanesians of British New Guinea* (Cambridge 1910),
p. 547.

11. SACRED DRESS

(a) *The Dress of Sanctity*

One of the longest and most varied chapters in the history of dress is that dealing with the garb of permanent sacred grades, priestly, royal, and the like, and of temporary sacredness, as in the case of worshippers, pilgrims, and victims. Some examples have been incidentally noticed; a brief reference to certain types must suffice here. In ancient India the ascetic had to wear coarse, worn-out garments, and his hair was clipped. The hermit wore skins or tattered garments—the term may include bark—or grass-cloth—and his hair was braided. The *Snātaka* wore clothes not old or dirty. He wore the sacred string. He was forbidden to use garments, shoes, or string which had been worn by others. The student for his upper dress wore the skin of an antelope or other animal, for his lower garment a cloth of hemp, or flax, or wool. He wore the girdle of a Brāhman, a triple cord of *Muñja* grass. A *Kṣatriya* wore as his cord a bow-string; a *Vaiśya* a cord of hemp.[1] The religious character of this caste-system renders the inclusion of the four last grades convenient.

Temporarily, in worship and on pilgrimage, the ordinary member of an organized faith assumes a quasi-sacerdotal character. For the *hajj* to Mecca the Musalmān must wear no other garments than the *iḥrām*, consisting of two seamless wrappers, one passed round the loins, the other over the shoulders, the head being uncovered. The ceremony of putting them on at a pilgrims' " station " is *al-iḥrām*, " the

[1] *The Laws of Manu*, vi. 44, 52, 6, 15; iv. 34-36, 66.

making unlawful " (of ordinary garments and behaviour
and occupations). The ceremony of taking them off
is *al-iḥlāl*, " the making lawful." The *hajjī* shaves
his head when the pilgrimage is over.[1] According to
some, the *iḥrām* is the shroud prepared in the event
of the *hajjī's* death.[2] More likely it is preserved and
used as a shroud when he dies.

The most important item in the costume of Japanese
pilgrims is the *oizuru*, a jacket which is stamped with
the seal of each shrine visited. "The three breadths
of material used in the sewing of this holy garment
typify the three great Buddhist deities — Amida,
Kwannon, and Seishi. The garment itself is always
carefully preserved after the return home, and when
the owner dies he is clad in it for burial." [3]

The dress of worshippers varies between " decent
apparel " and garments of assimilation to the god or
the victim or the priest. As in the case of Baal-
worship, the garments were often kept in the shrine
and assumed on entrance. In certain rites both
Dionysus and his worshippers wore fawn-skins. The
Bacchanals wore the skins of goats. The veil of the
worshipper has been referred to. In the earliest
Christian period a controversy seems to have taken
place with regard to female head-dress during worship. In the modern custom the male head-dress
is removed, the female is retained. Academies sometimes preserve the rule of a special vestment for worshippers, whether lay or priestly.

[1] E. Sell, *The Faith of Islam* (2nd edition, 1896), pp. 279-289.

[2] Sir R. F. Burton, *Personal Narrative of a Pilgrimage to Al-Medinah and Mecca*
(1898), i. 139.

[3] B. N. Chamberlain, " Notes on Some Minor Japanese Religious Practices,"
Journal of the Anthropological Institute (1893), xxii. 360.

It has been noted that the dress of *jogleors*, trouba-dours, and *trouvères* was an assimilation to the sacer-dotal.[1] From the same mediæval period comes the record of " singing robes."

(b) Priestly and Royal Robes

The dress of the sacred world tends to be the re-verse of the profane. Apart from the impulse—to be traced in the mentality of medicine-men—to im-press one's personality upon the audience by the fantastic and the grotesque, there is here the ex-pression of the fundamental opposition between natural and supernatural social functions. The garb of Tshi priests and priestesses differs from ordinary dress. Their hair is long and unkempt, while the lay fashion is to wear it short. The layman, if well-to-do, wears bright cloth; the priest may wear only plain cloth, which is dyed red-brown with mangrove-tan. Priests and priestesses, when about to communicate with the god, wear a white linen cap. On holy days they wear white cloth, and on certain occasions, not explained, their bodies are painted with white clay. White and black beads are generally worn round the neck.[2] The Ewe priests wear white caps. The priestesses wear steeple-crowned hats with wide brims. Priests wear white clothes. Priestesses wear " gay cloths " reaching to the feet, and a kerchief over the breast.[3] The survival of some antique mode often suffices, through various accidents and modifications, for the

---

[1] H. Spencer, *Principles of Sociology*, iii. 222.

[2] A. B. Ellis, *The Tshi-speaking Peoples of the Gold Coast of West Africa* (1887), pp. 123-124.

[3] *Id.*, *The Ewe-speaking Peoples of the Slave Coast of West Africa* (1890), pp. 143, 146.

11

priestly garb, other than sacerdotal vestments. Thus, the *ricinium*, a small antique mantle, was worn by the *magister* of the *Fratres Arvales* and by *camilli* generally.

The history of the dress of the Christian priesthood is a striking example of this. Here also we find the principle of opposition to the lay-garb. The democratic and non-professional character of primitive Christianity may be seen in the fact that in A.D. 428 Pope Celestinus censured Gallican bishops who wore dress different from that of the laity. They had been monks, and retained the *pallium* and girdle instead of assuming the tunic and toga of the superior layman. It is curious that the social instinct towards differentiation of dress to mark differentiation of social function was resisted so long. But in the sixth century the civil dress of the clergy automatically became different from the dress of the country, since, while the laity departed from the ancient type, the clergy withstood all such evolution. Thus, in the Western Empire the clergy retained the toga and long tunic, while the laity wore the short tunic, trousers, and cloak of the Teutons, the *gens bracata*. Gregory the Great would have no person about him clad in the " barbarian " dress. He enforced on his *entourage* the garb of old Rome, *trabeata Latinitas*. This cleavage was gradually enforced, and from the sixth century onwards the clergy were forbidden by various canons to wear long hair, arms, or purple, and, generally, the secular dress.

The characteristic garb of the Christian clergy, both civil and ecclesiastic, was the long tunic. Originally it appears to have been white. Then its evolution divided ; the alb derived from it on the one side, the civil tunic in sober colours on the other.

For the civil dress the dignified toga was added to constitute full dress; for use in inclement weather the *casula* or *cappa*, an overcoat (*pluviale*) with a cowl, was adopted. The last-named garment similarly divided into the ecclesiastic *cope*, and the civil over-cloak. The long tunic still survives in three forms —the surplice, the cassock, and the frock coat. Its fashion in the last instance superseded the toga, which again survives in the academic gown.

The evolution of vestments is in harmony with the psychology of dress generally, and in many aspects illustrates it forcibly. With the vestment the priest puts on a " character " of divinity. By change of vestments he multiplies the Divine force, while showing its different aspects. The changing of vestments has a powerful psychical appeal. The dress is a material link between his person and the supernatural; it absorbs, as it were, the rays of Deity, and thus at the same time inspires the human wearer. The dress is accordingly regarded not as an expression of the personality of the wearer, but as imposing upon him a super-personality. This idea is implicit in every form of dress. Dress is a social body-surface, and even in sexual dress, military uniform, professional and official dress the idea that the dress has the properties of the state inherent in it is often quite explicit. Further, the dress gives admission to the grade. In particular cases of solemnity a dress serves to render the person sacrosanct. Thus the Australian messenger is sacred by reason of his red cap.[1]

A temporary sacred garment may even be used sacrificially. At the Zulu festival of the new fruits, the king danced in a mantle of grass or of herbs and

[1] J. Fraser, *Aborigines of New South Wales* (Sydney 1892), p. 31.

corn leaves, which was then torn up and trodden into the fields.[1] In such cases there is perhaps a reverse assimilation of virtue from the sacred person.

Royal dress in civilization tends to combine the principles of military dress and the tradition of the long robes of ancient autocracy. The subject needs a special analysis. The distinctive head-dress, the crown, probably is an accidental survival of a military fillet, confining the long hair which among the Franks was a mark of royalty.[2] But its significance is in line with the general principle, and it is eventually an affirmation of the dignity of the head, the crown of the human organism.

Among the earliest cultures, social authority tends to adopt a specific garb. The headmen of the Nāgas wear a special dress.[3] The priest-king of the Habbes wears a distinctive costume.[4] The Nyasaland tribes commission the man who buried the dead chief to cover the new chief with a red blanket. " This he does, at the same time hitting him hard on the head." [5]

Ideas of purity readily attach themselves to priestly and royal garments. In the following case there seems to be some survival from Zoroastrianism. Among the Kafirs of the Hindu Kush, men preparing for the office of headman wear a semi-sacred uniform which may on no account be defiled by coming into contact with dogs. These men, *kaneash*, " were nervously afraid of dogs, which had to be fastened up whenever

[1] J. Shooter, *The Kafirs of Natal and the Zulu Country* (1857), p. 27 ; N. Isaacs, *Travels and Adventures in Eastern Africa* (1836), ii. 293.

[2] Sir J. G. Frazer, *Early History of the Kingship* (1905), p. 198.

[3] T. C. Hodson, *The Naga Tribes of Manipur* (1911), p. 24.

[4] L. Desplagnes, *Le Plateau central nigérien* (Paris 1907), pp. 321-322.

[5] H. S. Stannus, " Notes on some Tribes of British Central Africa," *Journal of the Royal Anthropological Institute* (1910), xl. 321.

one of these august personages was seen to approach. The dressing has to be performed with the greatest care in a place which cannot be defiled with dogs." [1]

Other less prevalent details of royal raiment are such as the girdle and the veil. In ancient Tahiti the king at his investiture was girded with a sacred girdle of red feathers, which was a symbol of the gods.[2] In Africa veiling the face is a general custom of royalty.[3] The pall of European monarchs, originally bestowed by the Pope, typifies their sacerdotal function. There is a tendency for each article of a royal panoply to carry a special symbolism, significant of the kingly duties and powers, just as the articles of the sacerdotal dress express Divine functions and attributes.

(c) The Dress of the Gods

Sir James Frazer has shown reason for believing that the costume of the Roman god and of the Roman king was the same. Probably the king was dressed in the garments of Jupiter, borrowed from the Capitoline temple.[4] In the earlier theory of society the gods are a special class or grade in the community. Their dress has not infrequently been an important detail in the social imagination, and has even formed a considerable item in the national budget. In so far as they stand for super-humanity, it goes without saying that their raiment is the costliest and finest that can be obtained.

Amongst the Nahuas, clothes were not the least important material both of sacrifice and of ministra-

[1] G. S. Robertson, *The Kafirs of the Hindu Kush* (1898), i. p. 466.

[2] W. Ellis, *Polynesian Researches* (1829), ii. 354-355.

[3] Sir J. G. Frazer, *The Golden Bough* (3rd edition, 1911-1915), iii. 120-122.

[4] *Id.*, *Early History of the Kingship* (1905), p. 197.

tion to the gods. "The finest cotton and woollen stuffs are not only employed in their clothing, but are lavishly burnt in their sacrifices." [1] The gods of Peru had their own herds of llamas and pacos, whose wool was woven for their robes,[2] and virgin-priestesses spun and wove it and made it up into dress.[3] The Vedic gods wore clothes.[4] The Egyptian [5] and Chaldæan [6] priests dressed their gods and performed their toilet, as Hindu priests do now. The ancient Arabs clothed idols with garments.[7] In Samoa sacred stones were clothed ; [8] and the images of the ancient Peruvians wore garments.[9]

The most artistic of races preserved for a long time the non-æsthetic but anthropomorphic custom of clothing statues with real clothes. The image of Apollo at Amyclæ had a new coat woven for him every year by women secluded for the work in a special chamber.[10] Every fourth year a robe woven by a college of sixteen women was placed on the image of Hera at Olympia. Before starting work they purified themselves with water and the blood of pigs.[11] The image of Asklepios at Titane wore a mantle and a shirt of white wool.[12] Zeus in an oracle commanded the Athenians to give Dione at Dodona new clothes.[13]

---

[1] E. J. Payne, *op. cit.*, i. 435.　　　[2] *Ibid.*, i. 437.

[3] *Ibid.*, i. 508, 510 ; ii. 541.

[4] H. Oldenberg, *Die Religion des Veda* (Berlin 1894), pp. 304, 366-367.

[5] G. Maspero, *The Dawn of Civilization* (2nd edition, 1896), pp. 110, 679.

[6] C. J. Ball, " Glimpses of Babylonian Religion," *Proceedings of the Society of Biblical Archæology* (1892), xiv. 153-154.

[7] J. Wellhausen, *Reste arabischen Heidentums* (2nd edition, Berlin 1897), iii. 99 ; cp. Isaiah, xxx. 22.

[8] G. Turner, *Samoa a Hundred Years Ago and Long Before* (1884), p. 268.

[9] J. de Acosta, *The Natural and Moral History of the Indies* (1880), ii. 378.

[10] Pausanias, *Græciæ Descriptio*, III. xvi. 2, xix. 2.

[11] *Ibid.*, V. xvi.　　　[12] Sir J. G. Frazer's Pausanias, ii. 574-575.

[13] *Hyperides*, iii. 43, 44.

The image of Hera at Samos possessed a wardrobe of garments, white, blue, and purple ; some the worse for wear.[1] The bronze statue at Elis of a man leaning on his spear, called the Satrap, wore a garment of fine linen.[2] The image of Brauronian Artemis on the Acropolis was covered with many robes, offered by devout women. The same was the case with the image of Ilithyia at Ægium.[3] The magnificent robe, first used as a sail for the sacred ship and then presented to the image of Athene at the Panathenæa, is famous. The image was the old wooden Athene Polias of the Erechtheum. It was clothed in the robe. This was woven every fourth year by two Arrhephoroi.[4]

The dress of the god not seldom becomes a thing in itself, just as the dress of a priest or a king may itself be his substitute. The Polynesians employed *tapa* in many ritualistic ways. Idols were robed in choice cloths. Every three months they were brought out, exposed to the sun (the term for this being *mehea*), re-anointed with oil, and returned to their wrappings. The god Oro was supposed to be contained in a bundle of cloths.[5] Matting and sinnet were similarly used. Papo, the Savaian god of war, was " nothing more than a piece of old rotten matting about 3 yards long and 4 inches in width." Idols were covered with " curiously netted sinnet," just as was the ὀμφαλός at Delphi. In Mangaia the gods were well wrapped in native cloth ; one god was " made entirely of sinnet." [6]

---

[1] G. Curtius, *Inschriften von Samos*, pp. 10-11, 17 ff. (a list is given).

[2] Pausanias, VI. xxv. 5.   [3] *Ibid.*, I. xxiii. 9 ; VII. xxiii. 5.

[4] Sir J. G. Frazer's Pausanias, ii. 574-575.

[5] W. Ellis, *Polynesian Researches* (1829), i. 335 ; J. Cook, *Voyages* (1790), p. 1542 ; J. Williams, *Narrative of Missionary Enterprises in the South Sea Islands* (1838), p. 152.

[6] J. Williams, *op. cit.*, p. 375 ; W. Ellis, *op. cit.*, i. 337 ; W. W. Gill, *Myths and Songs of the South Pacific* (1876), p. 107 ; *id.*, *Jottings from the Pacific* (1885), p. 206. Sinnet or sennit is plaited palm-leaf strips.

The Tahitian word for sinnet is *aha*, and the first
enemy killed was called *aha*, because a piece of sinnet
was tied to him.[1]

The term " ephod " in the Old Testament apparently bears three meanings. (1) It is part of the
high priest's dress. Worn over the " robe of the
ephod," it was made of gold, threads of blue and
scarlet, and fine linen. Its shape and character are
doubtful. Held at the shoulders by two clasps, it
was bound round the waist with a " curious " girdle.
(2) The term seems to be used for a garment set apart
for priestly use only. (3) There is the ephod which
is an image or its equivalent. Passages like Judges
viii. 26 make it difficult to interpret it as a garment.
But, apart from questions of verbal interpretation,
which in some cases are very obscure,[2] it is possible
to regard the ephod as a worshipped garment, the
practice being found elsewhere, or as a garment en-
closing or covering an image.[3]

Various divine objects, symbols, or emblems may
be clothed. In Uganda a jar swathed in bark-cloth,
and decorated so as to look like a man, represented the
dead king.[4] The Bhagats make an image of wood
and put clothes and ornaments upon it. It is then
sacrificed.[5] Such cases involve impersonation. Even
an emblem like the Cross, when veiled on Good Friday,
or sacred centres like the Ka'ba and the ὀμφαλός,
when clothed, decorated, or veiled, acquire a certain

---

[1] Davies, *Dictionary of the Tahitian Dialect* (1857), *s.v.*

[2] Judges xvii. 3.

[3] S. R. Driver, in *Dictionary of the Bible*, *s.v.* ; I. Benzinger and L. Ginsberg, in
Jewish Encyclopedia ; *s.v.* Exodus xxviii. 6, xxix. 5, xxxix. 2, Leviticus viii. 7 ; Josephus,
Antiquitates Judaicæ, III. vii. 5.

[4] Sir J. G. Frazer, *The Golden Bough*, iv. 201.

[5] E. T. Dalton, *Descriptive Ethnology of Bengal* (1872), pp. 258-259.

personal quality. The line is not always easily drawn between covering and clothing.

In the highest stages of theistic imagination the dress of a god tends to be metaphorical. He is clothed with the blue sky (as Christ in Burne-Jones's picture of the Second Advent), with light, with clouds, or with thunder, with majesty, power, and splendour.

(d) The Dress of Victims

By dressing an inanimate object, an animal, or a plant, a human quality is placed upon it. It thus becomes a member of society, by which capacity its saving force is enhanced. It does not follow that being so garbed it is a substitute for a previous human sacrifice. Even gifts may be so personalized. The Malays dress and decorate buffaloes which are presented as a gift.[1] But the principle is remarkably dominant in the case of sacrifices and effigies.

There are cases of a reverse impersonation. After killing a bear, the Koriaks dress a man in its skin, and dance round him, saying that they had not slain the bear.[2] When Nutkas had killed a bear they put a chief's bonnet on its head and offered it food.[3]

Ordinary impersonation is more frequent. Russian peasants dress up a birch tree in woman's clothes.[4] At the Little Dædala the Platæans dressed a wooden image made roughly from a tree, and decorated it as a bride.[5] The last sheaf of corn and similar representa-

---

[1] W. W. Skeat, *Malay Magic* (1900), p. 39.

[2] A. Bastian, *Der Mensch in der Geschichte* (Leipzig 1860), iii. 26.

[3] *A Narrative of the Adventures and Sufferings of John R. Jewitt* (Middletown 1820), p. 117.

[4] W. S. Ralton, *Songs of the Russian People* (2nd edition, 1872), pp. 234-235.

[5] Pausanias, *Græciæ Descriptio*, ix. 3.

tions of the corn-spirit are dressed in women's clothes
at European harvests.[1] The old Peruvians had a
similar rite, and dressed a bunch of maize in women's
clothes.[2] The effigy called "Death," torn in pieces
by Silesian villagers, is dressed in their best clothes.[3]
The image of "Death" in Transylvania is dressed in
"the holiday attire of a young peasant woman, with
a red hood, silver brooches, and a profusion of ribbons
at the arms and breast."[4] The Iroquois sacrificed
two white dogs, decorated with red paint, wampum,
feathers, and ribbons.[5] The human scapegoat of
Thuringia was dressed in mourning garb.[6] The scapegoat of Massilia was dressed in sacred garments.[7] The
human victims of the Mexicans were dressed in the
ornaments of the god, in gorgeous attire. In some
cases, when the body was flayed, a priest dressed himself in the skin to represent the deity.[8] The human
victim of Durostolum was clothed in royal attire to
represent Saturn. The mock-king in various lands is
dressed in royal robes, actual or sham.[9] The reasons
for the various dresses just enumerated are sufficiently
clear.

Dress, by personalizing a victim, provides a convenient method of substitution. When the oracle
ordered the sacrifice of a maiden, a goat was dressed
as a girl and slain instead.[10] Such cases may be ætio-
logical myths, but they may well have actually occurred.

---

[1] Sir J. G. Frazer, *The Golden Bough*, vii. 140 ff.

[2] *Ibid.*, vii. 172 ff.

[3] Reinsberg-Düringsfeld, *Das festliche Jahr* (Leipzig 1873), p. 80.

[4] Sir J. G. Frazer, *op. cit.*, iv. 247 ff.   [5] *Ibid.*, viii. 258 ; ix. 127, 209.

[6] Aeneas Sylvius, *Opera* (Bâle 1571); p. 423.

[7] Servius on Virgil, *Æneid*, iii. 57.

[8] Sir J. G. Frazer, *op. cit.*, ix. 275 ff.   [9] *Ibid.*, iv. 148 ff. ; ix. 403 ff.

[10] Eustathius on Homer, *Iliad*, ii. 732.

It does not follow, however, as has already been urged, that all cases of a humanly clothed animal or vegetable victim represent substitution for an originally human sacrifice.

The principle of assimilation to a particular environment, which is the focus of the ceremony, has striking illustrations. In a folk-drama of Moravia, Winter is represented by an old man muffled in furs, and wearing a bearskin cap. Girls in green danced round a May-tree.[1] A common practice in European and other folk-custom is to dress a person representing the spirit of vegetation in flowers or leaves. " In time of drought the Servians strip a girl to her skin and clothe her from head to foot in grass, herbs, and flowers, even her face being hidden behind a veil of living green. Thus disguised she is called the Dodola, and goes through the village with a troop of girls." [2] A remarkable case is seen in Sabæan ritual. When a sacrifice was offered to " the red planet Mars," as Longfellow calls it, the priest wore red, the temple was draped with red, and the victim was a red-haired, red-cheeked man.[3] The girl-victim sacrificed by the Mexicans to the spirit of the maize was painted red and yellow, and dressed to resemble the plant. Her blood being supposed to recruit the soil, she was termed *Xalaquia*, " she who is clothed with the sand." [4] The similar victim of the Earth-goddess occupied her last days in making clothes of aloe fibre. These were to be the ritual dress of the maize-god. The next victim, a man, wore the female victims' skin, or rather

---

[1] Sir J. G. Frazer, *op. cit.*, iv. 257.   [2] *Ibid.*, i. 273.

[3] D. Chwohlsohn, *Die Ssabier und der Ssabismus* (St. Petersburg 1856), ii. 388-389.

[4] E. J. Payne, *op. cit.*, i. 422-423.

a portion of it, as a lining for the dress she had woven.[1]
The victim of Tezcatlipoca was invested for a year
with the dress of the god. Sleeping in the daytime,
he went forth at night attired in the god's robes, with
bells of bronze upon them.[2]   At the festival of Toxcatl,
Tezcatlipoca's image was dressed in new robes, and
all the congregation wore new clothes.[3]

12. SOCIAL CONTROL OF DRESS

Dress expresses every social moment, as well as
every social grade.   It also expresses family, municipal,
provincial, regional, tribal, and national character.
At the same time it gives full play to the individual.
A complete psychology of the subject would analyse all
such cases with reference to the principle of adaptation.

The least reducible of all distinctive costumes are
the racial and the sexual.   For instance, as we have
already rites in another connexion, the Hindu fastens
his jacket to the right ; the Muslim to the left.[4]   In
European dress the male fashion is to fasten buttons
on the right, the female on the left.   Where a division
is central, the former still has the buttons on the right
side, the latter on the left, the respective garments
thus folding over in opposite directions.   The larger
differences are obvious, and need not be repeated.

A remarkable tendency is observable at the present
day, which is due to increased facilities of travel and
inter-communication, towards a cosmopolitan type of
dress, European in form.

The sense of solidarity distinguishing social from

---

[1] E. J. Payne, *op. cit.*, i. 470.
[2] *Ibid.*, i. 480 ; E. B. Tylor, *Anahuac* (1861), p. 236.
[3] E. J. Payne, *op. cit.*, i. 487-488.
[4] W. Crooke, *Things Indian* (1906), p. 163.

individual life is sometimes expressed, as culture
advances, in laws referring not only to the preserva-
tion of social grades as such, but to their economic
delimitations. Various particular reasons which do not
call for examination here have been the immediate
inspiration of sumptuary laws in various races and
nations. The sumptuary law proper is often combined with regulations of grade-fashion.

One of the earliest "laws" of the kind is to be
found in the *Lī-kī* of the Chinese.[1] The Koreans
have strict sumptuary laws relating to dress. "The
actual design of the dress is the same for all classes;
but it is the material of which it is made and its colour
that are affected by the law. The lower and middle
classes may wear none but garments of cotton or hemp;
while silk is the prerogative of the officials, who have
the right also of wearing violet, which is a sign of good
birth or officialdom." The dress itself, usually white,
consists of an enormous pair of trousers, tied under
the armpits, and two or more coats reaching to the
ankles. The sleeves of these are large, like those of
the Japanese *kimono*. The poor wear sandals, the rich
leather-lined shoes. In wet weather work-people
wear wooden clogs, in shape like the French *sabots*.[2]
Silk, according to Zoroastrian law, "is good for the
body, and cotton for the soul." The former is derived from a "noxious creature"; the latter acquires
from earth and water, which when personified are
angels, part of their own sacredness.[3] The Koran
forbids men to wear silk or gold ornaments. The

---

[1] *Sacred Books of the East*, xxvii. 238.
[2] H. S. Saunderson, "Notes on Corea and its People," *Journal of the Anthropological Institute* (1895), xxiv. 302-303.
[3] *Sacred Books of the East*, xxiv. 49.

Prophet forbade also the wearing of long trousers
"from pride." His injunction was : "Wear white
clothes . . . and bury your dead in white clothes. . . .
They are the cleanest, and the most agreeable." [1]

The military Dorian State passed laws against
luxury in female dress. The Solonian legislation
apparently followed its example. The *lex Oppia*
of the Romans forbade, *inter alia*, the wearing by
women of a dress dyed in more than one colour, except at religious ceremonies. The Emperor Tiberius
forbade the wearing of silk by the male sex. Philip
the Fourth enacted a law against luxury in dress.
The law of the Westminster Parliament of 1363 was
concerned chiefly with regulating the fashion of dress
of the social orders. The law passed in 1463 (3 Edw.
IV. c. 5) regulated dress generally on the lines of the
Mercantile Theory of Economics, as had been the
case, though less explicitly, in the previous English
sumptuary legislation. Luxury in dress (so the theory
was applied) merely increased the wealth of other
countries. A Scottish law of 1621 was the last of the
kind.[2]

It is natural that social resentment should follow
breaches of the most characteristic of all social con-
ventions. The mere fact of strangeness as disturbing
the normal environment is enough. Thus, in children
and uneducated persons, "anger may be aroused by
the sight of a black skin or an oriental dress or the
sounds of a strange language." [3] In accordance with
this essentially social instinct, the *Lī-kī* denounces

---

[1] *Hidayah*, iv. 92 ; *Dictionary of Islam*, *s.v.* "Dress."

[2] Guizot, *Civilization* (1846), ch. 15.

[3] E. Westermarck, *The Origin and Development of the Moral Ideas* (2nd edition,
1912-1917), ii. 227.

the wearing of strange garments as a sin, adding that
it "raises doubts among the multitudes." The
offence was punishable with death.[1]

Various ideas of personal dignity are apt to be
outraged by such breaches. Even in low cultures,
carelessness in dress reflects upon both subject and
object. Unless a Masai girl is well dressed according
to native ideas, and anoints herself with oil, she is
not admitted into the warriors' kraals,—a social
privilege,—and is regarded as outcast.[2] In view of
such social feeling, it is not surprising that in countries like India there is no liberty of the subject as
regards dress. Nor is there actually any more liberty
in the matter for members of European or American
societies. Decency, essentially a social idea, has here
its widest meaning : to contravene any unwritten law
of dress is an offence against decency—in itself an
adaptation to environment and state.

[1] *Sacred Books of the East*, xxvii. 237.
[2] A. C. Hollis, *The Masai* (Oxford 1905), p. 250.

II. DRINKS, DRINKERS, DRINKING

THE sensation of thirst is the psychological correlate of the metabolic functions of water. In direct importance drink comes next to air and before food. Thus in social psychology drink has played a more important part than food, especially since the primitive discoveries of fermentation and distillation made alcohol a constituent of drinkables. After being weaned from his mother's milk—a drink which is also a complete food—man finds a "natural" drink in water. But, as experimentation in food-material proceeded, the sensation of thirst was supplemented by the sense of taste. The resulting complex "sense of drink" was satisfied by a series of discoveries which gave to drinkables certain properties both of food and of drugs.

Before they were corrupted by European spirit, the Eskimo drank chiefly iced water, which they kept in wooden tubs outside their houses.[1] But on occasion they drank hot blood, and melted fat. An observer states of the New Hebrideans : "I have never seen a native drink water (or indeed use it for any purpose). When thirsty, a young coco-nut is split, and then with the head thrown back the whole of the milk is literally poured down the throat, without so much as one gulp. . . . The avoidance of the most obvious

---

[1] F. Ratzel, *The History of Mankind* (1896-1898), ii. 116.

[drink], fresh running water, which is in great abundance, and generally excellent, is very curious." [1]

1. FERMENTED DRINKS

(a) Beers

It is impossible to trace with precision the order of discovery and invention. Probably one of the earliest steps was the use and storage of fruit-juices. In time the practice of storage would lead to the discovery of fermentation. The use of corn for the preparation of fermented liquor is perhaps almost as early as its use for food. Cereal agriculture itself " received a powerful stimulus from the discovery that infusions of corn, like drinks made from the juices of fruits and the sap of trees, acquire an intoxicating quality by fermentation. . . . In most parts of the Old and the New World the produce of cereal agriculture was from an early period largely consumed in the manufacture of some species of beer . . . the early cultivators drank it to excess." [2]

The use of malted grain is probably later than the simpler principle of infusion. The term beer is generally employed to include the products of both. In the majority of early beers, such as the Mexican and Peruvian *chicha*, infusion only is used.

In Eastern Asia an intoxicant made from rice is very general. *Oryza glutinosa* is frequently used for it. The manufacture among the Dayaks is as follows. The rice is boiled, placed in pots with yeast, *ragi*.

[1] B. T. Somerville, " Ethnological Notes on New Hebrides," *Journal of the Anthropological Institute* (1894), xxiii. 381-382.

[2] E J. Payne, *History of the New World called America* (Oxford 1892-1899), i. 363-364

This stands for some days exposed to the sun. Then water is added, and the mixture is allowed to ferment for two days. It is then strained through a cloth. This drink is the *tuwak* of the Dayaks, the *tapai* of the Malays, the *badag* of Java. A similar drink is made by the Buginese and Makassars, called *brom*. These drinks are extremely intoxicating.[1] The rice beer, *zu*, of the Nāgas is said to be soporific rather than intoxicating.[2] This is also largely the case with barley-beers in all their varieties. " The liquor which plays so important a part in the daily life of the Garo is always brewed and never distilled. It may be prepared from rice, millet, maize, or Job's tears." [3] Many aboriginal tribes of India drink rice-beer.[4] The term *samshoo* or *samshee*, in China, includes rice-beer. *Saké* or *saki*, the national drink of the Japanese, is made from the best rice-grain by fermentation. It has a slightly acid taste, and is of the colour of pale sherry. Inferior varieties are *shiro-zaké* (white *saké*), and a muddy sort, *nigori-zaké*. There is a sweet variety, *mirin*.

Beer made from varieties of millet (*Andropogon sorghum vulgaris*) is the chief African drink. Its use extends from the Kafirs to the Egyptians. Under the name of *pombe* it is familiar throughout Central Africa.[5] In Egypt it is known as *durra*-beer. Besides

---

[1] Wilken-Pleyte, *Handleiding voor de vergelijkende Volkenkunde van Neder-landsch-Indië* (Leyden 1893), p. 9.

[2] T. C. Hodson, *The Nāga Tribes of Manipur* (1911), p. 7.

[3] A. Playfair, *The Garos* (1909), p. 52.

[4] C. A. Sherring, "Notes on the Bhotias of Almora and British Garhwal," *Memoirs of the Asiatic Society of Bengal* (Calcutta 1907), i. 102 (in the second pagination of pp. 93 ff.).

[5] L. Decle, " The Watusi," *Journal of the Anthropological Institute* (1894), xxiii. 422 ; F. Ratzel, *op. cit.*, ii. 357.

durra-beer, the Nubians and Abyssinians make a sour beer from oats.[1]

Where barley is the staple grain for beer manufacture, rye is sometimes used to make a coarser variety. Wheat is occasionally used. In Germany it was once largely employed in what was known as *Weissbier*.

A grain as important regionally as rice and millet for the manufacture of beer is maize (*Zea mais*). Occasionally used in the Old World, as in parts of Africa, it is the staple grain for beer in America, its use extending from the Chaco Indians to the Apaches in the North. The latter made much use of it in their ceremonial life. They called it *tizwin*, and flavoured it with various spices.[2] The Southern and Central America maize-beer is known as *chicha*—a name as familiar as is *pombe* in Africa. The fermented liquor, *chicha*, is an infusion of cooked maize in water. This is allowed to ferment. Its use was universal throughout ancient Mexico and Peru.[3] *Chicha* boiled down with other ingredients was a particularly strong intoxicant, used only at the *huacas*. To-day the Iquitos of the Amazons brew very excellent *chicha*, flavouring it with the young shoots of a plant which has the effects of an opiate.[4]

In Mediterranean and North European culture, barley has been the staple of beer. The ancient Egyptians made a beer, *zythum*, from barley. Dios-

---

[1] F. Ratzel, *op. cit.*, iii. 39.

[2] J. G. Bourke, "Distillation by Early American Indians," *The American Anthropologist* (1894), vii. 297 ; W. B. Grubb, *An Unknown People in an Unknown Land* (1911), p. 76 ; Sir E. F. Im Thurn, *Among the Indians of Guiana* (1883) p. 263.

[3] E. J. Payne, *op. cit.*, i. 364.

[4] Sir C. Markham, " A List of the Tribes of the Valley of the Amazons, including those on the Banks of the Main Stream and of all the Tributaries," *Journal of the Royal Anthropological Institute* (1910), xl. 103.

corides mentions ζύθος, κοῦρμι, and βρῦτον as being used in the Greek world. The Hebrews seem to have included beer in the term *shēkhār* (" strong drink "). Spanish beer (*celia* or *ceria*), Gallic beer (*cerevisia*), and an Illyrian beer were known to the Romans. Germany and England have always been famous for their beers, and in modern times their output is the most important. There was an old distinction between ale (beer without hops) and beer (the hopped liquor). Climate and water, as in the case of wine, have much to do with the production of varieties. English beer is quite a distinct variety from either the light or the dark beer of Germany. The Russian *kvass* is a beer of barley and rye, or of rye alone.

The geographical range of beer, including rice, maize, and millet, as well as barley and rye-beer, under the term, is precisely that of the respective cereals, covering the globe, except the Arctic and Antarctic parallels, and a narrow belt where the vine grows. In this belt, wine has always had precedence over beer and spirits, and it is not a luxury. In northern Europe, beer is more or less a " national " drink, and everywhere it is a comparatively cheap beverage. Its general characteristic as opposed to wine is that it has greater power of refreshment. Improved methods of storage have increased this since the time when beer had to be drunk as soon as it fermented.

(b) *Wines*

There is no reason why the term wine should not be retained to include the many varieties of liquor made by savage and semi-civilized races from the sap of trees. The *latex* of vegetable stems is sufficiently homologous with the juice of fruits, as that of the grape, to be classified with it in a genus distinct from fermented grain. It should be noted, however, that observers sometimes use the terms beer and wine indiscriminately, and do not always distinguish between fermented and distilled liquors.

As soon as vegetable juices, as distinguished from decoctions of grain on the one hand and infusions of leaves and berries on the other, are in question, the difference between the taste of grape-sugar, maltose, and thein is conspicuous. The character of wines may be described as sweet, that of teas as bitter, and that of beers as bitter-sweet. This permanent character is, as will be noted below, generally modified by art. The discovery of the drink-value of the sap of certain trees was not difficult. Those chiefly used are palms, sugar-canes, and agaves. In West Africa, palm-wine is the universal drink,[1] and it is commonly used all over the continent. The tree used is the *Raphia vinifera*, a bamboo-palm. The same tree is used for the purpose in Madagascar.[2] Palm-wine is the chief drink in most of the East Indian islands, Celebes, and especially the Moluccas; it is used to some extent in Java, Sumatra, Malaysia, and India. In the Moluccas the chief tree used is the *Arenga saccharifera*. The flower-stalk is tapped and the juice is fermented. Sweetness is sometimes corrected by adding bark. This drink, a typical form of palm-wine, is known as *sagero* in the Moluccas, *tuwak* in Malaysia and among the Bataks and Dayaks, and *legen* in Java.[3]

---

[1] F. Ratzel, *The History of Mankind* (1896-1898), iii. 110; E. Torday and T. A. Joyce, "Notes on the Ethnography of the Ba-Yaka," *Journal of the Anthropological Institute* (1906), xxxvi. 42.

[2] W. Ellis, *History of Madagascar* (1838), i. 210.

[3] Wilken-Pleyter, *op. cit.*, pp. 8-9.

It is the *toddy* of India, which is also made from the coco-palm and date-palm.[1] The *Borassus flabelliformis* is used in Leti, Moa, and Lakor.[2] This palm is the *Palmyra* of India and Africa. In view of the principle that adaptation to climatic conditions is partly effected by diet, it is noteworthy that the people of Tenimber and Timorlaut say that it is impossible to live in these islands without drinking a sufficiency of palm-wine.[3] The Guaraunos of the Orinoco made a fermented drink from the Mauritia palm.[4] The *gwy* of British Guiana is from the *æta* palm.[5] The not distant relative of these palms, the sugar-cane (*Saccharum officinarum*), is an obvious source of drinkables. In Burma, Assam, and Tong-king a fermented drink is made from it together with pine-apple juice.[6] The A-kamba make a fermented liquor from the sugar-cane and dried fruits.[7] The A-kikuyu ferment the juice of the sugar-cane.[8]

The ancient Mexicans were very skilful in the preparation of fermented liquors. The chief source of material was the *maguey*, the false or American aloe (*Agave Americana*), the fermented sap of which forms *pulque*. Like palm-wine, *pulque* is obtained by tapping the flowering stalk of the aloe. The sap can be drawn off three times a day for several months, one plant yielding perhaps several hogsheads. To increase its intoxicating qualities, various roots are added. In

---

[1] Rājendralāla Mitra, *Indo-Aryans* (Calcutta 1881), i. 418.

[2] J. G. F. Riedel, *De sluik- en kroesharige rassen tusschen Selebes en Papua* (The Hague 1886), pp. 15, 382-383, 434.

[3] *Ibid.*, p. 83.   [4] E. J. Payne, *op. cit.*, i. 309.

[5] Sir E. F. Im Thurn, *op. cit.*, p. 268.   [6] F. Ratzel, *op. cit.*, i. 361.

[7] C. W. Hobley, *The Ethnology of A-Kamba and other East African Tribes* (Cambridge 1910), p. 31.

[8] W. S. and K. Routledge, *With a Prehistoric People, the Akikuyu of British East Africa* (1910), p. 62.

appearance it resembles milk and water, or soapsuds, and it tastes and smells like rotten eggs. In 1890, 75,000 tons of *pulque* were carried on the main line of the Mexican railway—twice as much as the weight of any other commodity.[1]

The North American Indians made a fermented liquor from maple- and birch-sugar.[2]   In England the sap of these trees, as also of the ash and spruce, has been used for the same purpose. Spruce-" beer " (the German *Sprossenbier*) is common in northern Europe—a decoction of the young leaves of the spruce-fir. Cider is a fermented liquor made from apples.

The geographical range of the grape-vine makes two narrow belts round the world, extending, roughly, from parallel 30° to 50° N. and S.   But various conditions have limited its successful exploitation even here, and its most effective range is confined to southern and central Europe and parts of western Asia. In Italy, Spain, Portugal, Greece, and southern Europe generally the vine grows easily. In northern France and Germany it needs very careful culture. The southern wines, it has been noted, possess a larger proportion of sugar, but often are inferior in bouquet to those of the north.   France, the Rhine districts of Germany, Spain, Portugal, Italy, Sicily, parts of Austria-Hungary, and Madeira produce the best wines of the world. Xeres and Oporto have given their names to famous wines of Spain and Portugal. The sack drunk in old England was a sherry.   The Johannisberg vintages of Germany and the Tokay vintages of Hungary are particularly famous.   The once famous Canary is still produced in the Canary

[1] E. J. Payne, *op. cit.*, i. 374-375.   [2] F. Ratzel, *op. cit.*, iii. 430.

Islands. Greece, Algeria, and Russia make fair wines, and wine is now increasingly grown in Australia, South Africa, and America. In Persia the wines of Shirāz, the produce of an excellent variety of vine, are still famous. In the Græco-Roman world the vines of the Greek Islands, such as Chios, Lesbos, and Cos, produced the most valued wines. The Italian wines never attained their standard of excellence. A good deal of must was used by peasants, and wine turned sour was a favourite drink, and formed part of the rations of troops. The various Græco-Roman drinks were used in Palestine.

2. DISTILLED DRINKS

Distillation, the process of evaporating a fermented liquor, and thus separating alcohol, has been known in the East, especially in China, from the remotest antiquity. It is an invention difficult to trace to its source, but it seems to be attested for a few peoples at the stage of the lower barbarism, and in the higher stages of barbarism it is very generally known. Some of the more primitive American Indians seem to have been acquiainted with the process.[1] A primitive form of distillation was found by Cook in the Pacific Islands. It was known to, but little used in, the ancient Mediterranean civilization.

It is recorded that in the twelfth century the Irish distilled whisky, *uisge-beatha* = *aqua vitæ*, " the water of life." In British Central Africa " spirits used to be made by distilling from beer and banana- and palm-juice by means of a pot and a gun-barrel." [2] But the

---

[1] J. G. Bourke, " Distillation by Early American Indians," *The American Anthropologist* (1894), vii. 297.

[2] H. S. Stannus, " Notes on some Tribes of British Central Africa," *Journal of the Royal Anthropological Institute* (1910), xl. 322.

process is rare in Africa.   In the East it is very common.
The Korean native spirits are distilled from rice or
millet, and vary in colour, from that of beer to that of
pale sherry.[1]   The Chinese distil spirits from millet
and maize,[2] but chiefly from rice.   Rice-spirit and
distilled palm-wine are largely drunk in the East.   In
Sumatra rice-beer is distilled into a spirit.[3]   In South
India this is also used.   *Arrack* proper is a spirit distilled
from palm-wine.   In the Moluccas it is termed *koli-*
water.   *Sagero* from the *Arenga saccharifera*, or *Boras-*
sus flabelliformis, is distilled in a primitive fashion.[4]
Arrack, distilled from *toddy*, or from rice, is largely
drunk in India by the lower classes.   It is the *surā* of
the ancient Hindus.   Various peoples, such as the
Malagasy, distil spirits from the juice of the sugar-
cane,[5] a primitive form of rum.

In modern European civilization the use of spirits
has increased, relatively, more than that of beers and
wines.   The Russian *vodka* is distilled from rye, an
inferior sort from potatoes.   Scotland and Ireland
are famous for their whiskies, France for its brandy
of Cognac, Holland for its schnapps, or hollands, a
form of gin.

Portugal and Spain produce a true brandy known
as *aguardiente*.   Brandy proper is chiefly made in
France.   It is distilled from grape-juice alone.   Factitious or " British " brandy is, like gin, made from

---

[1] F. Ratzel, *op. cit.*, iii. 470.

[2] H. S. Saunderson, " Notes on Corea and its People," *Journal of the Anthropological Institute* (1895), xxiv. 308.

[3] J. W. Boers, " Oud volksgebruik in het Rijk van Jambi," *Tijdschrift voor
Neêrlands Indië* (1840), XXIV. i. 569.

[4] Wilken-Pleyte, *op. cit.*, p. 9 ; J. G. F. Riedel, *op. cit.*, pp. 83, 123, 291, 320,
434.

[5] W. Ellis, *op. cit.*, i. 210 ; Rājendralāla Mitra, *op. cit.*, i. 397.

"silent," or unflavoured, whisky. Whisky is made from a fermented infusion of grain, chiefly barley, sometimes rye, malted or unmalted. Rum in its varieties is made from molasses, and can be produced wherever sugar-cane grows. Its chief seat of manufacture is the West Indies. Germany and Russia produce potato brandy from the *fecula* of potatoes.

Mediæval Europe was rich in the lore of making cordials and essences. To the earliest period of the Middle Ages belong the terms *aqua vitæ* and *elixir vitæ*. The search of alchemy for elixirs of life and youth probably gave some impetus to industrial invention.

Civilized taste has declared against the fermented drinks included in the term "mead." Fermented liquors made from honey have been largely used from the earliest barbarism. The Bogos and Abyssinians make a variety of mead.[1] What is commonly styled honey-"beer" often is merely a sweet fermented liquor; but true honey-wine is reported for the Hottentots,[2] Feloops,[3] and A-kamba.[4] Certain peoples have made fermented liquors from saccharine substances produced from plant juices by evaporation. Such are recorded for ancient Syria, made from wine and palm-wine. In Yucatan a fermented liquor was made from *metl*, honey, and in Peru from that obtained by boiling the berries of *Schinus molle*.[5] Honey-mead, *madhu* (= Gr. μέθυ), whatever its nature, is

---

[1] F. Ratzel, *op. cit.*, iii. 211.

[2] Mungo Park, *Travels in the Interior Districts of Africa* (1860), i. 7.

[3] T. Hahn, *Tsuni-Goam, the Supreme Being of the Khoi-Khoi* (1881), p. 38.

[4] C. W. Hobley, *The Ethnology of A-Kamba and other East African Tribes* (Cambridge 1910), p. 31.

[5] E. J. Payne, *History of the New World called America* (Oxford 1892), i. 377-378, quoting authorities.

recorded for ancient India. It is said to have been superseded by *soma*.[1]

●

3. INFUSIONS

Tea, coffee, and cocoa are stimulants, without the specific effects of alcoholic drinks. Their properties are due respectively to the alkaloids thein, caffein, and theobromin. The use of these infusions and decoctions has increased enormously in modern times. It is significant that China has never been addicted to the use of alcoholic liquor, and that coffee is chiefly grown in Muhammadan countries. Ancient Mexico seems to have had a hard struggle against the national abuse of intoxicants, and its successful crusade was largely due to the presence of cocoa.

The tea-plant (*Thea chinensis*) is a native of China and Assam. Its cultivation in India and Ceylon is only very recent, but has assumed enormous propro-tions, chiefly in N.E. India and Assam, and S. India, as in Travancore. Used for centuries in Russia, which derived good tea from China since its connexion with the East, tea is now drunk practically all over the world. Even a people like the savages of the New Hebrides are fond of tea, coffee, and cocoa, provided there is plenty of sugar. But the wilder natives still prefer the milk of the coco-nut.[2] The distinction between black and green tea is due to different methods of drying the leaf. The use of tea among European peoples is relatively recent, while for China it has

---

[1] A. A. Macdoneil, *Vedic Mythology* (Strassburg 1897), p. 114.

[2] B. T. Somerville, "Ethnological Notes on New Hebrides," *Journal of the Anthropological Institute* (1894), xxiii. 382.

been traced back to the beginning of the third millennium B.C.

Tradition assigns the discovery of coffee to Abyssinia. It was introduced into Arabia in the fifteenth century, and into Turkey in the sixteenth. In the seventeenth century its use gained a footing in England and France. The coffee of the New World, deriving from one plant sent to Surinam from Amsterdam in 1718, is now the largest production, Brazil supplying the greater part. Arabia, North Africa, and the East Indies are the other great coffee-regions. It is grown also in Southern India. The best Arabian coffee is grown in Yemen. Besides the infusion of the roasted berry, there is a coffee prepared from the leaves. The green shoots are dried in the sun, and then roasted and powdered. The resulting beverage is the *kishr* of Yemen, the *wedang kopie* of Java, and the *kawah* of Sumatra. The aroma is regarded as being superior to that of ordinary coffee from the berry.[1]

The tree from which cocoa and chocolate are made is indigenous to Central and South America. It was cultivated by the Mexicans, and from them the beverage was introduced to Europe by the Spaniards. The Mexican cocoa was prepared by mixing the cacao-seed into a paste with maize. Diluted with hot water, and churned into a thick froth, which was the actual beverage, it was drunk when cold only. The Spaniards introduced the practice of drinking it hot. Vanilla was usually added as a flavouring. Chocolate, as thus drunk by the ancient Mexicans, was successful owing both to its aroma and to its fatty constituents.

---

[1] Wilken-Pleyte, *Handleiding voor de vergelijkende Volkenkunde van Nederlandsch-Indië* (Leyden 1893), p. 8 ; F. Ratzel, *op. cit.*, i. 433, iii. 211, 334.

It was known to be a nerve stimulant.[1]   In modern times the fat is removed by the screw-press ; this and the addition of sugar render it more palatable.   Ben-zoni (1519-1566) describes it as a drink more fit for pigs than for human beings ; Linnæus named it *Theobroma* ("food of the gods"), *Theobroma cacao*. It contains the same powerful alkaloid as the kola-nut. As a beverage in Western civilization it is only less important than coffee and tea.

4. OTHER DRINKS

Drinks prepared from roots are not numerous. Some have been incidentally referred to ; others are the *kava* of Polynesia, the *paiwari* of Guiana, and the *mishla* of the Mosquitos.   The root of the sweet potato (*Batatas edulis*) is occasionally used.[2]   *Paiwari* and *mishla* are made from *cassava* (manioc), the root, or bread made therefrom, of the *Manihot utilissima*, which in another form is the tapioca of commerce.

With *mishla* we approach a class of drinks which become pre-eminently social both in preparation and in use.   One noteworthy detail reflects the character-istics of communal life, and also illustrates the stage of culture in which the preparation of commodities is *ad hoc*, and storage and artificial production are at a minimum.   This is the fact that the communal drink is prepared only for special feasts, which are, however, frequent, and is all consumed.

The *mishla* of the Mosquito region includes all kinds of strong drink, but particularly that prepared

---

[1] E. J. Payne, *op. cit.*, i. 380.
[2] Sir E. F. Im Thurn, *Among the Indians of Guiana* (1883), pp. 263, 268.

from *cassava* or manioc.[1] The famous *kava* of Polynesia and Melanesia is in many regions becoming
obsolete, owing to the introduction of European
drinks. The *soma* of the ancient Indians, and the
identical *haoma* of the ancient Parsis, are the most
conspicuous examples of the communal drink becoming
religious, and being apotheosized.[2] *Amrita*, the nectar
conferring immortality, was produced, along with
thirteen other valuable entities, from the churning
of the milky ocean. It was, however, an unguent
rather than a drink.[3] The Homeric *ambrosia* was
the food of immortality ; the *nectar* was the drink of
the gods. Sappho and Anaxandrides speak of ambrosia
as a drink; it is also employed an as unguent like
the Vedic *amrita*. Alcman speaks of nectar as a food.
Later, it was a synonym for wine, and acquired the
special connotation of fragrance. The Homeric nectar conferred immortality ; hence it was forbidden to
men. It was described as ἐρυθρόν, and, like Greek
wine, was mixed with water. Apparently by etymology
(νή and root of κτείνω) its meaning is the same as
that of ambrosia.

5. TENDENCIES OF EVOLUTION

The evolution of taste is perhaps not altogether
a sociological, but partly an ontogenic process. It is
correlated with the evolution of manufacture. One
or two tendencies may be observed. For example,
man's drinks tend to the condition of water. Thus,

---

[1] H. A. Wickham, " Notes on the Soumoo or Woolwa Indians," *Journal of the Anthropological Institute* (1895), xxiv. 203-204, 206-207.

[2] J. Eggeling, in *Sacred Books of the East*, xxvi. Introduction ; A. A. Macdonell, *op. cit.*, pp. 104, 110-111.

[3] Sir M. Monier-Williams, *Brāhmanism and Hindūism* (4th edition, 1891), p. 108 ; *cp.* Crawley-Besterman, *Studies of Savages and Sex* (1929), pp. 187 ff.

many beverages of primitive peoples are prepared in
a thick soup-like form. Chocolate, for example, was
drunk very thick.[1]   In Tibet and many Mongol districts tea is prepared with butter. Turkish coffee is
characterized by the inclusion of grounds. English
beer has passed from a muddy consistency to a sparkling
clearness. The thick sweet character of *pulque* resembles the inspissated must of Græco-Roman wine
production. The ancient wine itself in its ordinary
form was very thick, almost of the consistency of
treacle, and probably for that reason it was generally
drunk diluted with water. The sparkling nature of
the best water has during the last century been suggested
both in wines and in water by the method of efferves-
cence.   First applied to the wines of Champagne, it was
adopted for certain of the Rhine vintages. The production of artificial mineral waters, in which an access
of carbonic acid gas causes sparkling, is characteristic
of the last half-century. One result of fermentation is
thus obtained, without, in the case of mineral waters,
any fermentation at all.

Another tendency is towards the reduction of
sweetness. Old wines in which no sugar is left have
been preferred in recent centuries. Such, however,
have a corresponding excess of alcohol. Dryness in
modern wines is increasingly sought after. Thick,
sweet, drinks, like mead and malmsey, are typical
in barbarism, and in ancient and mediæval culture.
Malmsey, the French *malvoisie*, was originally a Greek
wine, and carried on the tradition of the thick wines
of ancient Greece. The Greeks themselves corrected
sweetness by various methods, among them being the

[1] H. A. Wickham, *op. cit.*, xxiv. 207.

use of salt water. Savagery and barbarism had no lack of experiments in the production of varied flavours, if not of the correction of sweetness.

The rice-beer of the Nāgas is flavoured with jungle herbs, such as *Datura*,[1] while the neighbouring Garos dilute theirs with water.[2]   The natives of the Moluccas correct the sweetness of their *sagero* by adding barks of a bitter flavour.   The addition of hops to barley-beer gives it a tonic and more refreshing character.   In old English life spices were largely used in both ale and wine.   Mulled drinks were taken hot.

A similar tendency, found very early in culture, is to be noted in the preference for sour milk.

6. ANIMAL DRINKS

Drinks, other than milk and blood, produced from animal substance, are in the lower cultures not merely soups or broths, but actual beverages.   The credit of the invention and use of the only animal spirit known to the world belongs to the Tatar tribes of Asia.   Their *koumiss*, distilled from the milk of their mares, has been known since Greek times.

Human milk is the natural food of the human infant.   Though differing in some important respects, the milk yielded by various animals is a satisfactory diet for children, and, especially in its products, a valuable food for adults.   The use of milch-animals was a great step towards civilization.

When Dayaks kill a pig or an ox, which is done to music and singing, they scramble for the blood. Men, women, and children drink of it ; they smear

[1] T. C. Hodson, *The Nāga Tribes of Manipur* (1911), pp. 60-61.
[2] A. Playfair, *The Garos* (1909), p. 52.

themselves all over with it, and behave like maddened animals, burying their faces in the bleeding carcasses.[1] Blood, in fact, is to the savage " a perfectly natural food ; scarcely less so, perhaps, than milk, which is nothing but blood filtered through a gland." [2]

7. DRINKING CUSTOMS AND IDEAS

The natural care bestowed upon the preparation of drinkables is guided and developed by growing intelligence, and inspired at certain stages of culture by religious emotion. The Hindu is very particular as to the water he drinks. It must be ceremonially pure, though not necessarily chemically pure. It has to be very carefully fetched. If the carrier touches or comes near an out-caste or anything impure, the water is thrown away, and the vessel broken, or scoured with sand and water.[3] The kings of ancient Persia had their drinking water brought from particular rivers, expecially the Zab.[4]

Water, in Zoroastrianism, is sacred. It is a " dress for breath," physiologically and physically. It is a sin to drink water in the dark, or to pour it away.[5] Water is the " dark spirit " ; for sacrifice it is more valuable than spirituous liquors.[6]

---

[1] " Iets over de Daijakkers," *Tijdschrift voor Neërland's Indië* (1838), I. i. 44.

[2] E. J. Payne, *op. cit.*, i. 393. See, for further instances, C. New, *Life Wanderings and Labours in Eastern Africa* (1873), pp. 189, 397 ; A. C. Hollis, *The Masai* (Oxford 1905), pp. 257, 317-318 ; De Goguet, *The Origin of Laws* (Edinburgh 1761), ii. art. 3 ; W. Blackmore, " The North-American Indians," *Journal of the Ethnological Society of London* (1869), i. 313 ; H. Ward, " Ethnographical Notes relating to the Congo Tribes," *Journal of the Anthropological Institute* (1895), xxiv. 292.

[3] J. E. Padfield, *The Hindu at Home* (2nd edition, Madras 1908), pp. 41-42 ; Dubois-Beauchamp, *Hindu Manners, Customs, and Ceremonies* (3rd edition, Oxford 1906), p. 187.

[4] F. Ratzel, *op. cit.*, iii. 401.   [5] *Sacred Books of the East*, i. 74 ; iv. p. lxii.

[6] *Ibid.*, xxiv. 292 ; xxvii. 435.

A good deal of myth has gathered about the palm-wine tree (*Arenga saccharifera*) in the East Indies. Many stories are told of how the juice of the nut has brought the dead to life again.[1] The Dayaks of South-East Borneo figure palm-wine as milk, flowing from the tree as if from a woman.[2] The Niasers hold that a palm-tree planted by a woman yields more sap than one planted by a man. A folktale runs that a woman after delivery, feeling she was about to die and not wishing her babe to starve, cut off one of her breasts. Out of this grew the palm-wine tree.[3] In Angkola a woman prayed to be turned into a tree. When she died the *Arenga* tree came from her navel, the opium plant from her forehead, the *pisang* from her feet, milk from her breasts.[4]

Besides the stimulating and expansive properties of wine and spirits, the process of fermentation has naturally engaged the popular mind. A good deal of superstition is, no doubt, to be referred to speculation upon this mysterious change. Among the Masai, " when honey-wine is to be brewed, a man and a woman are selected for the purpose, neither of whom has had sexual intercourse for two days. A tent is set apart for them to live in until the honey-wine is ready for drinking (six days), during which time they may not sleep together. As soon as the honey-wine is nearly ready they receive payment, and go to their respective homes. Were they to have sexual intercourse during the six days that the honey-wine is brewing, it is believed that the wine would be un-

---

[1] A. C. Kruijt, *Het Animisme in den Indischen Archipel* (The Hague 1906), p. 150.
[2] *Ibid.*, p. 153.
[3] H. Sundermann, *Die Insel Nias und die Mission daselbst* (Barmen 1905), p. 412.
[4] A. C. Kruijt, *op. cit.*, p. 153.

drinkable, and the bees that made the honey would fly away." [1]

The ultimate reason for such a rule is probably merely an unconscious impulse towards concentration of purpose and avoidance of anything that might divert attention. The prohibition is particularly enforced in delicate operations. From the original impulse would develop ideas about the danger of mixing interests, no less than material ; and, later on, ideas of sympathetic influence, among which may be some comparison of the sexual function with the process of fermentation. In old Mexico the men who prepared *pulque* might not touch women for four days previously ; otherwise the wine would go sour and putrid. [2] The brewing of beer (*sheroo*) is regarded by the Kachins " as a serious, almost sacred, task ; the women while engaged in it having to live in almost vestal seclusion." [3]

In the Mexican example may be seen a possible explanation of the way in which a comparison of the processes of fermentation and of sex was applied. Mixing of personality has attached to itself various terms and ideas of " impurity." Similarly the ingestion of leaven has been regarded as resulting in an impure condition of the material acted upon. Leaven itself is a symbol of corruption. Thus, an impure state in the persons engaged may induce a similar impurity in the object of their labours. Conversely, in other circumstances, it may expedite a desired change, as from barrenness to fertility.

---

[1] A. C. Hobbs, " A Note on the Masai System of Relationship and other Matters connected therewith," *Journal of the Royal Anthropological Institute* (1910), xl. 481.

[2] B. de Sahagun, *Histoire générale des choses de la Nouvelle-Espagne* (Paris 1891), p. 45.

[3] J. Anderson, *From Mandalay to Momien* (London 1876), p. 138.

A similar objection to mixture may be seen in
an Australian custom. If we compare with it the
rule of the Timorese priest [1] which forbids him in
war-time to drink cold water, and orders him to drink
hot water only, so as not to cool the ardour of the
warriors, we may see how a rule arising naturally
from an aversion to anything exciting or disturbing,
when important operations are in progress, may be
sophisticated subsequently. The Australian case shows
an earlier stratum of psychosis. The Euahlayi people
believe that, if a medicine-man have many spirits in
him, he must not drink hot or heating drinks. These
would drive them away. Also, spirits would never
enter a person defiled by the white man's " grog." [2]
The Zambesi rain-maker, in order to keep his spirits
with him, never touches alcohol.[3]

When the savage has reached the idea of a spirit
informing his own organism, he has usually also reached
the idea that heating or spirituous liquor is itself
possessed of a spirit. Thus, if he wishes to concentrate the attention of his own spirit, he must, in sober
earnest, refrain from mixing it with others.

The care bestowed on the preparation of liquors
is also evidenced in the ceremonial handselling of the
new wine. Thus, among the Mexicans, the priest of
the god Ixtlilton, a healer of children, invested with
the god's robes, opened the new wine annually in the
houses of the people, and ceremonially tasted it.[4]

---

[1] H. O. Forbes, " On some Tribes of the Island of Timor," *Journal of the Anthropological Institute* (1884), xiii. 414.

[2] K. L. Parker, *The Euahlayi Tribe* (1905), p. 46.

[3] *Missions catholiques* (1893), xxvi. 266.

[4] H. H. Bancroft, *The Native Races of the Pacific States of North America* (San
Francisco 1882), iii. 410.

New liquor is made by the Nāgas at the feast of *Reengnai* in January. This is a *genna*, or occasion of taboo, and men carry their own water for the rice-beer, and during the manufacture men and women eat separately.[1]

From this " tasting " develops the sacrifice of the first-fruits of the vine. The Romans sacrificed the first of the new wine to Liber ; until this was done, the new wine might not be generally drunk.[2]

The mechanism of drinking as practised by Europeans is more or less identical with that of eating. The liquid does not fall down the pharynx and œsophagus, but each gulp is grasped by the tongue and passed down. Thus a man is able to drink while standing on his head. Many peoples, however, either have not reached this method or have modified it. (The " lapping " method of Gideon's three hundred [*Judges* vii. 5-6] was not " as a dog lappeth," but consisted merely in using the hand as a cup.)

The wild men of Malaysia drink by throwing the water from the hand into the mouth. The Orang Laüt do this with unerring aim, at a distance of more than a foot, without splashing. Even children are expert. A mother gives her infant water by dripping it from her hand.[3] A New Hebrides native throws his head back, and literally pours the liquid down his throat without gulping.[4] The ordinary drink in Oceania is the juice of the half-ripe coco-nut. The nut is held up and the juice allowed to fall into the

---

[1] T. C. Hodson, *op. cit.*, p. 171.

[2] Festus, *De verborum significatione, s.v.* " Sacrima " ; Pliny, *Historia naturalis*, xviii. 8.

[3] W. W. Skeat and C. O. Blagden, *Pagan Races of the Malay Peninsula* (1906), i. 110-111.

[4] B. T. Somerville, " Ethnological Notes on New Hebrides," *Journal of the Anthropological Institute* (1894), xxiii. 382.

mouth. It is unmannerly to touch the shell with
the lips.[1] The Lake Victoria tribes drink their beer
through a tube.[2] In the Hindu ritual of meals,
food is eaten with the right hand, but water is drunk
with the left; the vessel is taken up with the left
hand. The vessel must not touch the lips. It is
held a little way above the upturned mouth, and the
water is poured from it into the mouth. To allow
the vessel to touch the lips would be indecent.[3] The
Fijians never put a vessel to the lips when drinking.
They regard it also as objectionable for several persons
to drink out of the same vessel.[4] A Maori chief would
not touch a calabash with his hands when drinking;
he held his hands close to his mouth, and another man,
a slave, poured the water into them. It was a grave
crime to let any one use a cup rendered sacred by
having touched his lips.[5]

Muhammad forbade drinking water in a standing
posture. Three breaths are to be taken before a draught,
for the reason that thus the stomach is cooled, thirst is
quenched, and health and vigour imparted. Drinking
from the mouth of a leather bag was forbidden. " He
who drinks out of a silver cup drinks of hell-fire."
The faithful may not drink out of green vessels, large
gourds, or vessels covered with pitch, the last being
used for wine. During the fast of Ramadān it is

---

[1] F. Ratzel, *The History of Mankind* (1896-1898), i. 259.

[2] C. W. Hobley, *The Ethnology of A-Kamba and other East-African Tribes* (Cambridge 1910), p. 31.

[3] J. E. Padfield, *op. cit.*, p. 41 ; Dubois-Beauchamp, *op. cit.*, p. 183.

[4] C. Wilkes, *Narrative of the United States Exploring Expedition during the Years 1838-1842* (Philadelphia 1845), iii. 115.

[5] F. Shortland, *The Southern Districts of New Zealand* (1851), p. 293 ; W. Colenso, " The Maori Races of New Zealand," *Transactions and Proceedings of the New Zealand Institute* (1868), i. 43.

held that even to swallow saliva between sunrise and
sunset is a sin.[1]

The natural tendency against mixing reappears
in the custom of not eating and drinking at the same
time. This is only partially identical with physiological law, since certain foods require a liquid vehicle,
and certain drinks stimulate digestion. When eating
rice the Malagasy drink water. But otherwise they
rarely drink at meals.[2] The Hindu does not drink
until the meal is finished.[3] The natives of Borneo
usually drink only after they have finished eating. " They contend that by abstaining from taking
liquid with their food they prevent indigestion." [4]
In British Central Africa the native drinks between
meals, but chiefly water.[5] The Akikuyu never drink
at meals, but drink at any time when thirsty.[6] The
Abyssinians drink nothing at meals.[7]

Eating, especially in the somewhat rapid method
used by early peoples, is hardly compatible with
conversation; hence many rules against eating and
talking at the same time. Drinking does not labour
under this disability. When drink is alcoholic, there
is still less restraint of the tongue. In fifteenth century England " people did not hold conversation

---

[1] T. P. Hughes, in *Dictionary of Islam*, *s.v.* " Drinkables "; A. Leared, *Morocco and the Moors* (1876), p. 204.

[2] W. Ellis, *History of Madagascar* (1838), i. 190-210.

[3] Dubois-Beauchamp, *op. cit.*, p. 183.

[4] C. Hose, " The Natives of Borneo," *Journal of the Anthropological Institute* (1894), xxiii. 160.

[5] H. S. Stannus, " Notes on some Tribes of British Central Africa," *Journal of the Royal Anthropological Institute* (1910), xl. 322.

[6] W. S. and K. Routledge, *With a Prehistoric People, the Akikuyu of British East Africa* (1910), p. 61.

[7] F. Ratzel, *op. cit.*, iii. 228.

while eating, but the talk and mirth began with the liquor." [1]

When existence, as in the middle stages of social evolution, is threaded with superstition, methods of drinking and habits associated with drinking are either emphasized or inverted on special occasions which call for peculiar regard. As already suggested, it is probable that the ultimate psychological reason for these taboos is merely the instinct for concentration and the exclusion of foreign and disturbing interests. Ideas of supernatural danger are developed later, in order to give an explanation of the instinctive rule. Possibly the arbitrary prohibitions of " individual " taboos are due to the same instinct ; at any rate, the observance of such prohibitions helps to form the sense of responsibility.

On the Gold Coast, among individual taboos is the prohibition against drinking palm-wine on certain days of the week.[2] During a *genna* in January the Kabuis forbid young men to drink anything outside the house. On the occasion of the erection of a village monument the villagers may not use drinking-cups, but have to drink from leaves.[3] Among individual taboos of the Bangala are, " You must not drink native wine except through a reed, and never straight out of a vessel of any kind." [4] The cook of the party on the *hiri*, or trading expedition of the Massim, may not drink water, but only coco-nut milk.[5] A Massim

---

[1] T. Wright, *Domestic Manners in England* (1862), p. 396.

[2] C. H. Harper, " Notes on the Totemism of the Gold Coast," *Journal of the Anthropological Institute* (1906), xxxvi. 184-185.

[3] T. C. Hodson, *The Nāga Tribes of Manipur* (1911), pp. 173, 182.

[4] J. H. Weeks, " Anthropological Notes on the Bangala of the Upper Congo River," *Journal of the Royal Anthropological Institute* (1910), xl. 366.

[5] C. G. Seligmann, *The Melanesians of British New Guinea* (1910), p. 102.

sorceress drinks no water, but coco-nut milk only for eight days, by which time she is sacred and able to heal the sick.[1]   In Celebes the priest who is responsible for the growth of the rice may not drink with any one or out of any person's cup.[2]   In South-East Australia a visitor to another tribe was under certain restrictions for a time. He was allowed to drink muddy water, three mouthfuls on each occasion. He had to drink these very slowly, or his throat would swell up.[3] The Thompson Indian girl, during the first four days of her seclusion at puberty, drank water, while otherwise fasting, from a birch-bark cup painted red. She sucked up the liquid through a tube made of the leg of a crane or swan ; her lips were not allowed to touch the surface of the water. Subsequently she was permitted to drink from streams and springs, but even here she had still to use her tube, otherwise the spring or stream would dry up.[4] The Tlingit girl in the same condition had to drink through the bone of a white-headed eagle.[5]

On his first campaign the North American brave was very sacred. Especially was it essential that no

[1] H. H. Romilly, *From my Verandah in New Guinea* (1889), pp. 94-95.

[2] W. Hoezoo, " Over het doen overkomen van inlanders naar Nedenland," *Mededeelingen van wege het Nederlandsche Zendelinggenootschap* (1867), xi. 126.

[3] A. W. Howitt, *The Native Tribes of South-East Australia* (1904), p. 403.

[4] J. Teit, " The Thompson Indians of British Columbia," *Publications of the Jesup North Pacific Expedition* (1898-1900), i. 311-317.

[5] G. H. von Langsdorff, *Reise um die Welt* (Frankfort 1813), ii. 114. Cp. for similar instances from other peoples, A. G. Morice, " The Western Dénés, their Manners and Customs," *Proceedings of the Canadian Institute* (1888-1889), vii. 162 ff. ; G. Hamilton, " Customs of the New Caledonian Women," *Journal of the Anthropological Institute* (1878), vii. 206-207 ; G. M. Dawson, " On the Haida Indians of the Queen Charlotte Islands," *Geological Survey of Canada, Report of Progress for 1878-1879* (1880), Appendix A, p. 131 ; Guis, " Les Canaques, ce qu'ils font, ce qu'ils disent," *Les Missions catholiques* (1898), xxx. 119.

one should touch his eating and drinking vessels. When on the outward journey warriors drank from one side only of the bowl; on the return, from the other. When within a day's march of home they hung their vessels on trees or threw them away.[1] In another account a functionary named *elissu* is mentioned. His duty was to hand to the warriors everything that they ate or drank; they were not allowed to touch these themselves.[2]

Among the Tring Dayaks mourners may not drink ordinary water, but only water collected in the leaves of creepers. This is called " soul-water." [3] Before setting out on a trapping expedition, the Carrier Indian abstains from drinking out of the same vessel as his wife.[4] In Chotā Nāgpur and the Central Provinces of India men abstain from alcohol and women when rearing silkworms.[5]

The last case may be compared with the Masai taboo during the making of wine. There chastity is observed in order that the wine may not be spoiled. If the reason be that by magical " sympathy " a sexual process may taint the wine, that reason and any idea of the sympathetic action of alcohol on the larvæ can hardly apply to the Chotā Nāgpur taboo. Some

---

[1] *Narrative of the Captivity and Adventures of John Tanner during Thirty Years Residence among the Indians* (New York 1830), pp. 122-123.

[2] J. Adair, *The History of the American Indians* (1775), p. 380. Cp. for further instances from other peoples, D. Kidd, *The Essential Kafir* (1904), pp. 309-310; S. Hearne, *A Journey from Prince of Wales's Fort in Hudson's Bay to the Northern Ocean* (1795), p. 204; F. Russell, " The Pima Indians," *Annual Report of the Bureau of Ethnology* (1908), xxvi. 204-205.

[3] A. C. Kruijt, *Het Animisme in den Indischen Archipel* (The Hague 1906), p. 282.

[4] A. G. Morice, " Notes Archæological, Industrial and Sociological, on the Western Dénés," *Transactions of the Canadian Institute* (1892-1893), iv. 107.

[5] *Indian Museum Notes* (Calcutta 1890), i. 3, p. 160.

explanation more in accordance with the evolution of mind seems to be required.

In the following, ideas of sympathetic adaptation appear. During the preliminary ceremonies for making rain among the Arunta no water may be drunk, else the magic would fail [1]—no doubt because of the premature use of liquid. So in Java, when proceedings are taken to prevent the fall of rain, the person interested may not drink anything while the ceremonies are in progress,[2] otherwise the rain would at once commence. Conversely, medicine-men sometimes drink, and generally cultivate wetness, when making rain.

Permanent caution in the act of drinking is often found in the case of important persons, and sometimes it is a social habit. Africa is remarkable for such observances. In the Congo State " there is hardly a native who would dare to swallow a liquid without first conjuring the spirits. One of them rings a bell all the time he is drinking; another crouches down and places his left hand on the earth; another veils his head; another puts a stalk of grass or a leaf in his hair, or marks his forehead with a line of clay. This fetish custom assumes very varied forms. To explain them, the black is satisfied to say that they are an energetic mode of conjuring spirits." When a chief drinks he rings a bell at each draught : and at the same moment a boy brandishes a spear in front of him, " to keep at bay the spirits which might try to sneak into

---

[1] F. J. Gillen, " Notes on some Manners and Customs of the Aborigines of the McDonnel Ranges belonging to the Arunta Tribe," *Report on the Work of the Horn Scientific Expedition to Central Australia, Part iv, Anthropology* (1896), pp. 177 ff. ; Sir W. B. Spencer and F. J. Gillen, *The Native Tribes of Central Australia* (1899), pp. 189 ff.

[2] G. G. Batten, *Glimpses of the Eastern Archipelago* (Singapore 1894), pp. 68-69.

the old chief's body by the same road as the *massanga* (beer)." [1]

When the King of Loango " has a mind to drink, he has a cup of wine brought ; he that brings it has a bell in his hand, and, as soon as he has delivered the cup to the king, he turns his face from him and rings the bell, on which all present fall down with their faces to the ground, and continue so till the king has drunk." The king would die if he were seen in the act of drinking.[2] When Winwood Reade offered the King of Canna a glass of rum, the monarch hid his face and the glass under a towel.[3] When the King of Dahomey drinks in public, a curtain is held up to conceal him. Bowdich describes the scene when the King of Ashanti drank wine ; music played, and the soldiers, brandishing their swords with the right hand, covered their noses with the left, singing meanwhile the monarch's victories and titles, as he drank behind an extemporized curtain. A man of consequence never drinks before his inferiors without hiding his face. It is said in Ashanti that an enemy can most easily impose a spell on the faculties of his victim when drinking. A son of the King of Congo was put to death for having accidentally seen his father drink. A Pongo chief never drinks in the presence of others except behind a screen.[4] When the King of Unyoro in Central Africa went to the royal dairy to drink milk, the men

---

[1] Sir J. G. Frazer, *The Golden Bough*, iii. 120, quoting *Notes analytiques sur les collections ethnographiques du Musée du Congo. I. Les Arts, Religion* (1902-1906), p. 164.

[2] Sir J. G. Frazer, *op. cit.*, iii. 117-118, quoting authorities.

[3] W. W. Reade, *Savage Africa* (1863), pp. 184; 543.

[4] J. L. Wilson, *Western Africa* (1856), pp. 202, 308, 310 ; Sir R. Burton, *A Mission to Gelele, King of Dahome* (1864), i. 244 ; W. W. Reade, *op. cit.*, p. 53 ; T. E. Bowdich, *Mission from Cape Coast Castle to Ashantee* (1873), pp. 438, 382.

dispersed and the women covered their heads. No
one might see him drink. A wife handed him the
milk-bowl, but turned her face away.[1] The Thompson Indians believe that enemies can injure a man
by magic when he drinks.[2] A Warua when drinking
holds a cloth before his face. The habit is particularly
strong in the presence of a woman. " I had," says
Cameron, " to pay a man to let me see him drink ; I
could not make a man let a woman see him drink." [3]

In these cases the development takes the form of
a real, though secondary, sense of modesty. Von
den Steinen found in Central Brazilian tribes a sense
of modesty, attended by shyness and blushing, exhibited when alimentary functions were in progress,
a sense as keen as that shown by the majority of the
human race in the matter of sexual functions.[4] In
similar rules cited below there may be seen not merely
habits of etiquette, but a sense of modesty and a law
of decency, involving the fear of exciting disgust.
The idea that such practices hinder the entrance of
evil influences, or prevent the soul from escaping,[5] is
a later sophistication, and cannot explain their origin.

When the Indian of Cape Flattery falls ill, he
often ascribes it to a demon which entered his body
when he was drinking at a stream.[6] Bulgarians before drinking make the sign of the Cross, to prevent

---

[1] Sir J. G. Frazer, *op. cit.*, iii. 119, quoting J. Roscoe.

[2] J. Teit, " The Thompson Indians of British Columbia," *Publications of the
Jesup North Pacific Expedition* (1898-1900), i. 360.

[3] A. L. P. Cameron, " On the Anthropology of Africa," *Journal of the Anthropological Institute* (1877), vi. 173.

[4] K. von den Steinen, *Unter den Naturvölkern Zentral-Brasiliens* (Berlin 1894),
passim.

[5] Sir J. G. Frazer, *op. cit.*, iii. 120.

[6] J. G. Swan, " The Indians of Cape Flattery," *Smithsonian Contributions to
Knowledge* (1870), xvi. 77.

the devil entering the body with the drink.[1] Devout
Russians used to blow on the glass to drive Satan from
the liquor.[2] Conversely, the soul may be tempted
to remain, though the mouth is dangerously open,
by offering it a share in the beverage. When the
hair of the Siamese boy is cut, there is a danger lest
the *kwun*, the guardian spirit of the head, may de-
part. It is enticed and captured; then coco-nut
milk is presented to it. This is drunk by the boy, and
thus by absorbing the drink of the *kwun* he retains the
kwun itself.[3]

Rules of drinking, more or less impregnated with
superstition, occur all over the world. In Wetar it
is a serious offence to use a chief's drinking-cup.[4] A
Maori who drank from the cup of a man who wished
him ill became bewitched.[5] The Niam-niam, who
are said to be " particular at their meals," that is, to
observe alimentary decency, wipe the rim of a cup
before passing it on.[6] Great care was taken by the
Fijians that no one should touch the king's cup-
bearer. They regarded it as objectionable for several
persons to drink out of the same vessel, and held that
pollution was carried by saliva.[7] The civilized man
has the same instinct of isolation and of excluding
foreign elements from his drinks.

Contact with particular persons is avoided. According to the rules of Kafir *hlonipa*, relatives of a

---

[1] S. G. B. St. Clair and C. A. Brophy, *A Residence in Bulgaria* (1877), p. 14.

[2] G. A. Erman, *Travels in Siberia* (1848), i. 416.

[3] E. Young, *The Kingdom of the Yellow Robe* (Westminster 1898), pp. 64-65.

[4] J. G. F. Riedel, *De sluik- en kroesharige rassen tusschen Selebes en Papua* (The Hague 1886), p. 455.

[5] J. S. Polack, *Manners and Customs of the New Zealanders* (1840), i. 263, 280.

[6] G. Schweinfurth, *The Heart of Africa* (2nd edition, 1874), ii. 19.

[7] C. Wilkes, *Narrative of the United States Exploring Expedition during the Years 1838-1842* (Philadelphia 1845), iii. 115, 349.

husband will not drink milk at any kraal connected with the wife, nor will the wife's relatives at a kraal connected with the husband. For some time after marriage the wife will not use milk. The principle is that she was paid for with cattle, and would be *insila* (defiled) if she consumed her own purchase. After a visit to her father, from whom she brings a goat or an ox, the taboo is removed. The animal is slain, and the defilement passes from the milk into the animal. She has " cleaned her spoon." [1]

In the above case we have probably little more than a phase of etiquette. In others there is a distinct fear of contamination resulting in various conceptions of real or imaginary injury. In Tonga, inferior persons might not drink in the presence of superiors,[2] and the various " ranks " could not drink together.[3] In India, water cannot be accepted by high-caste from low-caste persons.[4] Even Pahariahs will not drink with Keriahs.[5] Among the Nāgas, with whom village feuds are frequent, one village may often be found refusing to drink from a running stream which supplies another.[6] New Guinea natives refused to drink water offered to them by Europeans.[7]

In cases like the last there is perhaps no definite conception, merely a vague uneasiness about the un-

[1] D. Leslie, *Among the Zulus and Amatongas* (2nd edition, Edinburgh 1875), pp. 173, 196.

[2] J. S. C. Dumont d'Urville, *Voyage pittoresque autour du monde* (Paris 1834-1835), ii. 77.

[3] W. Mariner, *An Account of the Natives of the Tonga Islands* (3rd edition, Edinburgh 1827), ii. 234.

[4] Sir M. Monier-Williams, *Brāhmanism and Hindūism* (4th edition, 1891), p. 453.

[5] V. Ball, *Jungle Life in India* (1880), p. 89.

[6] T. C. Hodson, *The Nāga Tribes of Manipur* (1911), p. 8.

[7] C. N. B. von Rosenberg, *Der malayische Archipel* (Leipzig 1878), p. 478.

familiar. A similar sensitiveness occurs in the case of unfamiliar or untested drinks. When the Eskimo find a new spring, an *angekok*, or the oldest man present, drinks of it first to rid the water of any *torn-garsuk*, or malignant quality which might make them ill.[1] Similar ideas are connected with the hospitable practice of " tasting," though it is not clear that they are the primary reasons of the custom (see below). At palm-wine drinkings the Kruman hostess takes the first and last drink herself, in order to " take off the fetish." [2] The same notion may be involved in the ceremonial tasting by an official of the new wine and the new fruits (see above). In Eastern Central Africa, at beer-drinkings given by the chief, the priest or " captain " of the chief tastes the liquor, to show the guests that it is not poisoned.[3] New Guinea natives taste the water they offer to a stranger, to prove that it is free from poison.[4] Among the Zulus it is not etiquette to offer beer to anyone without first tasting it.[5]

Drinking with a woman is avoided by many peoples in various stages of evolution. The Beni-Harith would not take drink from the hands of a woman on any consideration.[6] An artificial horror is generated in such cases. The Muskhogeans held it equivalent to adultery that a man should take a pitcher of water from the head of a married woman. It was permissible for him to drink if the woman removed the pitcher

[1] H. Egede, *A Description of Greenland* (2nd edition, 1818), p. 185 ; D. Cranz, *The History of Greenland* (1820), i. 193.

[2] J. L. Wilson, *Western Africa* (1856), p. 124.

[3] D. Macdonald, *Africana* (1882), i. 191.

[4] C. H. B. von Rosenberg, *op. cit.*, p. 470.

[5] D. Leslie, *op. cit.*, p. 205.

[6] W. R. Smith, *Kinship and Marriage in Early Arabia* (1885), p. 312.

herself, and retired after setting it on the ground.[1]
Following another line of thought, the Arunta hold
that a draught of woman's blood will kill the strongest
man.[2]

Among the Kafirs and the Bahima a menstrua-
ting woman may not drink milk; if she does, the cows
will be injured. She is restricted to beer.[3]   At his
daughter's first period, however, a Kafir father sets
apart an old cow for her exclusive use, and its milk
constitutes her only food.[4]   After being delivered,
the Greenland mother observes taboos. She has a
water-pail for her own use ; if anyone else drinks
from this, the rest must be thrown away.[5]   Pliny
mentions the belief that, if a menstrous woman touches
wine, it turns to vinegar.[6]   " In various parts of
Europe it is still believed that if a woman in her courses
enters a brewery the beer will turn sour ; if she touches
beer, wine, vinegar, or milk, it will go bad."   In Calym-
nos a menstrous woman " may not go to the well to
draw water, nor cross a running stream, nor enter the
sea.   Her presence in a boat is said to raise storms." [7]

On the face of these customs and ideas there is a
regard both for the woman's own safety and for that
of others.   She is rendered harmless by being insulated,
and at the same time is removed from danger.   It
has been further suggested, for the explanation of
similar cases, that any taint of sexual functions may

---

[1] J. Adair, *The History of the American Indians* (1775), p. 143.

[2] F. J. Gillen, *op. cit.*, p. 182.

[3] J. Macdonald, " Manners, Customs, Superstitions, and Religions of South
African Tribes," *Journal of the Anthropological Institute* (1891), xx. 138.

[4] J. Roscoe, " The Bahima, a Cow Tribe of Enkole in the Uganda Protectorate,"
Journal of the Anthropological Institute (1907), xxxvii. 107.

[5] H. Egede, *op. cit.*, p. 196.

[6] Pliny, *Historia naturalis*, vii. 64-65 ; xxviii. 77 ff.

[7] Sir J. G. Frazer, *The Golden Bough*, x. 96-97.

injure the milk of cows, and that the sympathetic link between the milk and the cow may be snapped by any process which converts the milk into another substance, such as curds.   Members of the " sacred world " may therefore use these substances without injuring their source.   On this principle the Wanyamwesi practice of mixing vaccine or human urine with milk has for its object the safeguarding of the source.[1]

The Jbāla of Northern Morocco believe that a murderer is permanently unclean.   " Poison oozes out from underneath his nails ; hence anybody who drinks the water in which he has washed his hands will fall dangerously ill." [2]   Among the Zulus a wounded man may not touch milk till a ceremony has been performed.[3]

The sources of contamination dangerous to drinkables are almost universally the same.   There are some variations, as perhaps the law of Muhammad that a vessel from which a dog has drunk is to be washed seven times before it is used by human beings.[4]

A universal source of contamination is death. After a death the Zulus drink no milk for a day ; the mourners not for some time.   Widows and widowers apparently are permanently forbidden its use.[5]   A Nandi who has handled a corpse may not drink milk until he has been purified.[6]   The Déné who has

[1] Sir J. G. Frazer, " Folk-lore in the Old Testament," *Anthropological Essays presented to Edward Burnett Tylor* (Oxford 1907), pp. 163-164.

[2] E. Westermarck, *The Origin and Development of the Moral Ideas* (2nd edition, 1912-1917), i. 378.

[3] N. Isaacs, *Travels and Adventures in Eastern Africa* (1836), i. 203-205.

[4] T. P. Hughes, *Dictionary of Islam, s.v.* " Drinkables."

[5] Sir J. G. Frazer, " Folk-lore in the Old Testament," pp. 160-161.

[6] A. C. Hollis, *The Nandi* (Oxford 1909), p. 70.

touched a corpse has to drink out of a special gourd.[1] In the same circumstances the Thompson Indian has to spit out the first four mouthfuls whenever he drinks.[2]

For the classification of the various magical properties of drinks the Zulu theory is instructive. But neither here nor elsewhere can a line be drawn between inherent and acquired characteristics. The Zulus logically distinguish between two complementary species of magical drinks. These are " black " and " white," negative and positive. The former removes, for instance, everything that causes a man to be disliked ; the latter gives him " brightness," and produces liking and admiration in others. The former is emetic in its operation. The ejected matter is placed in the fire ; thus the " badness " is consumed. The white drink, when used, for instance, to command the affections of a girl, or to conciliate a great man, should contain some object that the person referred to has worn next the skin.[3]

Drinks of the first class have the properties of liquids when used for washing ; those of the second have the positive qualities, stimulant or nutritive, which drinks share with food and drugs. A distinction is clearly to be drawn between the latter class and drinks which have been contaminated by alien or dangerous substances.

Just as mythology developed the generic idea of drink into a water of life or of immortality, so it has developed the idea of cleansing into a water of

---

[1] C. Hill-Tout, *The Far West, The Home of the Salish and Déné* (1907), pp. 193-194.

[2] J. Teit, *op. cit.*, i. 331 ff.

[3] H. Callaway, *The Religious System of the Amazulu* (Natal 1868), pp. 142-143.

oblivion. The "Drink of Forgetfulness" is found in Greek, Hindu, Norse, and other mythologies.[1]

In Fijian mythology the spirit of the dead man on his way to the other world drinks of a spring. As soon as he tastes the water, he ceases weeping, and his friends at home cease weeping, forgetting their sorrows. This savage Water of Lethe is called the *Wai-ni-dula*, the "Water of Solace." [2] The Fijian idea is significant when compared with certain ceremonial drinking which terminates mourning. Among the Kacharis of Assam an elder distributes to the mourners "the water of peace," *santi jal;* the drinking of this terminates the mourning.[3] The Kathkars effect "purification" after birth or death by means of water touched by a Brāhman.[4] In South India holy water is drunk to terminate mourning. In Roman Catholic ritual a sick man drinks water in which the priest has washed his hands.[5] At the end of mourning the Kaffir widow rinses her mouth with fresh milk.[6] Chaco Indians "purify" themselves after a funeral by drinking hot water and washing themselves,[7] cleansing thus both the outer and the inner man. In Central Africa the possessing spirit is driven out of a man by drinking an intoxicant. The Gonds believe they purify themselves by drinking

---

[1] W. Crooke, in *Folk-lore* (1898), ix. 121 ; G. W. Dasent, *Tales from the Fjelà* (1874), p. 71 ; M. Frere, *Old Deccan Days* (1868), p. 143.

[2] B. H. Thomson, " The Kalou-Vu (Ancestor-Gods) of the Fijians," *Journal of the Anthropological Institute* (1898), xxiv. 352.

[3] Sir J. G. Frazer, *Totemism and Exogamy* (1910), iv. 298.

[4] J. M. Campbell, " Notes on the Spirit Basis of Belief and Custom," *The Indian Antiquary* (1895), xxiv. 30.

[5] *Ibid.*, xxiv. 38.

[6] H. Lichtenstein, *Travels in Southern Africa* (1812-1815), p. 259.

[7] W. B. Grubb, *An Unknown People in an Unknown Land* (1911), p. 168.

spirits.[1] Among the Orāons a man is re-admitted
to caste after he has drunk the blood of a goat to wash
away his sin.[2] When the Bijāpur Bedars re-admit an
adulteress, they touch her lips with a red-hot twig of
Asclepias gigantea, and give her liquor to drink.[3] In
Mexico during the " bad days," which recurred every
four years, children were made to drink spirits.[4]

In these and similar cases there is a preference for
" strong " water, whether it be hot or spirituous,
or blood, or containing some added virtue. It is
difficult, therefore, always to distinguish " purification "
from the ingestion of virtue or *mana*. Many magical
drinks certainly have both negative and positive
properties. This is the case, whether literally by
acquisition or metaphorically by imagination, with
water itself. The Musalmān Nawab of Savanur drank
Ganges water only, not from piety, but because of
its medicinal properties. The water of which a
Brāhman sips thrice before a meal is " Vishnu's feet-
water." The Kenaras drink water in which the
priest has washed his feet.[5] In early England a cure
for demoniac possession was water drunk out of a
church-bell.[6]

From this aspect drinks are suitable for purposes
of consecration and institution. Their virtue gives
a vigorous set off in the new state. In old Scandinavia
the new king drank a horn of liquor before taking

[1] J. M. Campbell, *op. cit.*, xxiv. 30.

[2] P. Dehon, " Religion and Custom.s of the Uraons," *Memoirs of the Asiatic
Society of Bengal* (Calcutta 1907), i. 157.

[3] *Bombay Gazetteer*, xxiii. 94.

[4] H. H. Bancroft, *The Native Races of the Pacific States of North America* (New
York 1875-1876), iii. 376.

[5] J. M. Campbell, *op. cit.*, xxiv. 29-30.

[6] Sir E. B. Tylor, *Primitive Culture*, ii. 140.

his seat on the throne.[1] European monarchs after
coronation take the Sacrament.   So in Catholicism do
married couples. Interesting variants are the following.   In Avestan times the first food given to the new-
born child was the *haoma*-juice.[2]   Among the Tshi
peoples the father gives his son a name by squirting
rum from his mouth upon him.   Rum is poured out
on the ground for the ancestors on the same occasion.[3]
When a child is received into the Kok-ko of the Zuñi,
his " godfather " drinks " holy water " and gives it to
the child to drink. This godfather acts as a sponsor,
and takes the vows in place of the child.[4]   These customs explain themselves.

As part of his initiation the Southern Massim
boy drinks salt-water mixed with unripe mango-flesh.
He bathes in the sea, and drinks some sea-water.
Then he drinks some coco-nut milk. Whatever the
meaning of these drinks, they play a considerable
part in the process of man-making.[5]   In savage
pubertal ceremonies milk is sometimes drunk in connexion with a pretended new birth. Ancient religion had this fiction. After the new birth of the
taurobolium the initiate was fed on milk, like a new-
born babe.[6]

Ideas of invigoration are one of the most obvious
reactions to the effect of strong drinks. " Dutch
courage " has been an important factor in history.

---

[1] P. H. Mallet, *Northern Antiquities* (1770), p. 196.

[2] *Sacred Books of the East*, v. 322.

[3] A. B. Ellis, *The Tshi-speaking Peoples of the Gold Coast of West Africa* (1887),
p. 233.

[4] M. C. Stevenson, " The Religious Life of the Zuñi Child," *Report of the Bureau
of Ethnology* (1883-1884), v. 553.

[5] C. G. Seligmann, *The Melanesians of British New Guinea* (Cambridge 1910),
p. 495.

[6] *Fragmenta Philosophorum Græcorum*, ed. F. G. A. Mullach (1860-1881), iii. 33.

At a ceremony previous to war the Tobelorese give
their headmen palm-wine outside the temple. After
drinking the wine the generals run seven times round
the temple.[1] This custom is possibly a naive way of
inspiring the leaders of the people. Ancient classical
authors give several accounts of races whose practice
it was to go into battle drunk. " It is extremely
probable that the funeral sacrifice of men and animals
in many cases involves an intention to vivify the spirits
of the deceased with the warm, red sap of life." [2]
The shades in Hades renew their life by drinking
blood.[3] The offering of a drink is a frequent method
of animating a fetish, and is thus analogous to the
use of drink as an institutional rite. The Tshi negro
squeezes rum upon his new-made *suhman*, saying
" Eat this and speak." [4]

In metaphor and mythology drink plays a more
considerable part than food. From similes like " as
cold water to a thirsty soul " [5] to the metaphorical
description of Spinoza as " a God-intoxicated man,"
all the psychical reactions of drinks are expressed in
language.

In religion the story of wine constitutes a distinctly ideal element, and it is here that the function
of drink receives not only a sort of apotheosis, but perhaps a sound physiological explanation. The Vedic
gods were originally mortal ; immortality was acquired by, among other methods, the drinking of
soma.[6] Similarly the Homeric gods attained immor-

[1] A. C. Kruijt, *Het Animisme in den Indischen Archipel* (The Hague 1906), p. 409.

[2] E. Westermarck, *op. cit.*, i. 475.   [3] Homer, *Odyssey*, xi. 153.

[4] A. B. Ellis, *The Tshi-speaking Peoples of the Gold Coast of West Africa* (1887),
pp. 100-101.

[5] Proverbs xxv. 25.

[6] A. A. Macdonell, *Vedic Mythology* (Strassburg 1897), p. 17.

tality by drinking nectar and eating ambrosia.[1]   In
the mythology of ancient Babylonia, Hasisadra brought
into the ark a supply both of beer and of wine.[2]   According to the Mexicans, the first human beings created
by the gods fed on *pulque*.[3]

The sociological significance of orgiasticism has
been studied elsewhere.[4]

" Wine or spirituous liquor inspires mysterious
fear.   The abnormal mental state which it produces
suggests the idea that there is something supernatural in it, that it contains a spirit, or is perhaps
itself a spirit." [5]   The Siamese, intoxicated by the
spirit arrack, says he is possessed by the " spirit,"
in the Animistic sense, of the liquor.[6]   Thus the
juice of the grape is the blood of the vine, its soul or
life.   " The drinking of wine in the rites of a vine-god
like Dionysus is not an act of revelry, it is a solemn
sacrament." [7]

Some typical cases of the religious and social uses
of strong drink remain to be mentioned.   No attempt
is made to define stages of evolution.   The earliest
Brāhmanism used spirituous liquors in acts of worship.
Arrack was offered to the gods.   The *Sautrāmanī* and
Vājapeya rites were typical for the drinking of *surā*,
and the *soma* rite was in celebration of the *soma* itself.
The later Vedas prohibited the worshipper from
drinking the ceremonial liquor for a sensual purpose.
The Sāktas to-day have actually the same principle,

---

[1] Homer, *Iliad*, v. 339 ff. ; *Odyssey*, v. 99.

[2] G. Smith, *History of Babylonia* (1895), p. 41.

[3] H. H. Bancroft, *op. cit.*, iii. 347.

[4] Crawley-Besterman, *Studies of Savages and Sex* (1929), pp. 101 ff.

[5] E. Westermarck, *op. cit.*, ii. 344.

[6] Sir E. B. Tylor, *op. cit.*, ii. 181.

[7] Sir J. G. Frazer, *The Golden Bough*, iii. 248.

and purify the liquors before worship.[1]   The followers
of Zarathushtra have clung to the old way more
consistently than the Hindus.   Liquor-drinking forms
part of almost all Parsi ceremonies to-day.   Liquor
is specially consecrated on New Year's Day.[2]

The Eucharist in its early form has the mark of
a periodic wine-drinking, breaking up the " fast " of
work-a-day life.   It was necessary for organizers like
St. Paul to prohibit excess [3]—a fact which shows that
wine was freely taken.   The wine represented the
blood of Christ and conferred immortality.   In the
course of history the use of wine has been denied to
others than the celebrant, and in Churches which
allow all worshippers to partake of the chalice the wine
is not drunk but tasted.   The Hebrew Cup of Blessing
is an analogue of the Christian wine of the Eucharist.
The early Christians made a free communal use of
the sacred drink ; it was given to the dead ; vials of
it were placed in the grave, with cups inscribed with
toasts, such as " Drink and long life ! "

For very special offerings to a god the Bhils make
kuvari, " virgin liquor."   The distillers in this case
must bathe and wear newly washed clothes before
commencing operations.[4]

For special purposes, other than inspiration, a
priest may become intoxicated.   On certain days the
high priest of the Zapotecs was obliged to be drunk.
On one of these he cohabited with a Virgin of the
Sun.[5]

Gods reflect in an intensified form the ideals and

[1] Rājendralāla Mitra, *Indo-Aryans* (Calcutta 1881), i. 397, 407-408, 417 ff.

[2] J. M. Campbell, " Notes on the Spirit Basis of Belief and Custom," *The Indian Antiquary* (1895), xxiv. 319.

[3] 1 Corinthians xi. 20 ff.   [4] J. M. Campbell, *op. cit.*, xxiv. 320.

[5] H. H. Bancroft, *op. cit.*, ii. 142.

habits of their worshippers. If a god is housed, clothed, and fed, he is also supplied with drinks.

A difficult problem is presented by various customs of eating the dead. Their discussion belongs elsewhere; but they show variation even in the case of drinking. The Cocomas of the Amazons ground the bones of their dead to powder and drank this in their beer. They said " it was better to be inside a friend than to be swallowed up by the cold earth." [1] The Ximanas mingled the ashes of the dead with their drink.[2] Here there can be no survival of cannibalism. The Angoni make the ashes of the dead into a broth. This must be lapped up with the hand, and not drunk in the ordinary way.[3] The native practice, generally confined to the women, of drinking some of the fluids drawn from the decaying body of a dead relative is a commonplace of Australian anthropology.

As a preliminary to the problem may be mentioned the frequent occurrence of morbid perversions of appetite in cases of strong emotion. If such perversion be applied to a psychosis of affection or respect, the Australian and similar practices are more easy to understand. The Irish wake is a familiar example of the practice of drinking to celebrate death. In West Africa the Tshi people drink heavily during the fast which follows a death, and the mourners are generally intoxicated.[4] The same is the case among

---

[1] Sir C. Markham, " A List of the Tribes of the Valley of the Amazons, including those on the Banks of the Main Stream and of all the Tributaries," *Journal of the Royal Anthropological Institute* (1910), xl. 95.

[2] *Ibid.*, xl. 132.

[3] J. Macdonald, " East Central African Customs," *Journal of the Anthropological Institute* (1893), xxii. 111.

[4] A. B. Ellis, *op. cit.*, p. 156.

the Yorubas.[1]   But it is chiefly after the funeral that
drinking is the rule of the feast.

At funerals among the Woolwa Indians there is
much drinking of *mishla*.   A long line of cotton is
stretched, like a telegraph wire, from the house of
the dead, where the drinking takes place, to the burial-
ground where the body has been deposited.   " I
have seen the white thread following the course of
the river for many miles, crossing and re-crossing the
stream several times." [2]   As soon as a Bangala man
dies, the family gets in large supplies of sugar-cane
wine.   Dancing and drinking are carried on for three
or four days and nights, or until the wine is finished.[3]
The Guiana Indians drink and dance at the funeral
feast.[4]

Among the Tshinyaï of the Zambesi the native
beer, *pombe*, plays a considerable part in post-funeral
rites.   For the ceremony of *Bona*, a large quantity
is prepared.   Holes are bored above the grave and
pombe is poured in.   In one hole, in front of the
house where the grave is, the mourners wash their
hands with *pombe*.   As the procession retires, a widow
of the deceased (she is called *musimo*, the spirit), her
head covered with calico, constantly calls out for
pombe, which she drinks beneath the covering.   At
the house of the head widow a large hole is dug and
well cemented.   This is filled with *pombe*, and every
one lies down and drinks it without help of spoon

---

[1] A. B. Ellis, *The Yoruba-speaking Peoples of the Slave Coast of West Africa*
(1894), p. 156.

[2] H. A. Wickham, " Notes on the Soumoo or Woolwa Indians," *Journal of the
Anthropological Institute* (1895), xxiv. 207.

[3] J. H. Weeks, " Anthropological Notes on the Bangala of the Upper Congo
River," *Journal of the Royal Anthropological Institute* (1910), xl. 380.

[4] Sir E. F. Im Thurn, *Among the Indians of Guiana* (1883), p. 225.

or vessel. A feast follows, consisting of *pombe* and meat.[1]

Various considerations, some of which are supplied in the above-cited cases, suggest that drinking at funerals and their anniversaries is motivated by a double impulse, or rather by two complementary impulses, namely, the desire to stifle sorrow, and the desire to give the dead a share in the good things of the world to which they still belong, though absent in the body. These two expressions of feeling, coupled with the " sympathy " shown by the community, render funeral drinking a typical case of social instinct. Secondary ideas necessarily supervene.

The universal employment of a drink of fellowship to institute and also to terminate a social process is found in the case of pubertal ceremonies, though rarely. The reason is that, in this case, the process does not include a pair of persons. In the case of marriage and covenants this essential condition of a social act is patent. It may be said that the reciprocal process in the former class is between the novice and the members of the social state to which he is admitted. And in many analogous cases this is recognized, though the mind in its more primitive stages is slow to recognize by concrete expression such abstract ideas as that of community. But in these stages the other member of the couple may be found in the " god-

---

[1] L. Decle, " The Watusi," *Journal of the Anthropological Institute* (1894), xxiii. 421. For further instances see H. S. Stannus, " Notes on some Tribes of British Central Africa," *Journal of the Royal Anthropological Institute* (1910), xl. 315 ; J. J. M. de Groot, *The Religious System of China* (Leyden 1892, etc.), i. 79, 141 ; W. Munzinger, *Ostafrikanische Studien* (Schaffhausen 1864), p. 473; J. Perham, " Sea Dyak Religion," *Journal of the Straits Branch of the Royal Asiatic Society* (Singapore 1884), xiii. 296 ff.; H. L. Roth, *The Natives of Sarawak* (1896), i. 208 ff. ; J. H. W. Sheane, " Some Aspects of the Awemba Religion and Superstitious Observances," *Journal of the Anthropological Institute* (1906), xxxvi. 153.

father " or sponsor, on the one hand, and individual
members either of the same or of the other sex, the
latter being the indirect objective of the initiation.
Thus among many early peoples the boys after initiation drink with the girls. Similar ceremonies are
performed in connexion with the sponsor. After
initiation the A-kamba youth makes honey-beer, and
gives it to the elder who looked after him during the
ceremonies.[1]   At the end of the *ntonjane*, the Kafir
ceremony performed to celebrate a girl's arrival at
puberty, the girl's nearest female relative drinks milk,
and then hands the bowl to the girl to drink.[2]   From
such practices there may easily develop ideas of taboo,
which is to be ended by drinking or by some other
rite of passage. Thus, in Central Australia the man
whose blood has been taken to supply another with
health or strength is taboo to him until he releases
him from the " ban of silence " by " singing over his
mouth." [3]

Marriage is universally the occasion of a social
feast, and the rite in which the bridal pair drink
together is one of the most prevalent methods of
tying the knot. There is thus both individual and
social drinking at weddings. Sometimes the latter
is not shared by the marrying parties ; sometimes the
individual drinking rite is extended to relatives ; and
sometimes it is carried out by them as sponsors for
the bride and bridegroom. Naturally there is considerable variation in the ritual of the act of union.

At Tipperah weddings the bride receives a glass
of liquor from her mother. She takes this to the

[1] C. W. Hobley, *The Ethnology of A-Kamba and other East Indian Tribes* (Cambridge 1910), p. 76.

[2] G. McCall Theal, *Kaffir Folk-lore* (1882), p. 210.

[3] Spencer-Gillen, *The Native Tribes of Central Australia* (1899), p. 462.

bridegroom, sits on his knee, and, after drinking some
of the liquor, gives the rest to him.[1] Among the
Kafirs milk from the bridegroom' scows is presented
to the bride. Her drinking of this milk renders
the marriage complete, and the tie indissoluble. The
guests exclaim, " She drinks the milk ! She has drunk
the milk ! " [2] Among the Nakri Kunbis of Thana
liquor is given to the pair when the wedding ceremony
is completed.[3] The girl relatives of the Khyoungtha
bride bar the entrance to the village against the bridegroom with a bamboo. Across this he has to drink
with them a " loving-cup of fraternity " before he
is allowed to enter.[4] At weddings in Morocco the
priest hands to the pair a cup of wine which he has
blessed. When both have drunk of it, the glass is
dashed to the ground by the bridegroom, with a
" covert meaning that he wishes they may never be
parted until the glass again becomes perfect." [5] In
the Manuahiki Islands the priest gives the man a coco-
nut containing its milk. The man drinks, and the
woman after him.[6] Among the Larkas a cup of
beer is given to each of the two parties ; they mix the
beer, and then drink it. This completes the marriage.[7]
In the Moluccas, Japan, Bengal, Brazil, Russia, Scandinavia, and many districts of Europe, the bridal pair
drink, as the marriage ceremony or part of it, wine or
beer from one vessel.[8] At Beni-Israel weddings the

---

[1] T. H. Lewin, *Wild Races of South-Eastern India* (1870), p. 202.

[2] H. Lichtenstein, *Travels in Southern Africa* (1812-1815), i. 262.

[3] *Bombay Gazetteer*, xiii. 129.   [4] T. H. Lewin, *op. cit.*, p. 127.

[5] A. Leared, *Morocco and the Moors* (1876), p. 37.

[6] G. Turner, *Samoa a Hundred Years Ago and long before* (1884), p. 276.

[7] H. B. Rowney, *Wild Tribes of India* (1882), p. 67.

[8] J. G. F. Riedel, *De sluik- en kroesharige rassen tusschen Selebes en Papua* (The
Hague 1886), p. 460 ; E. T. Dalton, *Descriptive Ethnology of Bengal* (Calcutta 1872),
p. 193.

bridegroom pours wine into the bride's mouth.[1]   In Korea [2] and China [3] the pair drink wine from two cups, which are tied together by a red thread.   In Christian countries the rite is separated from the marriage ceremonial proper, but is carried out indirectly when the pair receive together the wine of the Communion, which is to be partaken of immediately or soon after the marriage itself.   Among the Gonds the respective fathers of the bridal pair drink together.[4]

Drinking together at marriage is a rite which applies to two parties the principles of social drinking. Sharing in an act is a sort of reciprocity, and, together with interchange of gifts, constitutes the fundamental principle of society.   The more abstract ideas of similarity, union, and identity follow, and the simple ritual of sharing has a corresponding development. From the beginning there are also involved in the process, but unconsciously, the reactions to the physiological feelings of refreshment, and in particular to the effects of alcohol, which increase both self-feeling and altruism.

Pure altruism is the primary motive of many a custom which involves a simple sharing of drink. Here is the virtue of the man who gives a cup of cold water to a little one.[5]   The natives of India have the custom of erecting sheds for the giving of water or butter-milk to poor wayfarers.[6]

Secondary motives, such as a general desire to

---

[1] *Bombay Gazetteer*, xviii. 520.   [2] W. E. Griffis, *Corea* (1882), p. 249.
[3] J. Doolittle, *Social Life of the Chinese* (1866), i. 86.
[4] S. Hislop, *Tribes of the Central Provinces* (Nagpur 1866), App. i., iv.   On the subject generally see Crawley-Besterman, *The Mystic Rose* (2nd edition, 1926), i. 289 ff., 336; ii. 117 ff., 226.
[5] Matthew x. 42.
[6] J. E. Padfield, *The Hindu at Home* (2nd edition, Madras 1908), p. 190.

conciliate or a wish to avoid the injury of a curse or
an evil eye, come to obscure the primary. In the
procession preceding the circumcision of an Egyptian
boy is a servant carrying a skin of water and brass cups.
Now and then he fills a cup and offers it to a passer-
by. Another servant carries a tray with materials
for coffee. It is his business, when they pass a well-
dressed person, to fill and present him with a cup; the
person gives him something, perhaps a half-piastre.[1]
The analogy of other Egyptian customs suggests here
the avoidance of the evil eye.

Even towards slain animals and the human objects
of social resentment pure altruism is shown. Indians
of the Orinoco, after killing an animal, pour into its
mouth some liquor, "in order that the soul of the
dead beast may inform its fellows of the welcome
it has met with, and that they, too, cheered by the
prospect of the same kind reception, may come with
alacrity to be killed." [2]   One may take leave to assign
a worthier motive as the origin of this custom. Similarly, though primitive peoples share their drink
with the dead, some have learnt to explain the custom of placing such things in the grave as a method
of inducing the dead to be quiet, and not to come
and pester the living for anything they want.

The co-operative totems of Australia are perhaps
the earliest instance known of the principle of co-
operative industry elevated into a system. Among
the totems of the Central Australians is a water-totem.
A member of this may drink water when alone; but,

---

[1] E. W. Lane, *An Account of the Manners and Customs of the Modern Egyptians* (1836), ii. 279.

[2] A. Caulin, *Historia corographica natural y evangelica dela Nueva Andalucia, Provincias de Cumaña, Guayana y Vertientes del Rio Orinoco* (1779), p. 97.

if he is in company, it is necessary for him to receive
it, or the permission to take it, from an individual
who belongs not to that totem, but to a moiety of
the tribe of which the water-man is not a member—
a complementary moiety. The principle, according to
Spencer-Gillen, is that of mutual obligation between
complementary food-totems, regulating the supply of
food and drink.[1]

But the principle of reciprocal service is at the
root of all social phenomena. Some of its forms are
curious ; others seem totally unlike the original type.
Secondary ideas, once more, are responsible for these
fluctuations. An African wife drank the medicine
intended for her husband, in the belief that he would
be cured.[2] A similar notion is seen in the belief that
what a man drinks may affect the child whose birth
is expected. A further development is reached in
such customs as that of the Kwakiutl Indian, who,
after biting a piece of flesh from the arm of a foe,
drinks hot water in order to inflame the wound.[3]
At this stage of sophistication there is often a choice of
absurdities. The Indian might be supposed anxious
for his own digestion rather than for the increase of
suffering on the part of his foe.

Another case of the intrusion of a secondary idea
is to be seen in the Australian custom of drinking
human blood before starting on an *atninga* (avenging
expedition). " Every man of the party drinks some
blood, and also has some spurted over his body, so
as to make him what is called *uchuilima*, that is,

[1] Sir W. B. Spencer and F. J. Gillen, *The Northern Tribes of Central Australia*
(1904), p. 160.

[2] R. Moffat, *Missionary Labours and Scenes in Southern Africa* (1842), p. 591.

[3] F. Boas, " The Social Organisation and the Secret Societies of the Kwakiutl
Indians," *Report of the United States National Museum for* 1895, p. 440.

lithe and active.   The elder men indicate from whom
the blood is to be drawn ; and the men so selected
must not decline, though the amount drawn from a
single individual is often very great ; indeed, we have
known of a case in which blood was taken from a
young and strong man until he dropped from sheer
exhaustion." [1]

The beginning of a venture or expedition is universally celebrated by drinking, on the principle of
invigoration, as in the old English " stirrup-cup."
But in the Australian example a further notion has
come in.   If on such an occasion a man joined who
had some connexion with the tribe to be visited, he
was forced to drink blood with the party, and, " having
partaken of it, would be bound not to aid his friends
by giving them warning of their danger." [2]

The Indians of the Cordilleras drink of the water
of a river, and pray the god to let them pass over.
So did the old Peruvians.[3]   Dingan's army at the
banks of the Ubilinganto strewed charcoal on the
water, and then drank of it, " the object perhaps
being to deprecate some evil power possessed by the
river." [4]   More probably the aim is to adapt one's
self to the object by contact, to produce fellow-feeling
and sympathy by communion.

Ideas of union similar to those concerned in marriage ceremonies of drinking, but involving from the
outset, or at least producing, *ipso facto*, the secondary
ideas of mutual responsibility by means of inoculation,

---

[1] Sir W. B. Spencer and F. J. Gillen, *The Native Tribes of Central Australia*
(1899), p. 461.

[2] *Ibid., loc. cit.*   [3] Sir E. B. Tylor, *Primitive Culture*, ii. 210.

[4] H. Callaway, *Nursery Tales, Traditions, and Histories of the Zulus* (Natal 1868),
i. 90.

or ingestion of the other's substance, or a conditional curse, have built up what may be described as the legal forms of social drinking. " The drinking of human blood, or of wine mixed with such blood, has been a form of covenant among various ancient and mediæval peoples, as well as among certain savages." [1] " He who has drunk a clansman's blood is no longer a stranger but a brother, and included in the mystic circle of those who have a share in the life-blood that is common to all the clan." [2] Robertson Smith's induction is actually a tertiary stage of thought on the subject, but present and powerful in the social consciousness of Arabs and other peoples. Among other details in point is the fact that blood-brotherhood itself is often produced by drinking any substance other than blood.

The ordeal, often termed " drinking the oath," is a legal application of a secondary idea. To extract the truth from a man, the Negro dips a *bohsum* in rum. This rum is then offered to the man, and, if he lies, makes his belly swell. A man claiming a debt due to a deceased person drinks the water in which he has washed the corpse. In legal actions before the chief, the *odum* drink is drunk as an oath and ordeal. It is a poisonous emetic.[3] A Masai accused of a crime drinks blood, and repeats these words : " If I have done this deed, may God kill me." [4]

Hospitality, a virtue of universal occurrence, is

---

[1] E. Westermarck, *The Origin and Development of the Moral Ideas* (2nd edition, 1912-1917), ii. 567.

[2] W. R. Smith, *Lectures on the Religion of the Semites* (2nd edition, 1894), p. 315.

[3] A. B. Ellis, *The Tshi-speaking Peoples of the Gold Coast of West Africa* (1887), pp. 197-198.

[4] A. C. Hollis, *The Masai* (Oxford 1905), p. 345. On the subject of oaths and ordeals generally see Crawley-Besterman, *Studies of Savages and Sex* (1929), pp. 219 ff.

often complicated by superstitious accretions due to
fear of the stranger within the gates.

As soon as a stranger enters the house of a Jivaro
or Canelo Indian, each of the women offers him a
calabash of *chicha*.[1] A guest is welcomed by the
Herero with a cup of milk.[2] These are simple acts
of fellow-feeling. It is particularly among Arab
races that the custom attains complexity.

Among the nomadic Arabs of Morocco, " as soon as
a stranger appears in the village, some water, or, if he
be a person of distinction, some milk, is presented to
him.   Should he refuse to partake of it, he is not allowed
to go freely about, but has to stay in the village mosque.
On asking for an explanation of this custom, I was
told that it was a precaution against the stranger ;
should he steal or otherwise misbehave himself, the
drink would cause his knees to swell so that he could
not escape.   In other words, he has drunk a conditional curse." [3]   Zaid-al-Khail refused to slay a
thief who had surreptitiously drunk from his father's
milk-bowl.[4]

Health-drinking, the *propinatio* of the Latins, has
some variations.   One form is the sharing of a drink ;
the person doing honour drinks first, and hands the
cup (in Greek life this became the property of the
person honoured) to the other.   Another is drinking
alone, with a look or a sentiment of goodwill towards
the person honoured.   The projection outwards of
the drinker's will is typified in many languages, as in

---

[1] A. Simson, " Notes on the Jivaros and Canelos Indians," *Journal of the Anthropological Institute* (1880), ix. 391.

[2] F. Ratzel, *op. cit.*, ii. 480.   [3] E. Westermarck, *op. cit.*, i. 590.

[4] W. K. Smith, *Kinship and Marriage in Early Arabia* (Cambridge 1885), pp.
149-150.

most of the customs, by emphasizing the fact that he drinks first. Among the Ba-Yaka and Ba-Huana the host drinks first, and the guest after him.[1] At Abyssinian mead-drinkings the host drinks first, by way of showing that the liquor is not poisoned. He notifies a servant which guests need their cups replenished. On receiving the drink, the guest rises and bows.[2] Among the Kafirs, it is not etiquette to give beer to a guest without first tasting it. This, according to the account given, is intended to safeguard the guest against poison.[3]

Terms like " pledge " connote the idea of guaranteeing goodwill. The poison-test is obviously not the origin of the custom of the host or pledger drinking first. When that custom took on secondary ideas, one of these would be the affirmation that what the host offers is his own, and that it is of his best.

In barbarism the drinking-bout so called is often the form of political discussion. The chief of the Akikuyu gives his people the news at beer-drinkings, to which he invites them.[4]

With agricultural drinking-feasts we return to man's immediate relations to intoxicating or refreshing drink. Drinking is a social rite in connexion with the ceremonial eating of the new crops. Lithuanian peasants observe a festival called *Sabarios*, " the mixing or throwing together," when the sowing of the new corn has taken place.[5] The Cheremiss

---

[1] E. Torday and T. A. Joyce, " Notes on the Ethnography of the Ba-Yaka," *Journal of the Anthropological Institute* (1906), xxxvi. 42, 279.

[2] F. Ratzel, *op. cit.*, iii. 228, 329.

[3] D. Leslie, *Among the Zulus and Amatangas* (Edinburgh 1875), p. 205.

[4] W. S. and K. Routledge, *With a Prehistoric People, the Akikuyu of British East Africa* (1910), p. 63.

[5] M. Prätorius, *Deliciae Prussicae oder Preussische Schaubühne* (Berlin 1871), pp. 60–64.

celebrate the baking of the first bread from the new corn by a ceremonial drinking of beer. " The whole ceremony looks almost like a caricature of the Eucharist." [1] In such rites there is the social consecration, implicit or explicit, of wine itself and its sources.

It is perhaps merely an abnormality that fasting among many peoples does not exclude drinking strong liquor. This is notably the case in West Africa. Spirits are largely drunk during the fast after a death, and mourners are generally intoxicated. During the fast-days of the yam harvest the people drink hard, and the king and chief distribute brandy and rum. [2]

For various obscure reasons, great personages of the sacred world are often restricted to pure water. The ancient kings of Egypt were restricted to a prescribed quantity of wine *per diem*. Plutarch says they never drank it at all, because it is the blood of beings who fought against the gods. [3] The chief of the Karennis of Burma " attains his position not by hereditary right, but on account of his habit of abstaining from rice and liquor. The mother, too, of a candidate for the chieftainship must have eschewed these things . . . so long as she was with child. During that time she might not . . . drink water from a common well." [4] The Bodia, or Bodio, the pontiff of the Grebo people of West Africa, may not drink water on the highway. [5] Here there is clearly

---

[1] J. G. Georgi, *Beschreibung aller Nationen des russischen Reichs* (St. Petersburg 1776), p. 37.

[2] A. B. Ellis, *op. cit.*, 229, 239 ; *id.*, *The Ewe-speaking Peoples of the Slave Coast of West Africa* (1890), p. 152.

[3] Diodorus Soculus, *Bibliotheca*, i. 70 ; Plutarch, *Isis et Osiris*, vi.

[4] *Indian Antiquary*, xxi. 317.

[5] Sir H. H. Johnston, *Liberia* (1906), ii. 1077.

a reference to " purity." Priests in Abyssinia drink neither wine nor mead.[1] Wine might not be taken into the temple at Heliopolis, and no one might enter the temple at Delos unless his system were free from wine.[2]

Asceticism naturally would interdict stimulating drinks, as it interdicts all tendency to expansion. " Water was the pure and innocent beverage of the primitive monks ; and the founder of the Benedictines regrets the daily portion of half a pint of wine, which had been extorted from him by the intemperance of the age." [3]

Many peoples, low in the scale of culture, emphasize by law the natural aversion of childhood, not to speak of womanhood, to intoxicants. The Akikuyu, for instance, allow no one to drink beer until he has reached the status of " elder." [4] The Chaco Indians forbid women and children, even youths, the use of intoxicants.[5] And we may suitably conclude with an allusion to the one really notable instance of such a prohibition in modern civilization, that of the United States of America.

[1] F. Ratzel, *op. cit.*, ii. 329.

[2] Plutarch, *op. cit.*, vi. ; G. Dittenberger, *Sylloge Inscriptionum Græcarum* (2nd edition, Leipzig 1898-1901), no. 564.

[3] E. Gibbon, *Decline and Fall of the Roman Empire*, ch. xxxvii.

[4] W. S. and K. Routledge, *op. cit.*, p. 62.

[5] W. B. Grubb, *An Unknown People in an Unknown Land* (1911), p. 184.

III. DRUMS AND CYMBALS

1. DEFINITIONS

THE drum is " a musical instrument of the percussive class, consisting of a hollow cylindrical or hemispherical frame of wood or metal, with a ' head ' of tightly stretched membrane at one or both ends, by the striking of which and the resonance of the cavity the sound is produced." [1] This definition hardly includes two types of drum which have played a more important part in social and religious evolution than any other—the incision-drum and the tambourine. The ordinary membrane-drum is composite in principle, combining in one structure the chief characteristics of both the tambourine and the homogeneous incision-drum. The actual genesis of the membrane-drum cannot be traced, though some speculations have been made on the suggestions supplied by various temporary drums and drum-substitutes. Clearly, like its two components, it has been independently invented by a fair proportion of the races of mankind.

2. DRUMMING

Methods directly or indirectly suggestive of drumming are either obvious or recondite to civilized experience. The Veddas have no musical instruments of any kind. In their dances they mark the

---

[1] *The New English Dictionary, s.v.* " Drum."

rhythm by beating with the hands their chests, flanks, or bellies.[1] The Andamanese women beat time for the dancers by slapping the hollow between the thighs, as they sit squatting on the heels, with the palm of the right hand, which is held at the wrist by the left.[2] The same method is employed among the Australian aborigines, whose women invariably form the orchestra.[3] This method is analogous to that of cymbals, as the Vedda method of beating the belly or chest is to that of the membrane-drum. Another method is common to several races. Thus, for an extemporized drum, the Chaco Indians, who also employ a far more highly developed drum, sometimes use a bundle of skins tied into a package. This they beat with a stick.[4]

In Australia the instrument, being the native rug or cloak of opossum-skin stretched across the hollow of the thighs, is analogous to the membrane of a drum. The women are said to keep faultless time.[5] At Australian corrobborees " the women of the tribe, who take the part of musicians, are seated in a semi-circle, a short distance from the large fire lit on these occasions, holding on their knees opossum rugs tightly rolled and stretched out. These are struck by the right hand, in time with the action of the master of the ceremonies, usually one of the old men. He carries in each hand a corrobboree stick, and these

[1] C. G. and B. Z. Seligmann, *The Veddas* (Cambridge 1911), pp. 214, 217.

[2] E. H. Man, " The Aboriginal Inhabitants of the Andaman Islands," *Journal of the Anthropological Institute* (1883), xii. 131.

[3] A. W. Howitt, " The Jeraeil, or Initiation Ceremonies of the Kurnai Tribe," *Journal of the Anthropological Institute* (1885), xiv. 304.

[4] J. W. Fewkes, " The Group of Tusayan Ceremonials called *Katcinas*," *Annual Report of the Bureau of Ethnology* (1897), xv. 276.

[5] K. L. Parker, *The Euahlayi Tribe* (1905), p. 122.

are struck together. . . . This use of the opossum
cloak and clanking of the sticks appears to be the most
primitive form of musical instrument, if it can be so
termed, amongst our aborigines." [1] Mitchell speaks
of the rolled opossum-skin rug as " the tympanum in
its rudest form." [2] In Western Victoria the rolled
rug contained shells, producing a jingling sound. [3]

The Samoans at their dances used stretched mats,
which were beaten with sticks, as well as the drum. [4]
This method may or may not involve the ideas of a
resounding cavity or vibrating membrane; for there
may be no cavity, or the mat may be spread on a
hard surface. But either cavity or membrane may
be supplied by the accident of imitating the making
of cloth. For beating bark into cloth the Polynesians
used a beam of wood with a groove on the lower side.
This rested on the ground, and a wooden mallet was
used to strike the bark. Owing to the groove, made
for the purpose of steadiness, " every stroke produces
a loud sound. . . . Heard at a distance, the sound
of cloth-beating is not disagreeable." [5] In Mangaia,
of the Hervey Islands, the cloth-beating mallet was
used for drums, and mimic cloth-boards were beaten
as drums at certain feasts. [6] The Bechuanas, who are
the finest leather-makers in Africa, use at initiation
feasts the method of the free membrane. An ox-
hide is held and tightly stretched by several men.

---

[1] R. Etheridge, " An Australian Aboriginal Musical Instrument," *Journal of
the Anthropological Institute* (1894), xxiii. 320-321.

[2] T. L. Mitchell, *Three Expeditions into the Interior of Eastern Australia* (1838),
ii. 5.

[3] J. Dawson, *Australian Aborigines* (Melbourne 1881), p. 80.

[4] G. Pratt, *Dictionary of the Samoan Language* (1878), *s.v.* " Tata."

[5] W. Ellis, *Polynesian Researches* (1829), i. 179, 184.

[6] W. W. Gill, *Myths and Songs from the South Pacific* (1876), pp. 259, 262.

This is beaten with sticks.[1] The process is a repetition
of one used in skin-preparation, here employed to
produce ceremonial music. In old days the Chippewa
made their war-drums by stretching a hide over
stakes driven in the ground, and binding it in place
by means of strong hoops.[2] Covering a pot or clay
cylinder with a head of skin is a common method of
making both permanent and temporary drums.[3]

3. THE DRUM, THE TAMBOURINE, AND THE CYMBAL

Among historical peoples the drum is of very great
antiquity. Its invention belongs to their pre-history,
its forms are the membrane-drum, tambourine, and
kettle-drum. It was known in Vedic India, and a
hymn in the *Atharvaveda* celebrates its praises.[4] The
earliest records of China are familiar with the drum.[5]
The tambourine and double-headed drum were used
by the Assyrians and Egyptians. The latter was
supported against the drummer's body and played
with both hands. Such an instrument is represented
in a relief of Ashurbanipal (668-626 B.C.), in which
women and children are clapping their hands.

Certain peoples, representing the lowest stages of
culture known, have failed to invent the drum, but
in savagery generally, in all the stages of barbarism,
and in civilizations like that of India, its use corresponds with its importance as the chief, and sometimes

---

[1] F. Ratzel, *The History of Mankind* (1896-1898), ii. 329.

[2] F. Densmore, *Chippewa Music* (Bureau of Ethnology, Bulletin 45, 1910), p. 11.

[3] See W. H. Holmes, "Aboriginal Pottery of the Eastern United States,"
Annual Report of the Bureau of Ethnology (1898-1899), xx. 34-35 ; L. Frobenius, *The
Childhood of Man* (1909), pp. 95-98 ; W. B. Grubb, *An Unknown People in an Unknown
Land* (1911), p. 178 ; F. Ratzel, *op. cit.*, ii. 329.

[4] A. A. Macdonell, *Vedic Mythology* (Strassburg 1897), p. 155.

[5] *Sacred Books of the East*, xxviii. 90.

the only, instrument of music.[1] The structural variations presented by the instrument are endless, but
the types are clearly marked. These are eight in
number.

(1) The incision-drum is a hollow cylinder, varying
in length from a few inches to twelve or more feet,
and in diameter proportionally. Made from a bamboo internode or hollow tree, the ends are closed by
the nodes or by the trunk sections. A narrow longitudinal slit, of varying length, but generally nearly
as long as the cavity, is made on one side of the drum.
Its width in the larger instruments is about three
inches. The tapering of the lips is important, for
the drumstick is applied to them, and the tones vary
according to the thickness of the substance struck.
This drum may be placed either in a vertical or in
a horizontal position. The best results are produced
from the latter.[2]

(2) The stamping-drum is a long hollow cylinder,
one end of which is closed and the other left open.
The " heading " of the closed end is either natural, as
the node of a bamboo, or artificial, as a " membrane "
of skin. This instrument usually has a handle, by
which the closed end is struck on the hard ground.

(3) The single-headed membrane-drum is a wooden
cylinder, whose length is not much more than its
diameter. The tightly stretched membrane of hide
is beaten with the fingers, the hand, or a stick. The

---

[1] See D. Cranz, *History of Greenland* (1820), i. 162 ; T. C. Hodson, *The Nāga Tribes of Manipur* (1911), p. 64 ; A. Simson, " Notes on the Napo Indians," *Journal of the Anthropological Institute* (1883), xii. 24.

[2] On this type of drum generally see the valuable paper by E. Nordenskiöld, " Ist die sogenannte Schlitztrommel in der neuen sowohl wie in der alten Welt selbständig erfunden worden ? " in *Ethnologische Studien*, ed. F. Krause (Leipzig 1929), pp. 17-28.

stick, usually knobbed, sometimes of a hammer-shape, becomes a heavy-headed club for the larger drums. The other end of the drum is closed.

(4) The double-headed membrane-drum is the single-headed with the closed end removed and converted into a " head." This drum is placed in a horizontal position and both heads are used.

(5) The friction-drum is (3) or (4) with a thong or cord stretched across the diameter of the head (one head in the case of the double-headed drum), or along its radius, being fixed in the centre. A small piece or splinter of wood may be inserted beneath the thong.

(6) The pot-drum is an earthenware vessel headed with a membrane.

(7) The kettle-drum is a metal vessel headed with a membrane. Both (6) and (7) are single-headed closed drums. Type (6) tends towards the hemispherical shape of body; (7) in its developed form is quite hemispherical.

(8) The tambourine is a head of membrane attached to a cylindrical rim. On this are generally hung pieces of metal, according to the *sistrum* principle. The membrane is struck by a stick, more usually with the hand.

" The drum," says Codrington, " in many forms, may be said to be the characteristic instrument of Melanesia." It is, however, absent from Florida and Santa Cruz. The incision-type is employed. A joint or internode of bamboo, or a tree-trunk of suitable size, for the largest, is selected, and a longitudinal slit of varying degrees of narrowness is made along one side. The lips of this slit are very carefully tapered; apparently the tone of the drum depends largely upon this detail. Small drums are held in the hands by dancers, but the large bamboo drums are held by an assistant. Most of these big drums have a special hut in which they are stored. They are valued very highly and certainly are in a sense sacred. They are described as " very resonant and well toned," and can be heard at a great distance.[1]

Big drums were made from hollowed trees throughout Polynesia. The lips being thick, and the whole instrument more or less a mere " dug-out," a heavy club was used by the drummer.[2]

The canoe-drum is a remarkable type, used in the Fiji Islands, Java, and Assam. A hollowed tree-trunk, often twenty-five or thirty feet in length, with closed ends tapering upwards, and an orifice along its upper length just wide enough to admit the body, is obviously both a canoe and an incision-drum of a large type. With two wooden mallets the operator beat on the lips of the incision, which were curved inwards. In Fiji these drum-canoes are the *lali*, and are kept in sacred houses.[3] The signal drums of New Pomerania and South Congo are identical. They are small, being not more than two feet in length.[4] The Malay peoples use a bamboo-stem with several internodes, each of which has the incision. As the diameter of the internodes increases, the scale, as with organ-pipes, descends.[5]

The Maori war-drum was of the incision type,

---

[1] R. H. Codrington, *The Melanesians* (Oxford 1891), pp. 336-337, 175, 332, 340.

[2] G. Brown, *Melanesians and Polynesians* (1910), p. 419.

[3] S. E. Peal, " The *Morong*, as possibly a Relic of Pre-Marriage Communism," *Journal of the Anthropological Institute* (1893), xxii. 252 ; L. Frobenius, *The Childhood of Man* (1909), pp. 83, 91 ; G. Brown, *op. cit.*, p. 419.

[4] L. Frobenius, *op. cit.*, p. 84.

[5] W. W. Skeat and C. O. Blagden, *Pagan Races of the Malay Peninsula* (1906), ii. 140.

but flat. It was hung from a cross-bar on a high scaffold, with the slit side underneath, and played from a platform half-way up the scaffold.[1] This *pahu*, hung in a sort of watch-tower, approximates in a fashion to the bell. In the Philippines the Jesuits have not only used old signal-drums of incised bamboo as church-bells, but have reproduced them in wood for the same purpose.[2] In the Tongan drums, from two to four feet in length, the chink ran nearly the whole length and and was about three inches in breadth. The drum being made from a solid tree-trunk, all the hollowing-out was done through the incision—a long and difficult operation. In playing this drum, the drummer with his stick, a foot long and as thick as his wrist, varied the force and rate of his beats, and changed the tones by beating "towards the end or middle of the instrument." This drum was the *naffa*, the *kaara* of the Hervey Islands.

In Tahiti the drum used was the upright one-headed closed drum. A tree-trunk section was hollowed out, leaving a closed base. Shark's skin was stretched over the open top. This was the *pahu* ; its sacred form was the *pahu ra*. One in Tahiti was eight feet high, and was beaten with two sticks. "The thrilling sound of the large drum at midnight, indicating a human sacrifice, was most terrific. Every individual trembled with apprehension of being seized."[3] The *kendang* or *gendang* of Indonesia, as used by Dayaks, Bataks, Macassars, Buginese and Javanese, in Borneo, and throughout the countries east of India, is of the Hindu type, a single-headed closed wooden drum,

[1] L. Frobenius, *op. cit.*, pp. 92-93.   [2] *Ibid.*, pp. 90-91.
[3] J. Cook, *Voyages* (1790), p. 1419 ; W. Ellis, *Polynesian Researches* (1829), i. 193, 195.

played with the fingers.[1] The American drum was either the pot-drum or the wooden single-headed membrane-drum.[2]

There is more variety of drums in Africa than elsewhere. Practically every form is found, and variations occur which are in some cases unique or extremely rare.[3]

The Baganda drum was made from a section of tree-trunk, conical in form ; the base of the cone alone was open. This was headed with a cow-hide, and this was the end kept uppermost. Some were ten inches high, others five feet, and four in greatest diameter. Some were beautifully decorated with cowries and beads. Except in the case of the very large drums, they were hung on posts, so as to get the full benefit of the sound. The skins were kept soft and elastic by being rubbed with butter.[4]

The essential character of the snare-drum and friction-drum is the presence of a string or thong of leather across the membrane or drum-head. A simple form is from British Guiana. A fine double thread, with a slip-knot in the centre, is stretched across the membrane. Before it is drawn tight, an exceedingly slender splinter of wood is secured in the slip-knot, so

---

[1] See F. Ratzel, *op. cit.*, i. 194 ; A. Playfair, *The Garos* (1909), p. 42 ; Wilken-Pleyte, *Handleiding voor de vergelijkende Volkenkunde van Nederlandsch-Indië* (Leyden 1893), p. 111.

[2] See Sir E. F. Im Thurn, *Among the Indians of Guiana* (1882), p. 309 ; A. C. Fletcher, " The Hako : a Pawnee Ceremony," *Annual Report of the Bureau of Ethnology* (1900-1901), xxii. pt. 2, 257 ; F. Densmore, *Chippewa Music* (1910), p. 12.

[3] For various African drums, see C. W. Hobley, *The Ethnology of A-Kamba* (Cambridge 1910), pp. 32-33 ; A. Werner, *The Natives of British Central Africa* (1906), p. 225 ; A. B. Ellis, *The Tshi-speaking Peoples of the Gold Coast of West Africa* (1887), p. 326 ; *id., The Yoruba-speaking Peoples of the Slave Coast of West Africa* (1894), p. 115.

[4] J. Roscoe, *The Baganda* (1911), pp. 26, 407-408.

16

as to rest on the membrane at right angles to the line
of the thread. The other head of the drum being
unaltered, the instrument gives two different sounds.
The friction-head produces, by the vibration of the
splinter against the skin, a "metallic sound." [1] In
another form the string extends along a radius only
of the membrane. [2] Such drums, besides producing
different tones from the two heads, can be muffled
by placing a wad beneath the string.

Small hand-drums are commonly used by various
peoples. [3] The old English tabor is a type of these.
The kettle-drum is not frequent. In the East the
gong is preferred.

The Greek and Roman drum (τύμπανον, *tym-panum*) comprised two varieties of the tambourine
type. The one was the flat tambourine; the cir-cumference was hung with bells. The other re-sembled the Lapp form, the under side being closed
by a convex hemispherical bottom. This variety was
also played with the hand like a tambourine. [4]

The Hebrew *tōph* (Greek τύμπανον, English Version
"tabret," "timbrel") was a simple tambourine, prob-ably without bells or rattles. The same Hebrew word
represents both the English, and probably there was
only one form.

The tambourine "which was once among the
chief instruments of the Lapland wizards is now a

---

[1] Sir E. F. Im Thurn, *op. cit.*, p. 308.

[2] H. Balfour, "The Friction-Drum," *Journal of the Anthropological Institute* (1907), xxxvii. 67.

[3] See G. Brown, *op. cit.*, p. 339; J. O. Dorsey, "Omaha Dwellings, Furniture, and Implements," *Annual Report of the Bureau of Ethnology* (1891-1892), xiii. 282; Skeat-Blagden, *op. cit.*, ii. 140; J. J. M. de Groot, *The Religious System of China* (Leyden 1892, etc.), i. 157.

[4] Pliny, *Historia Naturalis*, ix. 109.

great curiosity." Two types were in use. One was a wooden hoop strengthened with two cross-pieces and covered on one side with reindeer-skin ; the other was an oval box with a convex under-side, hewn out of a tree-trunk, and with a reindeer-skin head. In some there was a slit serving as a handle. Each tambourine had an " indicator " (*arpa*), consisting of a large iron ring, on which smaller rings were linked, for the purpose of divination by means of pointing to the symbols on the membrane. The hammer was made of reindeer-horn. The Lopars treated their tambourines with great respect, and kept them, with the indicator and hammer, wrapped up in fur. No woman dared to touch them.[1]

The cymbal varies in form, from a disk of metal to a shallow hemispherical or half-oval cup, with or without a flange. Cymbals were known in early India, and are still used by the Hindus in ordinary and temple orchestras.[2] The Garos use two sorts of cymbals : the *kakwa*, like the European, and the *nengilsi*, a smaller kind resembling in shape two small cups of brass.[3] The European type is derived from the Græco-Roman. These were quarter- or half-globes of metal with a flange. An older form is possibly indicated by the " bronze vessels " used in the ceremonial dismissal of family *manes* by the Roman *paterfamilias*. The Roman cymbals were either without handles or provided with a knob or ring or metal

---

[1] G. Klemm, *Kulturgeschichte* (Leipzig 1843-1852), iii. 90-99 ; J. Scheffer, *Lappoina* (Frankfort 1673), pp. 109-110, 130-131 ; V. M. Mikhailovskii, " Shamanism in Siberia and European Russia," *Journal of the Anthropological Institute* (1895), xxiv. 62, 126 ; W. Radloff, *Aus Siberien* (2nd edition, Leipzig 1893), ii. 18 ff.

[2] A. A. Macdonell, *op. cit.*, p. 134 ; J. E. Padfield, *The Hindu at Home* (Madras 1896), p. 182.

[3] A. Playfair, *The Garos* (1909), pp. 44-45.

handle ; others had a hole for the insertion of a cord. The unflanged, early Semitic type was also known. The Khasias use cymbals in combination with drums.[1] The Chinese drummer usually employs one pair of cymbals.[2] The Abyssinians have tambourines, cymbals, and various drums.

In modern European orchestras they hold a not unimportant place.

Only in the case of one people, the Hebrews, have cymbals attained independent importance. They were employed in dances and singing with the tōph, but in the Temple were used alone. The cymbals of the Hebrews (meṣiltayîm, ṣelṣelîm, κύμβαλα) were used in the temple-worship to mark time for chants. They were bronze " disks," held, one in each hand, and clashed together. Ṣelṣelîm is used only in 2 Samuel vi. 5 and Psalms cl. 5. In the latter passage the epithets " loud " and " high-sounding " are applied. It has been supposed, therefore, that the ṣelṣelîm were the conical flangeless cymbals, as used by the Assyrians, giving a highly-pitched note. In 1 Samuel xviii. 6 shālîshîm, κύμβαλα, cannot refer to cymbals. According to the Mishna and Josephus, one pair only was used in the Temple. It is not likely that κρέμβαλα, sistra, castanets are ever connoted by the terms meṣiltayîm and ṣelṣelîm. It is possible that in the case of the Temple cymbals one disk was fixed, and was beaten by the other like a clapper. In later Mishnaic the noun used is in the singular number. The cymbalists were Levites. In the Second Temple a special officer had the charge of the cymbals, which are stated to have been of great antiquity. Their sound is de-

---

[1] *Transactions of the Ethnological Society* (1869), vii. 309.
[2] J. J. M. de Groot, *The Religious System of China* (Leyden 1892, etc.), i. 157.

scribed as high, loud, and far-carrying. It has been suggested that the "tinkling cymbal" of St. Paul's simile implies the metallic spheres worn on bridles and by courtesans on their belts. This agrees better with the epithet ἀλάλαζον.[1]

The use of the drum as an instrument of society, and probably the art itself of drum-playing, have their highest development in Africa. The only national instrument that can approach the drum of the African is the pipes of the Scot. But the skill with the drum is more widely diffused among the Africans. Uganda in the old days supplies a typical example of a drum - conducted community. The chief drums of the Baganda were the royal, called *mujaguzo*, ninety-three in number. Fifty-one of these were small. They were guarded by a chief, *kawuka*, and his assistant *wakimwomera*. Drummers took their turn of a month's residence each year in the royal court for beating the drums. A particular drum belonged to each chieftainship. The numerous totem-clans, had each special drums; the leading members defrayed the expense. Every chief, besides his drum of office, had his private drum. This was beaten from time to time to ensure his permanent holding of office. Each clan had a special rhythm which was recognized.[2]

4. THE ART OF DRUMMING

Drum-playing calls for considerable executive skill, particularly on account of the rebound of the membrane. It is in the utilization of this rebound that

[1] Josephus, *Antiquities*, VII. xii. 3; *Mishna*, 'Ar. 13a; 1 Chronicles xvi. 42; Psalms cl. 5; 1 Corinthians xiii. 1; cp. 1 Chronicles xv. 16, 19, 28, xvi. 5, xxv. 6; 2 Chronicles v. 13, xxix. 25; Nehemiah xii. 27.
[2] J. Roscoe, *The Baganda* (1911), pp. 25-30.

the essence of the drummer's art consists. Even with the heaviest drums no great force is required. The weight of the blow varies as the thickness of the membrane. In the case of large incision-drums, where the body serves as a membrane, the lips are finely tapered, and very resonant notes are produced by the use of a light stick. Various forms of drum-stick have been mentioned incidentally.

The Baganda drummer used two short but heavy sticks, club-shaped. " The vibration from the large drums was so great that a man who did not understand how to beat them might have his shoulder dislocated by the rebound of the leather when struck. Music could be got from these drums, so much so that any one a mile away would scarcely believe that a drum, and not some other instrument, was being played." [1]   In the New Hebrides big wooden billets are used for beating the largest incision drums. High notes, in concerted music, are supplied by small horizontal incision-drums. These are beaten " in brisk syncopated time, to the loud boomings of the bigger drums." [2]

5. THE PSYCHOLOGY OF DRUMMING

For the psychological study of music by which the social and religious importance of the artistry of sound is destined to be explained, the music of drums and cymbals supplies unique data, and the drum-music of such races as the Central African, the American Indian, and his congener the Northern

---

[1] J. Roscoe, *The Baganda* (1911), pp. 26-27.

[2] B. T. Somerville, " Notes on some Islands of the New Hebrides," *Journal of the Anthropological Institute* (1894), xxiii. 11-12 ; *id.*, " Ethnological Notes on New Hebrides," *Journal of the Anthropological Institute* (1894), xxiii. 384.

Asiatic (the Melanesians are, artistically, in a lower class) forms one of the most indispensable documents.

The fact is that the music of the drum is more closely connected with the foundations of aurally generated emotion than that of any other instrument. It is complete enough in itself to cover the whole range of human feeling, which is not the case with its subordinate, the cymbals, while it is near enough to the origins of musical invention to appeal most strongly to the primitive side of man's nature. The investigator will need a long experience and adaptation to the atmosphere in which the vibrations of drum and tambourine produce their emotional waves. To compare, as an early explorer (Schweinfurth) did, the orchestral drum-music of negroes to " the raging of the elements let loose," is no longer an explanation of primitive music. To put it briefly—the emotional appeal of music is to a very large extent muscular. Rhythm is practically a neuro-muscular quality, and it is the fundamental form of musical sound. Most of our emotions tend to produce movement.[1] Harmonious rhythm in movement and action is the soul of society, as it is the soul of the dance.

" In all primitive music, rhythm is strongly developed. The pulsations of the drum and the sharp crash of the rattles are thrown against each other and against the voice, so that it would seem that the pleasure derived by the performers lay not so much in the tonality of the song as in the measured sounds arranged in contesting rhythm, and which by their

---

[1] J. B. Miner, " Motor, Visual and Applied Rhythms " (*Psychological Monographs*, v. 4, 1903); S. Wilks, in *Medical Magazine* (January 1894); W. Wundt, *Völkerpsychologie* (Leipzig 1904-1905), i. 265; R. Wallaschek, *Primitive Musik* (1893), *passim*.

clash start the nerves and spur the body to action, for the voice which alone carries the tone is often subordinated and treated as an additional instrument." [1] Helmholtz observed : " All melodies are motions. Graceful rapidity, grave procession, quiet advance, wild leaping, all these different characters of motion and a thousand others can be represented by successions of tones. And, as music expresses these motions, it gives an expression also to those mental conditions which naturally evoke similar motions, whether of the body and the voice, or of the thinking and feeling principle itself." [2]

To increase muscular power the strongest stimulus is muscular movement ; to produce emotional intoxication the combination of muscular movement that is rhythmical with rhythmical sound (or motion translated into music) is the most efficient. One great sphere of drum-music has been the social emotions. Not only military, religious, and sexual excitement, but every possible form of social orgiasticism has been fostered and developed by its influence. It is a significant coincidence that the boom of the modern cannon and the boom of a primitive drum mean war. In contrast to this large, impressive sound, which is so essentially organic in its nature and its production, may be placed the exclusively religious use of cymbals by the Hebrews, and the prominence of cymbal-music in the perverted sexualism of the cult of Attis.[3] These two last cases are isolated phenomena. The music of the drum is more completely human.

[1] H. C. Fletcher, " Love Songs among the Omaha Indians," *Proceedings of the International Congress of Anthropology* (Chicago 1893).

[2] *On the Sensations of Tone* (1885), p. 250.

[3] The general use of symbols in the worship of Dionysus and in the Eleusinian Mysteries belongs rather to the category of the impressiveness of noise, as such.

Lastly, the muscular appeal of the drum is made powerful by the very limitations of the instrument. The player is practically confined to rhythm, and the influential manipulation of this depends on his personality. He is one with his drum. It is this translation of human meaning and will into sound that explains the so-called " drum-language." Further, the player's muscular skill and muscular life are at their highest efficiency ; he is for his hearers an inspirer, a leader, and a prophet, the individual representative of the social body in movement and in emotion. It is on this principle that the drum in so many races gives the summons for all social functions. The blow of the drum-stick translates itself not merely into sound, but into a spiritual reverberation, an impulsive stroke upon the social consciousness.

The meaning of drum-sounds is thus of a universal, undifferentiated character ; they appeal primarily to the muscular sense, and secondarily to all that is built up on that foundation. An instance of the simplest possible application may be contrasted with others more or less elaborate. Explaining the route to Spirit-land to the soul of a dead chief, the Chippewa punctuates his words with sharp drum-taps.[1] " To a European," says Ellis, " the rhythm of a drum expresses nothing beyond a repetition of the same note at different intervals of time ; but to a native it expresses much more. To him the drum can and does speak, the sounds produced from it forming words, and the whole measure or rhythm a sense. In this way, when company drums are being played at an *ehsudu*, they are made to express and convey to the

[1] F. Densmore, *Chippewa Music* (1910), p. 54.

bystanders a variety of meanings. In one measure they abuse the men of another company, stigmatising them as fools and cowards ; then the rhythm changes, and the gallant deeds of their own company are extolled. All this, and much more, is conveyed by the beating of drums, and the native ear and mind, trained to detect and interpret each beat, is never at fault. The language of the drum is as well understood as that which they use in their daily life. Each chief has his own call or motto sounded by a particular beat of his drums." [1]

Klark declares that " the sound of the tambourine, the convulsive antics of the shaman, his fierce screams, his wild stare in the dim light, all strike terror into the hearts of semi-savage people, and powerfully affect their nerves." [2] The character of this tambourine-music has been thus described : After some preliminary sounds such as that of a falcon or a sea-mew, which concentrate attention, " the tambourine begins to make a slight rolling noise, like the buzzing of mosquitoes : the shaman has begun his music. At first it is tender, soft, vague, then nervous and irregular like the noise of an approaching storm : it becomes louder and more decided. Now and then it is broken by wild cries ; ravens croak, grebes laugh, sea-mews wail, snipes whistle, falcons and eagles scream. The music becomes louder, the strokes on the tambourine become confused in one continuous rumble ; the bells, rattles and small tabors sound ceaselessly. It is a deluge of sounds capable of driving away the wits of

---

[1] A. B. Ellis, *The Tshi-speaking Peoples of the Gold Coast of West Africa* (1887), pp. 326-327.

[2] V. M. Mikhailovskii, " Shamanism in Siberia and European Russia," *Journal of the Anthropological Institute* (1895), xxiv. 65.

the audience. Suddenly everything stops ; one or two powerful blows on the tambourine, and then it falls on the shaman's lap." [1]

6. SOCIAL FUNCTIONS OF THE DRUM

To peoples like the Central Africans, the drum, apart from its directly emotional use in social gatherings, as an instrument of social intoxication, plays the part of the church-bell, the clock, the town-crier, and the daily newspaper, besides being used for religious music and the exhortation of the sick.

In Africa (Lake Nyasa) the drum is used at dances, at feasts religious and secular, at wakes, by doctors at the sick-bed, by boatmen to time the paddles, and to send messages over the country.[2] Among the Woolwa Indians the drum is played when drink is offered to the guests at *mishla*-drinkings.[3] Of the Baganda drums, Roscoe writes : " The drum was indeed put to a multitude of uses, quite apart from music : it was the instrument which announced both joy and sorrow ; it was used to let people know of the happy event of the birth of children, and it announced the mourning for the dead. It gave the alarm for war, and announced the return of the triumphant warriors who had conquered in war. It had its place in the most solemn and in the most joyous ceremonies of the nation." The royal drums were beaten to

---

[1] Anonymous writer in the *Sibirskii Sbornik*, quoted by V. M. Mikhailovskii, *op. cit.*, xxiv. 94.

[2] H. S. Stannus, " Notes on some Tribes of British Central Africa," *Journal of the Royal Anthropological Institute* (1910), xl. 297, 333-334 ; J. H. Weeks, " Anthropological Notes on the Bangala of the Upper Congo River," *Journal of the Royal Anthropological Institute* (1910), xl. 380, 402, 404.

[3] H. A. Wickham, " Notes on the Soumoo or Woolwa Indians," *Journal of the Anthropological Institute* (1895), xxiv. 204.

announce the coronation of a king, and his entry into a new house, and also at the new moon. Drums were carried on journeys and beaten to encourage the walkers. A young man would beat the drum with his hands and sing meanwhile. " The people when carrying loads, or when on a march, loved to be accompanied by the drum, and if they had no drum they sang songs, and set the time for marching by the song." [1]

Its co-operative and socializing importance is here well suggested. Its most spectacular use is that of a postal, telegraphic, and telephonic service. The carrying power of these fine instruments renders communication very rapid. The big drum of the Anyanja can be heard at a distance of six miles.[2] The Chippewa drum, which is not two feet high, can be heard at a distance of ten miles.[3] As the drum-telephone is used to-day in Central Africa, it depends on an elaborate code, which to one reared in the atmosphere is perhaps more dependent on social understanding and mutual recognition of " tone-variations " than on a colourless translation of sounds into letters. At any rate, throughout a very large tract of Central Africa, daily by means of the drum two or more villages exchange their news. Travellers, even Europeans, have obtained food and lodgings by its means. The notes used can be imitated by tapping the cheek when the mouth is open.[4] An apt method is here implied for native practice, since it is the aperture or incision-drum that is used for the sound-messages. Dennett's account of actual messages sent by drum is

---

[1] J. Roscoe, *The Baganda* (1911), pp. 25, 27, 29.

[2] H. Werner, *The Natives of British Central Africa* (1906), p. 225.

[3] F. Densmore, *op. cit.*, p. 12.   [4] L. Frobenius, *op. cit.*, pp. 84-85.

all the more valuable because it is free from any attempt to heighten the effect.[1] He notes that this system gives the key to a perennial puzzle, revived during the Boer War, How does news travel among the natives in the speedy way it does ? The drum-message system is found in New Guinea, and among the Jivaros of South America, the old Mexicans, and some Indians of the North-West. It is particularly developed in Oceania, the countries north-west and north-east of New Guinea, especially New Pomerania. Signalling by means of the incision-drum, but without any highly developed code, was used in Borneo, Java, the Philippines, New Zealand, the New Hebrides, Fiji, and the Hervey Islands.[2]

7. THE SACREDNESS OF DRUMS

Throughout Melanesia, drums are part of a rich man's establishment. The top of these drums is fashioned into a grinning face. When the drum is an image of a venerated ancestor, the taps are made on the stomach.[3] In Melanesia, ancestor-worship is linked to the civil and military authority by these instruments, half-drum and half-image. It is natural also for rulers and important persons to collect round them as many sources of *mana* as possible, though they may leave the more recondite applications of supernatural power to the shamans. In the Upper Nile regions the " sacred " official drums hang in front of the chief's house, or under the sacred tree of the village. They are regarded with awe.[4] The regalia of a chief

---

[1] R. E. Dennett, *At the Back of the Black Man's Mind* (1906), pp. 77 ff.

[2] F. Ratzel, *op. cit.*, i. 37, ii. 22 ; L. Frobenius, *op. cit.*, pp. 86-93.

[3] R. H. Codrington, " Religious Beliefs and Practices in Melanesia," *Journal of the Anthropological Institute* (1881), x. 295.

[4] F. Ratzel, *op. cit.*, iii. 39.

are, as it were, his *sacra*. These may come to be
identified with the mysterious power of his office.
In other cases, the drum may be regarded as the mouthpiece of a god or spirit, as containing the voice of the
god or the god himself. This voice, in the lower cultures, derives impressiveness not from stillness or
smallness, but from loudness and resonant power.

Some miscellaneous examples are appended of
the beliefs and ritual connected with the sacredness
of drums.

The regalia of Malay States includes the court and
official drums, which are sacred. The royal drums of
Jelebu are said to be "headed" with the skins of
lice, and to emit a chord of twelve different sounds;
the royal trumpet and the royal gong also emit the
chord of twelve notes. The Sultan of Minang-kabau
wakes daily to the sound of the royal drum (*gandang
nobat*). These drums are regarded as having come
into existence by their own will. "Rain could not rot
them nor sun blister them"; any person who even
"brushed past them" would be felled to the ground
by their magic power. In the State drum of Selangor
resided the *jin karaja'an*, or "State demon"; and
powerful *jinn* dwelt in the other royal drums.[1]

Each temple and house of a chief in West Africa
has a tall drum (*gbedu*) covered with carvings. This
drum had a protecting spirit, that, namely, of the
slave who was sacrificed on it when it was made. It
is beaten only at religious ceremonies. Before being
struck, it receives an offering of blood and palm-wine,
which is poured on the carvings.[2]

[1] W. W. Skeat, *Malay Magic* (1900), pp. 25-28, 40-41.
[2] A. B. Ellis, *The Yoruba-speaking Peoples of the Slave Coast of West Africa*
(1894), p. 100.

Tane, the Polynesian god, was more or less represented by his sacred drum. These drums were often surmounted by carved heads; and possibly the evolution here is from drum to idol. While the drum retained its membrane, a connexion would be traced between its sound and the voice of the god.[1] When the special royal drum, *kaula*, of the Baganda received a new skin, the blood of the cow whose skin was used was run into the drum. Also a man was beheaded, and his blood was run into it. The idea was that, when the drum was beaten, the life of the man added fresh life and vigour to the king. When any drum was fitted with a new skin, the ox killed for the purpose also supplied the blood for pouring into the drum.

Every drum contained its fetish. Renewing the fetish was as necessary as renewing the skin, and the two operations were simultaneous. These fetishes were concrete objects of the familiar African type. It was not every man who knew how to make a drum-fetish. A characteristic drum-fetish was that of the drum of Dungu, god of hunting. It was composed of portions of every kind of animal and bird hunted; all kinds of medicines used in making charms for hunting; miniature weapons, and pieces of cord used in making traps. This fetish was fixed upright in the drum.[2]

The clan Gomba of the Baganda had a drum, *nakanguzi*. A runaway slave, if he reached its shrine, became the servant of the drum, and could not be removed. Any animal straying thither became the

---

[1] H. C. March, " Polynesian Ornament a Mythography : or, a Symbolism of Origin and Descent," *Journal of the Anthropological Institute* (1893), xxii. 314.

[2] J. Roscoe, *The Baganda* (1911), pp. 27-28, 312.

property of the drum, a sacred animal, free to roam.[1]
A criminal among the Marotse of Africa escapes punish-
ment if he can reach and touch the drums of the king.[2]

In Vedic India the drum was not only beaten, but
invoked, to drive away danger, demons, and enemies.
It was used in sacrifices, and in battle ; the warrior
offered it worship. Before being played, a *mantra*,
or charm, was spoken into it.[3] The analogy between
thunder and the boom of the drum is obvious. Russian peasants used the drum to imitate thunder, by
way of a charm for the production of rain.[4] The
natives of Guiana prefer the skin of the baboon or
" howling monkey " for the heads of their drums,
believing that a drum so fitted possesses " the power
of emitting the rolling, roaring sounds for which this
monkey is celebrated." [5] The Timorese regard cymbals as the home of spirits.[6] Such beliefs are found
with all musical instruments.

The essential instrument of Christian temple-
worship has been, from a very early period, the organ.
No doubt an impulse of antagonism to pagan ritual
prevented the early Christians from adopting pagan
instruments. Only perhaps in Abyssinia, and in the
modern Salvation Army, has the drum found a place.
Drums do not appear to have been used by the Hebrews
in temple-worship. The usual drum, *tōph*, of the tam-

---

[1] J. Roscoe, *The Baganda* (1911), p. 167.

[2] A. St. H. Gibbons, *Exploration and Hunting in Central Africa, 1895-1896*
(1898), p. 129.

[3] A. A. Macdonell, *Vedic Mythology* (Strasburg 1897), p. 155 ; *Sacred Books of
the East*, xli. 23, 26, xlii. 77, 117, 130 ; H. Oldenberg, *Die Religion des Veda* (Berlin
1894), p. 39.

[4] W. Mannhardt, *Antike World- und Feldkulte* (Berlin 1877), p. 342.

[5] Sir E. F. Im Thurn, *Among the Indians of Guiana* (1883), pp. 308-309.

[6] J. G. F. Riedel, " Die Landschaft Dawan oder West-Timor," *Deutsche Geo-
graphische Blätter* (1887), x. 278-279.

bourine type, was used in processions, at weddings, and feasts, and to accompany religious music of a joyous and popular character.[1] But in the great Oriental religions, particularly in Hinduism and Buddhism, the drum has an important place in the temple-worship ; nor is it unknown in the worship of Islām. In lower cults the drum serves as a church-bell, an organ, and a direct vehicle of supernatural power.[2] The Baganda temple-drums were next in importance after the royal drums. Each had its particular rhythm and particular fetish. They were beaten at feasts and at the time of the new moon, warning the people of the monthly rest from work.[3] In New Guinea, drums are beaten to drive away the ghosts of men slain in battle ;[4] in New Britain, to stop earthquakes.[5] Demons are expelled by South African drummers.[6] In the Moluccas the drum is employed against evil spirits causing difficult child-birth.[7] In Central Africa demons are driven away with guns and drums at funerals and before death.[8] Dayak women and shamans alike use the drum to cure the sick.[9]

---

[1] 1 Maccabees ix. 39; Exodus xv. 20; Psalms lxxxi. 2; 2 Samuel vi. 5; 2 Chronicles v. 12-13.

[2] J. Mooney, "The Ghost-Dance Religion," *Annual Report of the Bureau of Ethnology* (1892-1893), xiv. 725; J. G. Kohl, *Kitchi-Gami* (1860), i. 59 ff.

[3] J. Roscoe, *op. cit.*, pp. 28, 297, 312.

[4] H. C. Haddon, *Head-hunters, Black, White, and Brown* (1901), p. 308.

[5] J. L. D. van der Roest, "Uit het Leven der Bevolking van Windessi," *Tijdschrift voor Indische Taal-, Land- en Volkenkunde* (1898), xl. 157-158.

[6] J. Macdonald, *Religion and Myth* (1893), pp. 100 ff.

[7] J. G. F. Riedel, *De sluik- en kroesharige rassen tusschen Selebes en Papua* (The Hague 1886), pp. 175, 265, 449.

[8] J. Macdonald, "East Central African Customs," *Journal of the Anthropological Institute* (1893), xxii. 114-115.

[9] G. A. Wilken, "Het Shamanisme bij de Volken van de Indischen Archipel," *Bijdragen tot de Taal-, Land- en Volkenkunde van Nederlandsch-Indië* (1887), xxxvi. 610.

17

In China, scapegoats are driven away to the music of drums.[1] Greek historians record the " disinfecting " of ambassadors by Turkish shamans by means of the drum ; [2] and the use of it to drown the cries of children offered to Molech.[3] The *ska-ga*, or shaman, of the Haidas undertakes to drive away the evil spirit which possesses the sick. His chief implements are the drum and the rattle.[4] The exorcism of an evil spirit causing disease is carried out by the Wanika medicine-man in the centre of a band, playing drums and shouting.[5] The Patagonian doctor beats a drum by the sick man's bed to drive out the spirit.[6] The Asiatic shamans use the drum to cause spirits both to appear and to disappear.[7]

There is always something very human about the use of drum-music, even when applied to spiritualities. At an Eskimo feast the drums are beaten softly when the traders' goods are brought in ; loudly when the guns are brought, so that the shades of animals present may not be alarmed.[8] For induction of spirits, the principle may be that of a summons or of an invitation.[9]

---

[1] J. H. Gray, *China* (1878), ii. 306.

[2] *Fragmenta Historicorum Græcorum* (Paris 1885), iv. 227.

[3] Plutarch, *De Superstitione*, xiii.

[4] G. M. Dawson, " On the Haida Indians of the Queen Charlotte Islands," *Geological Survey of Canada, Report of Progress for 1878-1879* (Montreal 1880), p. 122.

[5] J. L. Krapf, *Travels, Researches and Missionary Labours during an Eighteen Years' Residence in Eastern Africa* (1860), p. 189.

[6] M. Dobrizhoffer, *Account of the Abipones* (1822), ii. 262.

[7] J. Georgi, *Les Nations samoyèdes et mandshoures* (St. Petersburg 1777), p. 140.

[8] E. W. Nelson, " The Eskimo about Bering Strait," *Annual Report of the Bureau of Ethnology* (1896-1897), xviii. 383.

[9] H. S. Stannus, " Notes on some Tribes of British Central Africa," *Journal of the Royal Anthropological Institute* (1910), xl. 313 ; A. B. Ellis, *The Tshi-speaking Peoples of the Gold Coast of West Africa* (1887), p. 125 ; Sir E. F. Im Thurn, *Among the Indians of Guiana* (1883), p. 339 ; W. W. Skeat, *Malay Magic* (1900), p. 512 ;

An old Motu-motu man observed to Chalmers :
" No drums are beaten uselessly ; there are no dances
that are merely useless." The young men, for instance, are bidden to beat the drum and dance that
there may be a large harvest.[1] The Papuans' remark
applies universally. Tshi priests work themselves into
an inspired state by dancing to the music of the drums.
Each god has a special hymn accompanied by a special
beat of the drum.[2] In ancient Israel the priests prophesied to the music of harps, psalteries, and cymbals.[3]
Among the Chaco Indians the boys during initiation
are called " drums," from the fact that during this
period the village drums are beaten incessantly day
and night by relays of men. Among the Port Moresby
natives (New Guinea) the boys at initiation have only
one serious duty, which is for each to make his drum.
They are taboo, and live in the forest until the drums
are completed ; this may be a week or a month. Several
boys go together. " A straight branch is selected and
cut to the requisite size ; this is next scraped with
shells till the orthodox shape is arrived at ; finally,
the cavity is carefully and laboriously burnt out."
During the whole period they observe minute rules :
if they were seen by a woman " the drum would have

J. A. Kruijt, *Het Animisme in den Indischen Archipel* (The Hague 1906), p. 445 ;
J. H. Meerwaldt, " Gebruiken den Bataks in het maatschappelijk leven," *Mededee-
lingen van wege het Nederlandsche Zendeling genootschap* (1907), li. 98 ; G. A. Wilken,
loc. cit. ; J. H. W. Sheane, " Some Aspects of the Awemba Religion and Superstitious
Observances," *Journal of the Anthropological Institute* (1906), xxxvi. 132 ; J. H. Weeks,
" Anthropological Notes on the Bangala of the Upper Congo River," *Journal of the
Royal Anthropological Institute* (1910), xl. 372, 404.

[1] J. Chalmers, *Pioneering in New Guinea* (1887), p. 181.

[2] A. B. Ellis, *The Tshi-speaking Peoples of the Gold Coast of West Africa* (1887),
pp. 120 ff.

[3] 1 Chronicles xxv. 1-3 ; 2 Samuel vi. 5 ; W. B. Grubb, *An Unknown People in
an Unknown Land* (1911), p. 178.

to be destroyed, otherwise it would be certain to split, and would sound like an old cracked pot." If they eat fish the skin of the drum will burst ; red bananas cause a dull tone. They may not touch fresh water, but only that found in the stems of bananas, or coco-nut milk. Should they touch water inadvertently before the drum is hollowed out, they break it, crying : " I have touched water, my firebrand is extinguished, and I can never hollow out my drum." The sorcerers instruct them that water extinguishes the " fire " of the music ; a fish-bone tears the tympanum ; and the sight of a woman destroys the tone.[1]

The basket-drum of some American tribes recalls not only primitive substitutes for the drum, but cer-tain features of agricultural rituals. In their sacred rites the Navahos use an inverted basket in lieu of a drum. It is finely made by the women from twigs of sumach, wound in helix form, and when inverted the basket is nearly hemispherical. During cere-monies it is beaten with the sacred drum-stick. This is made according to elaborate rules from the leaves of *Yucca baccata*. The Navahos say, " We turn down the basket," when they refer to the commencement of a song; " We turn up the basket," when a song is finished. As it is raised, hands are waved in the same direction, to drive out the evil influence which the sacred songs have collected and imprisoned under the basket.[2]

It is no sacrilege to serve food in this sacred drum. To do so is common enough, but without ceremonial meaning. In Græco-Roman cults, such as the mysteries

[1] A. C. Haddon, *op. cit.*, p. 257.
[2] W. Matthews, " The Basket Drum," *The American Anthropologist* (1894), vii. 202-208.

of Attis, eating sacred food from the sacred drum and
cymbal was probably a reversion to primitive times,
when platter, drum, basket, and winnowing-fan were
interchangeable.

The use of the tambourine by the shamans of
Northern Europe and Asia is remarkable. This instrument and its shamanistic manipulation are found
in a belt which almost completely surrounds the world
in northern parallels, through Asiatic Russia, Greenland,
Northern America, and Lapland, and among Amer-
indians, Mongols, Tatars, and Lapps.[1] The structure of
this hand-drum has already been described. Those
used by Americans, Tatars, and Mongols have pic-
torial designs on the drum-head. The designs are
supposed to produce or modify the sounds, and each,
being thus a sort of word or sentence accompanied by
pure sound, has its particular influence on the spirits
who are invoked by the music.[2] The Lapp shaman's
drum has small brass rings fastened loosely on the
head. These move and dance over the designs inscribed when the head is beaten with the hammer;
and, according to their movements in relation to the
magic signs of sun, moon, and planets, the shaman
predicts the future.[3] The origin of this method,
which, it is to be noted, is always secondary to the
musical or " suggestive " use of the instrument, may
be from the following practice : the Yakut shaman
places a ring or coin on the palm of the inquirer's
hand, moving it about in various directions, and then

---

[1] V. M. Mikhailovskii, *op. cit.*, xxiv. 91, 93-94.

[2] G. Mallery, " Picture-Writing of the American Indians," *Annual Report of the Bureau of Ethnology* (1888-1889), x. 514.

[3] H. G. M. Murray-Aynsley, " Discursive Contributions towards the Comparative Study of Asiatic Symbolism," *The Indian Antiquary* (1886), xv. 67.

foretells the future.[1]   The Votyak *tuno* moved beans
on a table for the same purpose.[2]

It is suggestive of hypnotism rather than of music
to find that the drum is tuned up by holding it in
front of the fire.   A drum-stick or the hand is used in
playing.   The tambourine plays the main part in the
kamlanie, the invocation of spirits and subsequent
prophesying.   The Chukchi shaman in his *kamlanie*
taps the tambourine with a piece of thin whalebone.
The *kam* uses the tambourine in various ways, and
produces the most varied sounds.   The spectators
recognize the various rhythms, such as the tramping
of horses' feet, during which the *kam* is supposed to
be riding with his guards.   As he taps, he collects
spirits in the tambourine.   Sometimes during the collection of spirits the tambourine becomes so heavy
that the *kam* bows under the weight.[3]

Our survey shows us that it would probably be
no exaggeration to describe the drum as the most
widely-used and the most important and significant
of all musical instruments.

[1] V. M. Mikhailovskii, *op. cit.*, xxiv. 95.
[2] *Ibid.*, xxiv. 154.   [3] *Ibid.*, xxiv. 68, 72, 75-76.

INDEX

PRINTED IN GREAT BRITAIN AT THE UNIVERSITY PRESS, ABERDEEN